THE
MAGICAL
PERSONALITY

Who Do You Think You Are?

What's your magical personality: Dragon? Pegasus? Mermaid? Since personality is central to the success of magic and other goal-related activities, knowing your type—and its corresponding shadow—can give you insight into which methods and techniques work best for you, and why your magical work sometimes fails despite your best efforts.

Written by a psychologist and psychotherapist with extensive magical training, *The Magical Personality* is the only book to advance a new model of personality based on the ancient system of the four elements. Use the questionnaire to identify your strongest and weakest elements. Then discover your magical personality type—one of twelve types represented by the dragon, phoenix, wyvern, chimera, mermaid, satyr, centaur, wodwose, gryphon, pegasus, unicorn, and firebird.

Your primary element indicates the things that interest you most, as well as your greatest strengths. It also indicates the aspects of magical work for which you have the greatest natural affinity. Your secondary element indicates other strong character traits and areas of interest. Together these two elements comprise your primary personality type.

Next you'll identify your two weaker elements. These represent your shadow type, indicating the internal personal factors that may hinder your magical success. Learn how to use meditation, behavioral techniques, crystals, color correspondences, and ritual to strengthen the facets of your personality that may be holding you back from magical success.

Make the most of your magic and learn more about yourself with this guidebook to the mind.

About the Author

Mike Leslie holds master's degrees in occupational psychology and psychotherapy, and has worked in careers counseling, psychiatric nursing, and psychotherapy. Currently he is a psychiatric nurse with extensive experience in psychological assessment in both clinical and nonclinical settings. He lives in England.

To Write to the Author

If you wish to contact the author or would like more information about this book, please write to the author in care of Llewellyn Worldwide and we will forward your request. Both the author and publisher appreciate hearing from you and learning of your enjoyment of this book and how it has helped you. Llewellyn Worldwide cannot guarantee that every letter written to the author can be answered, but all will be forwarded. Please write to:

Mike Leslie
℅ Llewellyn Worldwide
P.O. Box 64383, Dept. 0-7387-0187-4
St. Paul, MN 55164-0383, U.S.A.

Please enclose a self-addressed stamped envelope for reply,
or $1.00 to cover costs. If outside U.S.A., enclose
international postal reply coupon.

Many of Llewellyn's authors have websites with additional information and resources. For more information, please visit our website at

http://www.llewellyn.com

Mike Leslie

THE
MAGICAL
PERSONALITY

IDENTIFY STRENGTHS & WEAKNESSES
TO IMPROVE YOUR MAGIC

2002
Llewellyn Publications
St. Paul, Minnesota 55164-0383, U.S.A.

First Edition
First Printing, 2002

Cover art © Eyewire
Cover design by Kevin R. Brown
Editing and book design by Rebecca Zins
Mythical creature illustrations by Eric Hotz

Library of Congress Cataloging-in-Publication Data
Leslie, Mike, 1956–
    The magical personality : identify strengths & weaknesses to improve your magic /
Mike Leslie.—1st ed.
    p.   cm.
Includes bibliographical references.
ISBN 0-7387-0187-4
1. Magic. 2. Typology (Psychology)—Miscellanea. I. Title.

BF1621 .L47 2002
133.4'3—dc21

2001050619

Llewellyn Publications
A Division of Llewellyn Worldwide, Ltd.
P.O. Box 64383, Dept. 0-7387-0187-4
St. Paul, MN 55164-0383, U.S.A.
www.llewellyn.com

Printed in the United States of America on recycled paper

Contents

Contents

Introduction

The idea for this book came from considering the traditional dichotomy between black and white magicians in myth and fantasy. Why this stark polarization? Why were black magicians only able to perform evil magic? Why were white magicians constantly at risk of going over to the dark side, while black magicians never seemed to be at risk of turning to the light? The simple answer is that some were good and some were evil. However, this answer is too simplistic and conveniently based on moral judgements regarding what these sorcerers did as a consequence of their inherent natures. In other words, some wizards (and by extension some people) are "born bad" and thus attracted to the black arts, while others are naturally good and hence given over to white magic. The alternative explanation is that some wizards begin as good but are somehow "turned" by a malevolent influence. Either way, the individual is not held responsible for his or her actions and choices. The implication is that nobody is a free agent.

Thinking about this in terms of magical intention, I was led to the idea of magical personality types. Basically, a magician is either black or white, according to the choice of magical aim. Success comes if the individual is suited to the nature of the goal, and such success generally leads to further work in the same vein. Everyone differs with respect to interest, aim, motivation, and skill. Generally speaking, therefore, you will be motivated to best employ your skills toward the aims that interest you most. Interest, motivation, and aims are features of personality. This reasoning is in line with modern personality theories as well as my own experience of magical work.

Anyone who has attempted to work magic will have been struck by the variability of outcomes. It seems that some goals are achieved with apparent ease while others remain stubbornly out of reach despite your best efforts. There are a number of factors that need to be taken into account when planning anything, and magic is no exception. The more ambitious the aim, the more things can go wrong; the more delicate the operation, the greater the skill required. Virtually anyone can heat a frozen pie, but making a soufflé requires culinary skill.

It ought to go without saying that in order to succeed you need to be interested and motivated. Consider the choice of occupation. People who enjoy practical work are attracted to things like carpentry and engineering. Similarly, people who enjoy working in a helping capacity may be motivated to become, for example, therapists or doctors. One of the principle aims of the career counselor is to identify these interests through the use of inventories, which frequently are based on theories of personality. Job satisfaction and motivation to succeed are related to the strength of interest, which in turn is related to personality. Ability, of course, is a separate matter. Many people harbor a desire to be an artist, for instance, but few have the ability to succeed with this ambition.

This reminds us that magic is also very much an art, and that different people possess different degrees of artistic or magical ability. I have often heard people say that they can't draw. They are wrong, of course, because everyone can draw, however badly. What they really mean is that they can't draw well, which is a different matter. I believe that the same is true of magic. Anyone can practice and achieve results, but there are only a few magical geniuses who are able to perform minor miracles. It is a truism that practice makes perfect, and that being gifted is of little value if those gifts are not developed. Even a poor artist can develop with practice, while many gifted people squander their talents through lack of application. Magic also needs to be worked at if results are to follow.

It helps to have an understanding of the factors that can help or hinder you in your efforts. The emphasis of this book is on your personal strengths and weaknesses, and how to identify and develop them. To this end I have drawn on both ancient and modern theories of personality and created a model that has particular relevance to the practice of magic. Having discovered your strengths, you will have a better idea concerning the type of magical aim with which you are most likely to succeed. Having identified your weaknesses, you will have a better idea of why you fail and how to overcome these deficits. Even if you do not intend to practice magic, this system will permit you to learn something about yourself and other people, and in what ways you may be open to personal development.

1

THE SCIENCE OF MAGIC

Before going into the main subject of this book—magical personality—it is apropos to begin by exploring the nature of magic itself. There are several ways to approach this task. Magic may be conceived as a goal, as a method of achieving a goal, and as the goal itself. It can therefore be viewed simultaneously as aim, process, and outcome.

There is also a difference between "high" and "low" magic. High magic is predominantly a structured method of personal and spiritual development. Low magic is predominantly concerned with the manipulation of the physical world in some way. This is what most people mean when they refer to magic, the casting of spells, and such like. Some high magicians even regard low magic, in all its forms, to be black magic. This is an extreme viewpoint that is difficult to uphold if healing and other beneficial outcomes are included. It does, however, indicate that the black versus white dichotomy is not so easily resolved as one might imagine.

Magic is not "magick." *Magick* is the spelling adopted by Aleister Crowley to distinguish his own magical system from what he considered to be the inferior methods that he was trying to supercede. Modern writers, almost without exception, use Crowley's spelling to refer to a set of concepts and methods of working that owe little or nothing to Crowley's own. For this reason I have stubbornly adopted the traditional spelling at the risk of appearing old fashioned and less "sexy" than my contemporaries.

This may seem pedantic to some. Call it magick if you wish. It is probably true that the people who are interested in the kind of ceremonial magic that was practiced by the Golden Dawn, or magick as practiced by Crowley, will not be offended. They are not much interested in the practice of magic as it is understood by the general reader of occult works, or by most New Age enthusiasts. It is this type of magic, the magic of spells and spellcasting, of hedge magic and obstacles to the success of this activity, that is the subject of this book.

One thing we can take from Crowley is the oft-quoted definition of magic as the art and science of causing change in conformity with the will. This notion of causing change in the physical world by nonphysical means immediately separates "high" from "low" magic, and leads us into the realm of ethics and black versus white magic, of which we'll read more later. Practitioners of high magic are those aforementioned ceremonial magicians whose principle aim is spiritual development, and for whom the casting of spells—the aim of which is to bring about changes in the physical world (rather than in oneself)—constitutes low magic.

The pejorative connotations of this term "low" are obvious, especially considering that some authorities view all but high magic to be black. That would make this book a work about black magic, but only if we adopt the same high opinions as these practitioners of high magic. However, most people do not regard the practice of low or practical magic as inherently bad. Much depends on intention and outcome, and as I have indicated, intent and success are functions of personality.

If magic is a means of producing change in conformity with the will, how is this achieved? Magic may be conceived of as an aim (like electricity), as a process (like the building of a circuit), or as an outcome (such as the lighting of a bulb). However, unlike electricity, magic does not fit into the generally accepted framework of modern science. The inverse square law, for instance, states that a light becomes weaker the farther away the light source becomes, and the weaker the gravitational pull between two bodies the farther apart they are. Magic seems to defy this basic law regarding weaker effects over increasing distances. Apparently magic remains as effective over a distance of a thousand miles as it does over a few feet. Moreover, magical intentions expressed today may not exert an effect until some months later, which means that magic does not even respect the time barrier.

Clearly this is anathema to classical physics but it is more understandable given the discovery of hitherto unknown properties of the universe, such as black holes and the peculiarities of subatomic phenomena that also seem to defy the accepted laws of time and space. It is more widely appreciated now that unscientific ideas can actually encapsulate profound truths about the universe. Up until about thirty years ago, though, science and spirituality did not mix. Since then the teachings of Eastern mystics, particularly those espousing Taoist and Buddhist philosophies, have been found to converge with modern scientific discoveries.

One of the implications of modern thinking is that we have the potential to know everything because we *are* everything. This rather bizarre claim can be understood through ideas such as those of Bohm and the implicate order. Put simply, the implicate order refers to the universe as an undivided whole, the ground from which springs the explicate order, the physical world we experience and are a part of. Because we are a part of this world we tend to regard it as the only world, and to be unaware of, or ignore, the invisible world beyond. Here we have an example of the ancient Hindu concept of *maya* (illusion) finding expression in modern thought. The Hindus long ago described the physical world as an illusion beyond which lies reality, poetically referred to as "the dream of Brahma." This suggests that the apparently solid world around us is no more than a dream dreamt by the divinity and that all will vanish when Brahma awakens.

Modern atomic theory (itself a rediscovery of an ancient Greek idea) shows the atoms that make up the stones and other physical things around us consist of almost nothing but empty space. The physical qualities of density, hardness, and so on are a product of the arrangement of atomic forces. At subatomic levels there is nothing at all that corresponds to physical matter, just forces in different patterns of relationship.

This makes the idea of a nonphysical reality easier to accept. It also makes the existence of an Otherworld easier to accept. The idea of the explicate order, beyond which lies the implicate order, is quite similar to the idea of the spiritual Otherworld lying beyond the physical world.

Consider also the idea of the holographic universe; this analogy is based on the discovery that if you break a holograph, you will have not fragments of the image but whole copies of it in miniature. The holographic metaphor is used here to express the idea that all parts of the universe are encapsulated within all parts of the universe—the whole can be found in each individual part. Now you can better understand how you can have the potential to know and influence everything—because everything is within you. This idea will be reinforced when we come to examine the psychology of magic. If you are particularly interested in the way modern scientific thought upholds magical philosophy, I recommend *Where Science and Magic Meet* by S. Roney-Dougal (1993), in which these theories, and much more besides, are described in a very readable fashion.

A magical model of the universe assumes that the physical world we inhabit is not only in contact with but partly overlaps this Otherworld of spirit. Later we will consider the central importance of psychology in relation to this worldview and to the practice of magic. For now let us assume that a very real world of spiritual forces coexists with the tangible world with which we are all familiar, and that this Otherworld can be accessed and its inhabitants contacted with the aim of gaining their cooperation. Traditionally the shaman was empowered to do just that, often with the aid of powerful hallucinogens such as peyote. As both Harner and Castaneda have pointed out, the use of drugs is far from necessary. A much safer and indeed preferable method is via the induction of a light trance state, similar to that achieved in meditation or during magic rituals.

Another useful concept that may help in understanding the notion of the Otherworld is that of the Australian Aboriginal Dreamtime, in which the universe was created in the distant past and continues to be created as life is lived. In another of those examples of ancient ideas rediscovered and expressed in modern thought, there is a similarity between this concept and that of phenomenologists who observed that the world is both a given and constantly created by each of us as we experience it. This in turn is upheld by ideas within modern physics, such as quantum theory, and in particular the Heisenberg principle. This refers to the realization that the observer, in some sense, creates what is observed. The experimenter is actually a factor in the experiment and cannot be excluded.

I would like to clarify at this point that the physical world is no less spiritual than the Otherworld. Personally I hold to a pantheistic spiritual outlook in which everything is divine, and it follows from this that the different worlds are different in kind, not different in substance. Just as Eastern religions postulate this basic belief, so various Western philosophers have drawn the same conclusion. Spinoza, for instance, reasoned that mind and matter are not independent substances, rather they are distinct attributes of a single, divine substance. All is one, and one is all.

One way to appreciate this is to consider everything in terms of spiritual energy and density. Just as there are three states of matter—solid, liquid, and gas, solid being the most dense—so are there states of being where the manifest world of form is most dense. The magical view is that because everything is an aspect of the divine, everything is animate and alive, even rocks. Rocks do not appear to be alive because we understand "alive" to be a strictly biological phenomenon that cannot apply to minerals. However, rocks are manifestations of the divine just like everything else in the manifest world, and they are alive in this spiritual sense. Mystics have for thousands of years postulated a series of levels of spiritual refinement with gross physical matter at the bottom, so to speak, rather like the result obtained from using a centrifuge. Beyond this level are found other, more refined levels that we do not ordinarily perceive.

Mainstream science continues to deny the possibility of magic as a force of nature. Physicists are understandably unwilling to give up a general principle such as the inverse square law that makes everything neat and rational, much as medieval thinkers were unwilling to give up the notion of crystalline spheres that encircled the Earth and were pushed around by fleets of angels. It is worth bearing in mind, however, that such intellectual revolutions do occur. Newtonian physics revolutionized scientific thinking in the seventeenth century, but they could not account for the observations made by Einstein in the twentieth century.

Newton wasn't wrong, of course, but his understanding was incomplete. It is possible that the physics of the future will accommodate forces such as magic. No scientist would assert that current models of the universe are final, and it is a commonplace that yesterday's magic becomes tomorrow's science—we need only look as far as planes and telephones for evidence of that. Magic is about the occult, the hidden and the unknown.

One of the aims of science is to disclose the unknown and then make it familiar through technological applications. Perhaps occultists, like the ancient philosophers of the Far East, are actually ahead of their time rather than the deluded primitives that they are often perceived as being.

2

THE PSYCHOLOGY
OF MAGIC

In a sense, magic is psychology. If thought is creative—referring to the conscious mind and the individual's part in creating his or her own personal reality—then magic is a means whereby creative thought and emotion are used to bring about objective changes via subjective experience. In line with the notion of the holographic universe, we are everything. The means by which we are able to access literally everything is via the Otherworld, and this is accessed via the unconscious mind—actually, "subconscious" might be more accurate because it emphasizes the accessibility of this layer of the mind to conscious reflection. Also, it would allow us to avoid the Freudian unconscious and the association with repression. However, the unconscious is generally understood to mean a part of the mind that lies outside of normal awareness and that extends to the borders of the collective unconscious, so I will retain this term.

Beyond the personal unconscious is the Jungian concept of the collective unconscious, with its collection of archetypes. As we shall see, modern magical theory lays heavy emphasis on both the personal and the collective unconscious to explain occult lore and the Otherworld of spirits. Indeed, Jung was of the opinion that the complexes and their associated archetypes would at one time have been referred to as spirits, and mental illness as possession by these spirits. The language of the unconscious, the collective unconscious, and also of magic is that of symbolism, and few have written so extensively on this subject as Jung. Jung has in fact been described as the nearest thing to a truly modern shaman that we have yet seen (Noel, 1997).

The abstract forces of the Otherworld are perceived by us in symbolic terms as beings with which we are familiar in our own physical world. This is why the shaman contacts power animals, although it should be obvious that there are no spectral bears or what have you roaming through spectral woods. The forces that we perceive creatively as bears, owls, and the like are real enough, but if we are to "see" them they need to adopt a form that is congruent with the power they represent. Thus, we associate Eagle with spiritual matters because it can fly high into the heavens, and consequently relevant powers are perceived as eagles. Owls are regarded as birds of the occult realms, and so forces relating to arcane knowledge are perceived by us as owls.

Sometimes these forces do not correspond to creatures with which we are familiar as living animals but as composites, and so they may be viewed as fabulous beasts, such as dragons and unicorns. Similarly, there may be communication with elementals, angels, and god-forms. These are the forces whose help is enlisted in the practice of magic. They are the agents of change, and each has qualities and characteristics that are pertinent to the magical goal. Symbols function as the link between the unconscious mind of the magician and the power that the symbol represents.

Because of Freud's influence, we are used to the idea of the unconscious affecting our lives in a detrimental way. Practitioners of psychosynthesis, on the other hand, encourage their clients to journey into the unconscious to make changes there that are intended to have a beneficial effect on the client's conscious life (Ferrucci, 1995). This technique bears more than a passing resemblance to the shamanic journey into the Otherworld, the purpose of which is to effect change in the "ordinary" world. This example from the field of psychotherapy seems to be another indication of the similarity between the Otherworld and the unconscious.

The practice of magic, then, involves the magician contacting and gaining the assistance of relevant forces to produce a tangible effect. Spiritual forces reflecting the magician's thoughts and desires gather around him or her in line with the principle of "like attracts like." Here is the key to the black versus white magician conundrum. Considered in this light, it is clear that the magical process begins even before the magician has cast the circle—before, in fact, she or he has taken up the practice of magic. The magician's psychology and especially his or her personality is the key to what forces you can most easily attract and with what you can most easily succeed. Choosing the right time and place, the right tools, the right method—these considerations follow from what has already begun. It is a sobering thought that your personality and the values to which you cleave attract comparable powers. It is also comforting, since it implies that a kind disposition will attract very few, if any, malignant entities, for example.

To return to the notion of magic as aim, process, and outcome . . . the aim is to bring about change; the method of bringing about this change involves entering the Otherworld to obtain help from the appropriate forces; and the outcome is expected to follow from the intention. The outcome may not be as intended, however, and indeed there may be no discernible outcome at all. Magic is an imprecise activity, and there are innumerable factors that can work against the successful completion of a spell. Later I will address the major extrinsic limitations pertaining to space and time before going on to the intrinsic personal factors that are the main focus of this book.

Before going on to either of these topics, however, I want to complete my consideration of psychological factors that impinge on the magical process. We can refer to two types of magical activity, passive and active. Both are employed in occult activities and people have different capabilities with respect to each, depending on personality. Examples of passive forms of divination include augury and precognition as experienced through dreams. Active forms of divination include the use of tools such as tarot cards, runes, the I Ching, and so on, in which answers to questions are sought. However, active methods such as these also require the development of a receptive frame of mind, so it is evident that even active methods succeed, paradoxically, through passive means.

Much the same can be said about ritual magic. Ritual is active, involving a clearly stated goal and a carefully choreographed set of procedures to follow. However, the following factors are essential to the success of the enterprise, and again the central importance of paradoxically passive techniques is emphasized. In the first place, you should not focus on what you want to achieve but rather *assume that the goal is already achieved.* The reason for this is that the subconscious responds to the present tense, so reference to the future works against the aim. This is the reason that the present tense is always used in hypnosis.

This focus on the present tense, as if the goal is already accomplished, is not easy and like any skill it needs to be practiced. It may help to link it with another important factor that may be described as "flow." Much has been written recently about this psychological frame of mind that has been known to psychologists for some time. Anyone who has acquired a skill can attest to the automatic quality of the behavior in question. For instance, you do not consciously think about moving your legs when you walk, you just walk. Similarly, if you play a sport, a musical instrument, or drive a car, you know that you cannot do it well if you constantly have to think about doing it.

Real skill has been developed when the behavior becomes automatic and you never have to think about it. Conscious thought interferes with the performance, so automaticity is essential. There comes a point when this is so total, when the performer is so engrossed in the activity, that a frame of mind is reached—called "flow"—when the performer has effectively entered into an altered state of consciousness. At this point true virtuosity is achieved; this is what sets the artist apart from the technician. If you can achieve an altered state you are in the Otherworld as well as this one; you are operating fluidly and automatically, engrossed in a performance celebrating a goal that has already been achieved.

In addition to these factors, and integral to them, is the use of simple, rhythmic patterns in the form of incantations, drumming, song, gesture, dance, and anything else that helps you to achieve the altered state of consciousness (ASC). Another important consideration is to enjoy what you are doing and not be too serious about it. To be serious means to be tense, and to be tense weakens the ASC. In light of the above, one possible approach to ritual is to treat it as a private theatrical performance that is designed not to bring something about but to celebrate something that has already happened.

This is like singing a song that tells a story and reflects the joy of something wonderful that has happened. You are not singing about what *will be*, but what *is*. Finally, it is worth mentioning the "release of effort" effect. This refers to how things happen just as you've given up hope. It's as if trying to achieve something actually prevents it from happening. When you stop trying and give up, the desired result follows. This paradoxical phenomenon emphasizes my point about passive magic working "behind" active magic.

As I have said, there are innumerable limiting factors that can work against successful outcomes. Some of these are external and relate to time and place, while others are internal and relate to the personal psychology of the magician. Of these two, the intrinsic psychological factors are undoubtedly of greater importance. In fact it could be argued that only psychological factors are operative. This does not mean that magic is a form of self-deceit that is entirely dependent on autosuggestion; remember that we need access to the Otherworld through the unconscious. The reason that the magician uses concentration, visualization, and emotion to such a large extent is because these techniques serve to enhance the receptivity of the unconscious mind. Yet there are still many instances of failure. These can usually be attributed to psychological variables, many of which remain unknown to us.

Happily, some of the most relevant psychological variables relate to our own personality, and, according to the principle of like attracts like, this in turn indicates the degree of affinity between the magician and the forces that are being called upon. Personality can also be seen to relate to different aspects of the magical process. Personality factors correlate with desire and motivation. Imagine, for instance, that your magical aim is monetary gain. You will experience far greater difficulty achieving this aim if you are not very acquisitive by nature (undeveloped Earth, in terms of the magical personality described later). Or imagine the somewhat unlikely scenario of trying to win the affections of someone that you don't like very much. If you're not motivated to succeed because your heart isn't in it, you'll fail.

This leads back to the consideration of black and white wizards that was the starting point for my thoughts on the magical personality. Myths and legends are full of examples of wholly good or wholly bad sorcerers. The reason why some were able to succeed exclusively with black or white magic lies with the personality of the practitioner. Outcome follows intent, and intent is allied to values and motivation. Well-meaning people will therefore have as much difficulty calling up sufficient negative energy in the performance of destructive acts as malevolent people will have performing altruistic acts. In each case, the intention is incongruent with the nature of the magician.

I do not therefore believe that people are inherently good or bad, nor that they are somehow turned toward (or away from) the dark arts by external agents in the form of the devil (to use a common example). A black magician is one that performs destructive magic. In this sense we all have the potential to be black or white magicians at any time. Even the best of us can become angry and say or do things in haste that we later regret. Herein lies the importance of personal development and an ethical code. You can't blame your genes or Beelzebub if you choose to follow a dark path, because it's your choice. You need to guard against your own feelings and desires, for these are the dark forces that may come to control you.

This brings me to the main focus of this book, the magical personality. This system is expressed in terms of the ancient theory of the four elements Earth, Air, Fire, and Water. If a description of something as deep and complex as the human personality in terms of only four factors seems hopelessly inadequate, be aware that many of the personality inventories most commonly used by psychologists are also often predicated on the basis of a few factors, usually four or five. The Myers-Briggs Type Indicator has been for many years widely used and respected as a tool in educational, counseling, and occupational psychology; based on Jung's original concept of psychological types, the MBTI has four dimensions. More recently, the "Big Five" theory of personality has become very influential and, as the name suggests, inventories based on this theory have five dimensions.

Even those models with larger numbers of factors are reducible to four or five more basic factors. The sixteen-factor personality measure (16PF) devised by Cattell can be reduced to a smaller number of most often four broad factors. One of the earliest of the modern personality theories and associated inventories is that of Eysenck, the EPI (Eysenck Personality Inventory), which is based on only three dimensions. The interesting thing here is that Eysenck began with the observation that since the time of the ancient Greeks, the same descriptions of personality occurred. The ancient Greeks offered four categories: melancholic, sanguine, choleric, and phlegmatic. These biological correlates of the four elements Earth, Air, Fire, and Water were used to "type" people—there was no room in this system to be, for example, mostly sanguine but also somewhat choleric and a little melancholic. You would be described entirely in terms of one of these four humors. The chart below shows the different factors for each model.

Model	Factors				
Big 5	Neuroticism	Extraversion	Openness	Agreeableness	Conscientiousness
MBTI		Extraversion/ Introversion	Intuition/ Sensing	Feeling/ Thinking	Judging/ Perceiving
16PF	Anxiety	Exvia	Intelligence	Cortertia	Superego
EPI	Neuroticism	Extraversion			Psychoticism
Greek		Choleric	Sanguine	Phlegmatic	Melancholic
Magical Personality		Fire	Air	Water	Earth

My model is also based on the four elements of the ancients, but is much more flexible and extensive in that it includes all four temperaments in different proportions to yield a range of types. There are good reasons for assuming that everyone exhibits all the qualities attributable to the elements to some degree. Air refers broadly to the intellect, to thinking, reasoning, and analytical ability; Water refers to the emotions, to empathy, compassion, and nurturance; Fire refers to energy, passion, drive, and enthusiasm; and Earth refers to stability, practicality, and organization. Few people can be described as having no intellect or no emotions. Even psychopaths have feelings, if only for themselves. In addition to the four elements with which we are familiar, the ancients also made reference to a fifth element called Quintessence. This was considered to be the basis of the unstable four elements, and the balancing principle that maintained a degree of harmony among them. I have incorporated this as a Quintessence ("Q") factor that allows a rough estimation of the degree of balance among the elements in a given individual's personality.

The Magical Personality model is constructed as follows: Most people will be characterized by a primary element, the one with which they feel most in tune. This element will, among other things, indicate what the individual shows most interest in, and the particular strengths associated with that element. It will in addition indicate those aspects of magical work with which she or he has greatest natural affinity. The secondary element indicates other relatively strong character traits and areas of interest.

Diagram 1: The twelve types and their primary element

The individual will feel at home with this element too, but not to such a great extent as with the primary element. Taken together, these two elements represent your primary type.

The tertiary element indicates characteristics that are not strongly represented in your personality. This will indicate abilities and areas of interest that you favor less. It also indicates magical intentions and methods of working with which you can expect to have less success. The last element indicates personal characteristics that are least evident in your makeup, and consequently interests and abilities that are least favored. It also points to magical intentions and aims that you should expect to have greatest difficulty achieving. Both these elements, being relatively undeveloped, will tend to operate unconsciously. Taken together, they represent your shadow type. In some ways these elements are the most important because they indicate the most potent limiting factors—in other words, your weaknesses as a magician.

There are twelve personality types arranged on a circle (see diagram 1), each represented by a mythical creature that symbolizes the qualities of that type. Once you have identified your primary and secondary elements, you can look at the description of the appropriate type. Then identify the third and fourth elements in your makeup and read the description of the appropriate shadow type. The overall extent to which the four elements harmonize is indicated by the Q factor.

Finally, I would like to mention the magical persona. In many books on magic, there are references to the magical personality. This is not the same as any of the magical personalities described in this book. It is more of an alter ego, a deliberately constructed "magical ideal" that the magician "becomes" in order to enhance the magical process. However, to call this a personality is something of a misnomer, since the term "personality" refers to an enduring set of personal characteristics. A persona (literally, "mask"), on the other hand, is like a role that is adopted when required.

There are sound psychological and magical reasons for creating a magical persona for yourself. In keeping with the theatrical origin of the term, the persona represents the character that the person is attempting to portray on the ritual stage, as it were. Watson (1996) describes the development of the magical persona in terms of strategies used by actors to get into a role. This is an excellent way of approaching the persona. It is your other self, the Magician, the powerful character you become when you engage in magical work. By adopting this role, you become what you intend to be: a powerful wizard whose spells are successful.

3

TIME AND PLACE

Many readers will already be familiar with the problems associated with timing and location of rituals, and you may prefer to skip this short section that I have included for the sake of completeness. Others may be new to the practice of magic and they ought to find this brief consideration of external factors of some interest.

Time

Traditionally, the timing of magical operations is of crucial importance. Supernatural stories always seem to include a black magician who has to perform a ritual that reaches a climax at a very precise moment when all planetary aspects are exactly right. Naturally this is the point where the good guys stop the bad guy at the last minute and foil his (sometimes her) plans to become all-powerful. The importance of temporal factors in magical operations vary but, in line with what I wrote earlier about the centrality of psychology to magical work, psychological factors are of greatest importance.

Planetary and other influences are held by most occultists to be highly influential. Generally speaking, there is a pattern of temporal "tides" that ebb and flow in cycles that last for minutes, hours, days, months, or years. The longest cycles are those of the distant planets, such as Uranus, but these are of least consequence in magical work. The shortest cycles are those of the moon as it passes through the various signs, but more important than this is the lunar cycle itself. Traditionally, constructive magic is performed as the moon waxes from new to full, with the greatest accumulation of power at the full moon. Magic designed to remove or reduce something is usually performed as the moon wanes from full to new. Even if the moon exerts no physical influence at all (and few occultists would argue in favor of this idea), the purely psychological effect of the moon's cycle should incline you wherever possible to adhere to traditional practice.

The yearly solar cycle begins at the winter solstice (around December 22), at which point the sun as a symbol of the life force itself is reborn and the year begins to wax, reaching full, as it were, at the summer solstice (around June 22). From this point on, the year is on the wane until the sun is reborn at the next winter solstice. As with the lunar cycle, the growing time of the year is most conducive to productive work, while operations aimed at reduction and removal are best performed as the year wanes. Also of importance are the festivals between the solstices. The equinoxes occur around March 21 and September 21, respectively, and are the peak points between the solstices, roughly equivalent to the waxing and waning moons. They are points of rising and falling power.

The old agrarian fire festivals occur as follows: February 1, Brigantia; May 1, Beltane; August 1, Lughnassadh; November 1, Samhain. These festivals used to be celebrated over a three-day period beginning on the eve of the festival and ending the day after it. Consequently, Samhain (Halloween) traditionally falls on October 31, although the pagan New Year actually began on November 1. The importance of these festivals is that they mark points throughout the year when the Otherworld is believed to be closer to our own, and magic is more likely to be successful. The close proximity of the Otherworld at these times is especially marked at Halloween, which is why we dress up as ghosts and ghouls and decorate the house in a creepy way. This is designed to confuse the spirits that cross over at this time. Halloween is the most powerful festival in this respect, followed by Beltane, although magical aims may also be favored by deities that are associated with particular festivals.

The days of the week are associated with particular planets and hence with particular magical intentions, and the same is true for the hours of the day beginning at sunrise, with another set of hours covering nocturnal workings. Finally, if you really want to take into account all the planetary influences that may impinge on your work, then you could cast a horoscope, paying particular attention to the position of relevant planets and the aspects between them. If you are interested in Feng Shui you may like to take account of temporal factors based on this system.

In practice it is often difficult to work at traditionally auspicious times. Circumstances may not permit you to work at the full moon, or your need to work may simply occur at an inopportune time. Even if you are able to work at the most propitious moment, there can still be unknown temporal influences at work that will prevent success of the operation. Undoubtedly the single best method of establishing whether or not the time is right for a given operation is to consult the I Ching, or Book of Changes. This is possibly the oldest book in the world, having existed in one form or another for about 4,000 years.

This remarkable work is not only the oldest book on the planet, it is an interactive text based on binary code—the same mathematical system on which modern computers are based. Chinese thought was less concerned with the cause and effect phenomena that have always been the primary focus of the West, but concentrated instead on the quality of temporal relationships. This was one of the things about the I Ching that impressed Jung and that agreed so well with his acausal connecting principle, better known as synchronicity.

The ancient Chinese conceived of different types of time: linear time, involving the process of cause and effect that was the central focus in the West; cyclical time, in which phenomena wax and wane; and "timeless time," in which all events coexist. According to the Chinese, this "timeless time" could on occasions intrude into "ordinary" time, thereby offering an opportunity to discover things past, present, and future. The I Ching is concerned with the patterns of time and the degree of harmony between these and a person's current focus of interest. Based on the premise that to be successful you should work in harmony with the prevailing time conditions (a time to reap and a time to sow), the I Ching purports to offer guidance on the correctness or otherwise of a proposed course of action.

The I Ching is approached as if it were a living sage from whom the student hopes to gain instruction. The book responds with answers phrased in terms of the correctness or incorrectness of the current time conditions in respect to the proposed activity. It may, for instance, indicate that the time is ripe for progress (hexagram 35), or for waiting (hexagram 5). It also offers advice, pointing, for example, to the overcoming of disharmony (hexagram 38), or a need for caution (hexagram 64). Probably the best introductory text is *The I Ching Workbook* by R. Wing (1979).

On a more mundane level, it goes without saying that you should choose a time when you will not be rushed, disturbed, disturbing to others, tired, or ill. It may sound obvious, but you should also choose a time when you are strongly motivated. This, in fact, is probably the most important time consideration of all, since emotional energy is essential to a successful outcome. The golden rule therefore is to work when you feel most strongly motivated to do so, because it is at this time that your emotional power is greatest. If you go about magical work half-heartedly, you may as well not bother.

A sense of urgency, on the other hand, can provide you with the energy that makes the difference between success and failure. Urgency is likely to be related to need, and a strong need is more likely to provoke an emotional reaction exhibited as drive. One thing needs to be stressed at this point—however angry you are, resist the urge to perform destructive magic. Once your temper has cooled, you will see the wisdom of not acting rashly in such matters. For one thing, you may regret what you have done in the heat of the moment, and secondly the force may rebound on you. Beware of what you wish for!

Space

The place in which you choose to conduct your magical operations is important for a number of reasons, and various limiting factors can readily be identified. Apart from a few obvious considerations like size, privacy, peace, and quiet, it would be ideal if the chosen working space was set aside exclusively for ritual. This is often impossible, and you may well have to make do with converting your bedroom or some other place that is usually used for more everyday things.

If you do have exclusive use of an appropriate working space, then decorate it according to your taste and preference, taking into account such factors as the elemental directions and consecrating it for magical work. This done, you should use the room exclusively for activities associated with your magical work and resist any urge to use it for other purposes. This will be your sacred space; over time it will become increasingly imbued with magical influences, and whenever you enter it you will undergo a psychological transformation in keeping with your magical persona. Indeed, it will be the home of your magical persona.

I think it is also well worth considering the energy patterns of the chosen working space. Probably the easiest way to do this, if you are not acutely sensitive to environmental qualities, is to employ the geomantic principles of Feng Shui. The practice of Feng Shui is, of course, an art in itself, and there are a confusing variety of approaches and schools of that can make the study frustrating. My advice is to choose a system that appeals to you for whatever reason and follow that one alone. In my experience, the simplest and most complete system can be found in *The Principles of Feng Shui* by S. Brown (1996).

The basic premise underlying Feng Shui is quite simple: Every living thing has an aura, an invisible energy signature that is unique to that organism. Feng shui operates on the basis that environments also have a unique energy pattern that may or may not match your own. The extent to which it does match will have implications for various life activities—you may find that your career or relationship areas are adversely affected, for example. The implications for magical work may also be profound, either enhancing or reducing your chances of success with respect to the given aim. Fortunately various cures are suggested for bad chi (or energy) that often involve little more than subtle changes, such as adding a crystal or repositioning a mirror. Using this system you can assess the Feng Shui of a district, house, room, or even a desk, and make appropriate changes as necessary.

4

THE MAGICAL PERSONALITY
TYPE QUESTIONNAIRE

I recommend completing the questionnaire before reading the descriptions of the different types so as not to influence your responses. Simply decide whether or not you agree with the statement, score the questionnaire as indicated, and enter the scores on the pentagram. Begin by reading the descriptions of the individual elements to get an idea of your personal strengths and weaknesses, then refer to the appropriate primary and shadow types.

Your scores on the personality indicator should be relatively high for two of the elements and relatively low for the other two. This is usually the case, and indicates that you are more in tune with the high-scored pair than with the low-scored pair. The high-scored pair indicates your primary type, the one that describes your preferences and your personal strengths with respect to magical work. The low-scored pair refers to your shadow sign and indicates your weaknesses, and consequently those areas that are most in need of development. The relative strengths of each element can be found by calculating the differences between them, while the overall level of harmony among elements is reflected by the Q score (see page 30). You may wish to work on developing the weaker elements in your personality makeup by using the exercises given later in this book.

Remember that there are no right or wrong answers in the questionnaire, only the ones that you feel are true of yourself. Mark the scale according to the extent to which you agree or disagree with the statement given, where:

-2 means that the statement definitely does not describe you at all

-1 means that the statement does not describe you well

0 means that the statement does not apply to you either way

1 means that the statement does describe you to some extent

2 means that the statement describes you very well

Readers may want to photocopy pages 28 and 29 prior to taking the questionnaire.

For readers with access to the Internet, the Llewellyn website, www.llewellyn.com, has an online version of the questionnaire. Click on "Magical Personality Questionnaire" at the home page for further instructions.

The Magical Personality Type Questionnaire

1. I am practical by nature.
2. I enjoy intellectual debates.
3. I often do things on the spur of the moment.
4. I spend a lot of time reflecting on things people have said or done.

5. I take pride in being forthright.
6. I am a very organized person.
7. I tend to be rather hot-headed.
8. I am very sensitive to other people's feelings.

9. I am not convinced by theory—I like to test things out in practice.
10. I often daydream.
11. I hate to be inactive—I am always on the go.
12. I am very sensitive to the atmosphere of my surroundings.

13. I try to be as specific as possible and I wish others would be, too.
14. I enjoy finding out about things, however obscure they are.
15. I feel rather lost if I'm not doing something.
16. I am very interested in mythology.

17. I prefer to use tried and tested methods.
18. I pride myself on my analytical abilities.
19. I tend to lose interest in things quickly and move on to something else.
20. I am a good listener.

21. I think that there's too much change for its own sake.
22. The facts matter more than how people feel about them.
23. I have good leadership ability.
24. I enjoy being with people, but I would prefer not to take the lead.

25. I always do things in a clear, orderly way.
26. I try to be firm but fair.
27. I am the life and soul of the party.
28. I hate to be pushy.

29. A realistic attitude is more important than being idealistic.
30. I can, if necessary, argue either side of an argument.
31. I always look on the bright side.
32. I pride myself on my empathic ability.

33. I enjoy working with my hands.
34. It is more important to be right than to be liked.
35. I am an optimist by nature.
36. I enjoy being helpful to others.

37. I prefer a slow but sure approach.
38. I learn something best by concentrating on the underlying theory first.
39. I often have several things going at once.
40. I don't mind putting myself out to help others.

41. People should live more in the present moment.
42. I need to see proof before I'll accept an idea as valid.
43. I am bored by details.
44. People try to take advantage of my good nature.

45. I tend to keep my feelings to myself.
46. I am good at working with numbers.
47. I constantly look ahead to new projects.
48. I sometimes feel neglected but would never say so.

49. I don't like to daydream—it's more important to get things done.
50. I enjoy science.
51. I am very assertive.
52. I am quite an emotional person.

53. I always speak plainly, and I wish others would, too.
54. I have a curious nature, and I enjoy learning about things.
55. I have a strong urge to succeed.
56. I have strong powers of intuition.

57. Seeing is believing.
58. I have a wide range of interests.
59. I am very strong-willed.
60. I am proud of my insightful nature.

61. I am, by nature, fairly restrained.
62. I like to plan things well in advance.
63. I am naturally outgoing.
64. The facts are less important than how people feel about things.

65. I learn best by doing.
66. I have a very active fantasy life.
67. I hate to be restricted to plans and schedules.
68. I am very good at reading people's body language.

69. I like the idea of being a farmer.
70. I like the idea of being a researcher.
71. I like the idea of being a sports coach.
72. I like the idea of being a therapist.

Score the completed questionnaire by writing the score for each question next to the appropriate question number below:

	Earth	Air	Fire	Water
Question No.	1	2	3	4
	5	6	7	8
	9	10	11	12
	13	14	15	16
	17	18	19	20
	21	22	23	24
	25	26	27	28
	29	30	31	32
	33	34	35	36
	37	38	39	40
	41	42	43	44
	45	46	47	48
	49	50	51	52
	53	54	55	56
	57	58	59	60
	61	62	63	64
	65	66	67	68
	69	70	71	72

Totals =

Earth =

Air =

Fire =

Water =

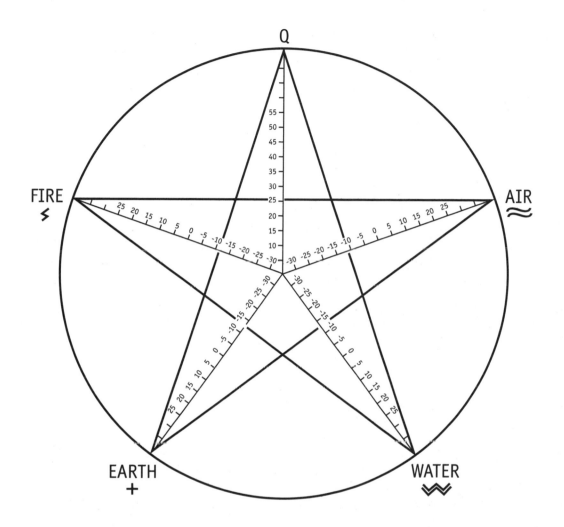

Diagram 2: The pentagram score sheet

Differences

	E	A	F	W
E	x	____	____	____
A	____	x	____	____
F	____	____	x	____
W	____	____	____	x

Q = Sum of differences ÷ 6

Type (see page 56):

Shadow (see page 122):

Find the differences between totals by subtracting smaller from larger pairs. In the case of negative totals, *add* the totals. Enter the differences between totals on the chart. Finally, add the differences and divide this total by 6 to obtain your Q score. The Q score should fall between 0 and 48, where:

    0 reflects no differences between elements

  12 reflects mild differences

  18 reflects moderate differences

  24 reflects strong differences

  48 reflects maximum differences

Lastly, plot your scores on the pentagram for a visual representation of your elemental makeup.

An example of this procedure is:

	Earth	**Air**	**Fire**	**Water**
Totals =	14	32	-2	27

Strongest pair = Air and Water = Unicorn

Weakest pair = Earth and Fire = Wodwose Shadow

Differences

	E	**A**	**F**	**W**
E	x	18	16	13
A		x	34	5
F			x	29
W				x

$$Q = \frac{18 + 16 + 13 + 34 + 5 + 29}{6}$$

= 16.666 (17 for simplicity)

In this example, Air is the strongest element, followed by Water. There is only a five-point difference between them, which is quite small. The weaker elements are Earth and Fire, with sixteen points between them, which is moderately large. Fire is the weakest element in the personality of this individual, and is the only one expressed as a negative number. This accounts for the huge differences, principally between Fire and Air, and is the single biggest reason for the moderately large Q score. Clearly this person needs to work on strengthening the Fire aspect of his or her nature if the inherent limitations are to be minimized.

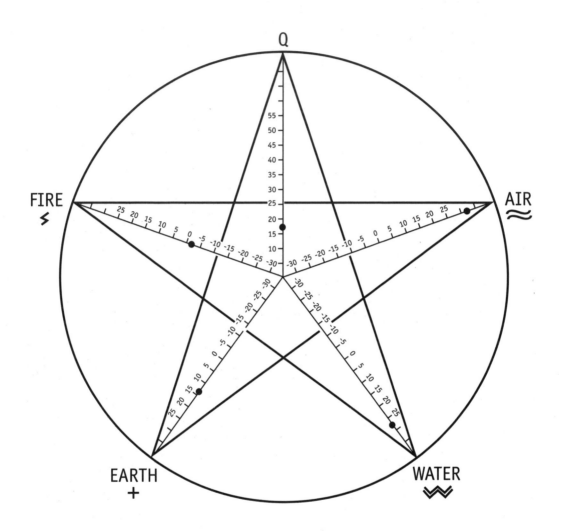

Diagram 3: Example score sheet

5

THE FIVE ELEMENTS

The ancient concept of the elements seems hopelessly anachronistic compared with the sophistication of modern chemistry, yet even in scientific terms the elements retain a certain validity as states of matter and energy. All matter exists as solid, water, or gas, depending on the temperature. A few substances skip the liquid state by sublimating from solid directly to gaseous form, but generally all modern elements exist in one of these three states. It is not difficult to find a correspondence between theses states and the ancient elements of Earth, Water, and Air (solid, liquid, and gas, respectively), while Fire represents energy itself.

Of course magicians are not concerned with equating the ancient concept of the elements with the elements of modern science. The five elements (including Quintessence) are representative of energy patterns and basic qualities that are found universally, including as psychological correlates. That is what this book is about. We are combinations of the elements in that we exist as physical beings in a physical universe (Earth); we are emotional (Water) but also rational (Air); and we are endowed with spirit (Fire). Psychologically each of us leans more toward some aspects of being—and away from others—and to different degrees, which is why we see such a range of individual differences. The following sections describe more fully the four elements mentioned above, plus the relatively neglected fifth element of Quintessence. Once you have identified your personal elemental makeup using the questionnaire, you should first read these descriptions to find in what ways you conform to the strengths (or lack of) related to each element.

Earth

This is the element with which each of us can most readily identify. We are physical beings who live on a planet actually called Earth, and we are undeniably tied to the physical world simply because we are composed from it. Each of us is Earth in this sense. Psychologically we are earthy or melancholic, as the ancients termed the psycho-physiological correlate. Melancholia reflects in a somewhat pejorative way certain characteristics of Earth types that make them appear dour and miserable, namely tough-minded, aloof, slow, and unimaginative. This is unfair because Earth types can just as easily be witty and fun loving (consider the earthy sense of humor that is a feature of some characters, and the association of music with the sign of Taurus, for example).

The apparent gloominess of Earth types is explained by their cautious natures, their realism, and their focus on technique and careful attention to detail. Add to this their forthright, outspoken tendency to call a spade a spade and it becomes clear where the Earth type's reputation for being dull originates. Earth types, therefore, are conventional, conservative, and not keen on change for its own sake, yet they are tenacious in their efforts to get things done *thoroughly*. This makes them extremely dependable. They like to see clear, tangible results for their efforts. As far as Earth types are concerned, they literally are their physical bodies.

Earth types rely heavily on their five senses, through which they perceive the "real" world of the here and now. They are therefore sensual and literal; they do not like imprecision because everything is clear-cut to them. They use words precisely, will give the exact time in minutes and even seconds, and expect other people to do the same. Everything is black and white to them, right or wrong, left or right. They are supreme pragmatists with brilliant but inflexible, highly organized systems. They believe absolutely in known laws and despise chaos, either physical or social. Since magic falls outside the laws of Newtonian physics, it cannot exist. Even if Earth types believed in personality types—and most will not even accept something as abstruse as psychology at all—they will not accept the idea of magic. If you are very earthy and you are still reading this book without sneering, you are unusual.

Earth types believe that if you want anything done, you should do it yourself. Moreover, you will only succeed through diligence and hard work. These types are consequently very disciplined and patient, efficient and reliable. They take great care over details. They are apt to be possessive over material things but also financially astute, although some would say stingy. They derive a sense of security from material things, including a home base that is to them what the shell is to the tortoise. Without it they are naked and vulnerable and will not survive. This ensures that they are home builders and homemakers. They love the comfort and security provided by this haven and will beautify it luxuriously, including the garden.

The flip side to the Earth type is an irrational fear of impending chaos that can lead to a compulsive, anxious undercurrent. Because they believe that they are their bodies, they naturally fear the inevitability of physical death, which they take to be final. They therefore suffer more than the other types from existential angst and would love to believe in a purely spiritual life beyond this one. This is not to say that they do not have spiritual beliefs, but they are more likely to accept the more literal versions of the afterlife described by orthodox religions. Often they will be atheists who do not believe in any kind of spiritual reality. This could make them immoral and self-serving were it not for a strong sense of duty and a desire to be seen as a pillar of society.

Their faults include a narrow outlook and especially an intolerance of theory, plus a tendency to reject anything that has no obvious practical value. They have a tendency to seize upon the first practical solution to a problem. They dislike fantasy, which is why they have a reputation for being dull. They can be tied to routine and may be stubbornly dogmatic. They often exhibit relatively poor social skills and may be socially isolated. They can be grasping and miserly. They may overindulge in physical pleasures of all kinds and value nothing else. On the other hand, they can be repressed and joyless.

They will carry a grudge for years and can be vindictive, even cruel. Typical preferred occupations of Earth types include builder, farmer, banker, accountant, and engineer.

Water

Water is the next most familiar element, partly because our bodies consist of around 80 percent water and two-thirds of the surface of the planet is covered in water. Water is the origin of life. We can live for some time without solid food but only a matter of days without water. Water relates to the unconscious, the primitive and instinctual. The other reason that Water is such a familiar element psychologically is because it is associated with the emotions and with nurturing. We are emotional beings long before we develop a mature intellect, and many people never mature beyond this stage of emotionalism. This does not mean that emotions are infantile—far from it. A major problem in our culture is that many people denigrate the intellect while others despise the emotions. This leads to an unbalanced adult pattern of either irrational, unstable emotion or cold, unfeeling intellect. Actually, thought and feeling interact harmoniously in the mature, balanced adult such that neither is isolated and compartmentalized. Water types are what the ancients referred to as phlegmatic.

The difference lies in mature as opposed to immature emotional reactions. Water types believe that what they feel is real. Emotions are inextricably linked with interpersonal relationships, and other people are of central importance to this type. They need to be constantly in relation, and fear being alone for too long because they feel that they do not exist without others. Their sense of security comes from relating with others in a loving, harmonious way. They are communal beings that live with and through others. They are aware of a sense of interconnection among people based on feeling. As a consequence, they are extremely perceptive regarding social relationships and nuance. They are sensitive to both social atmosphere and to people's feelings. They are empathic and caring, derive a sense of personal satisfaction and value from helping others, and are exactly the type of people that others turn to for emotional support.

Because feelings change constantly, Water types are also changeable. They are greatly influenced by impressions and are drawn to nonverbal means of expression, such as music and the visual arts. They tend to be highly imaginative and creative, with a strong aesthetic sense. Their homes are therefore often beautiful, dreamy places that radiate calm. They are sensual and have a natural feel for color, imagery, and symbolism. They are very receptive to symbolic communication and may expect other people to divine meanings in a similar way, as if they were mind readers. Water types seem to be unaware of boundaries, which is why they are so open to the occult. They are the most psychic and intuitive in the sense of being open to otherworldly contacts. These people often seem to be in another world, which they are to some extent. Although they are extremely sociable, they are prone to daydream and therefore appear distant at times.

Water types can be difficult, despite their innate sociability. Their changeable nature can show as neurotic moodiness and inconsistency. Their sensitivity can be all one-sided and they will appear highly insensitive toward others. This is complicated by an unreasonable attitude that is based exclusively on the validity of their own transient-feeling states. This means that they effectively operate a double standard that is intrinsically unfair. They can be irrational and will deal in lies and half-truths as if they were facts. They are quite capable of believing their own lies, and will be injured by heartless reference to the truth of a matter.

They can be opinionated, bigoted, prejudiced, and given to malicious gossip. At the same time as making themselves unpopular through a mixture of capriciousness and spite, they can be emotionally demanding and possessive, and they will make use of emotional blackmail as an effective first resort. They can also be seductive or smothering and feel resentful or rejected, depending on the people involved. They are given to wistful reflection on the past and on what might have been, or mawkishly sentimental over what has been left behind. They are not the most articulate of the types but express their feelings readily, if not always appropriately. Typical preferred occupations for Water types include counselor, therapist, nurse, and artist.

Air

Air is familiar to us as the gas that we breathe; we would die within minutes without it. Psychologically it refers to the human quality of reason and the intellect. Although human beings are innately gifted with intelligence, it is still an aspect that needs to be developed and honed over time. Unlike the emotions that are with us from birth and that generally need to be curtailed, the intellect is rudimentary at birth and needs to be encouraged. As stated above, thought and feeling interact to influence each other in the mature adult. Feeling is informed by reason, and reason is tempered by emotion. Unlike the constantly shifting emotions, however, reason is relatively stable. This quality is like the good seamanship that can guide us through emotional storms and without which we would be constantly adrift. It is what the ancients termed sanguine.

Air types, then, are characteristically reasonable, rational, logical, and lovers of truth. They value systems and concepts and think in abstract ways in a most objective manner. They are analytical, open to new ideas, and want to know about everything. They are curious about the world on a theoretical level and enjoy philosophical debate. They are the most gifted in terms of literary and verbal ability, being extremely eloquent in both their questions and their explanations. They demonstrate a ready understanding of very complex problems that they manage to comprehend on numerous levels. Among the types, they are the thinkers.

A capacity for abstract thought is what separates us from our animal cousins, and it is also the basis of civilization. Air types are therefore very interested in ethics and morality, with the problems of right and wrong, good and evil. They are humanitarian in outlook and recognize the uniqueness of individuals as well as their common needs and burdens. They have great integrity. They are the intellectuals and revolutionary thinkers that take the world forward because of their inventiveness and breadth of vision. They are also frequently misunderstood because they are ahead of their time and wrapped up in their own thoughts. It has been noted that these creative problem-solvers, the ones that come up with brilliant solutions and new ideas, are exactly the people who are sacked by companies for not toeing the line. The company thereby loses a valuable resource due to narrow-mindedness.

Air types have their faults, of course. An obvious one is intellectual snobbery and an attitude of superiority. They can be too distant and cold, too abstract in their concerns about the human race to notice the pain of individuals. They can be so divorced from feeling that they resemble psychopaths. Their feelings may be devalued and repressed to the point where an explosion is inevitable. On the other hand, they can be emotionally immature despite being intellectually advanced. In this case they are hypersensitive and need mothering. They are clingy and intense due to emotional vulnerability, and wide open to abuse from the unscrupulous. One problem is that they are too trusting. Despite being intellectually gifted, they can be extremely naïve and childlike. Their emotional sophistication can be inversely proportionate to their intellectual brilliance.

Typical preferred occupations of Air types include psychologist, writer, teacher, scientist, and surgeon.

Fire

Fire is pure energy manifesting as heat and light. The mastery of fire was one of the earliest major turning points in the history of our species. In myth, Prometheus stole fire from the gods and brought it to earth to be used by humans. It has always had an association with the divine, and its light symbolizes the divine spirit and the hope of salvation. Images of fire are often used to indicate urgency and intensity—for example, divine spark, fire of redemption, flame of desire, fire of passion, and so on. Psychologically, fire refers to drive, energy, and action. Without the motivating force of Fire, there would be no movement or progress. It was termed choleric by the ancients.

The qualities of the Fire type are therefore those of energy itself, namely restlessness, volatility, expansiveness, and transformation. Fire types are impulsive by nature and focus their energy passionately and intensely on a given project for a short period before losing interest and moving with equal intensity to something else. Their interest and enthusiasm resembles fire in the way they move rapidly from one thing to another. They hate to be constrained by anything but need instead to be free to express themselves and to experience new things. Routine stifles these people as effectively as lack of oxygen stifles fire.

They are creative people who love fantasy. They are not bound by time and space, having an outlook on life that is characterized by endless possibility and adventure. They are visionary travellers of both the physical world and the world of the imagination. If the Air types produce the theoretical basis and the Earth types are the builders, Fire types are the people who can bring the dream into being. For them, all things are possible. They take a broad-brush approach because details bore them, and anyway it is up to others to fill in the gaps. Fire types are natural leaders and enjoy being directive.

Like Water types, Fire types are therefore social creatures, but they are less helping than enabling. They are warm and outgoing, full of bonhomie, the proverbial life and soul of the party. This is the type who works hard and plays hard. Verbal communication is not a particular strength; they prefer action to words and gesture to sentiment. They are intuitive in the sense of being sensitive to subtle social cues. They like to

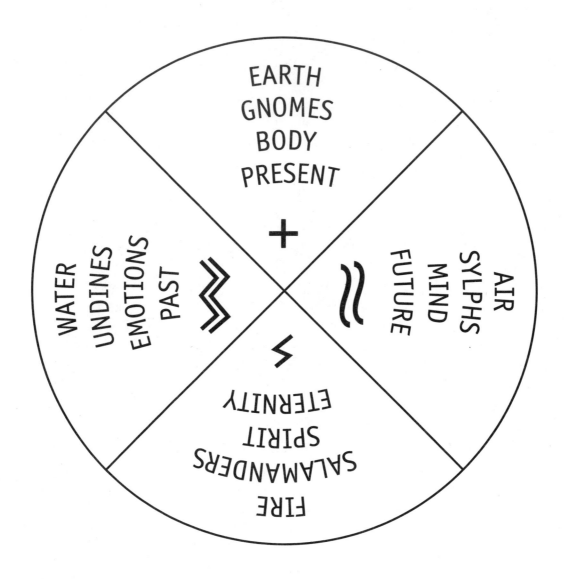

Diagram 4: The four elements

express themselves through dramatic display. They are the larger-than-life types who can fill a room with their presence and who inspire others to great achievements. They also tend to be lucky, which may be attributed to their optimism and the power of positive thinking. It is of course also true that they enjoy a gamble and may achieve more than others through sheer daring. In any event, they require constant stimulation of body and mind or they become as difficult as they are empowering.

Fire types are egocentric and can be extremely self-centered. Their courage can become recklessness that does not take into account the safety or needs of others. They can be unpredictable and even dangerous. Their need for constant stimulation can lead them into excessive drug and alcohol abuse, as well as potentially lethal forms of thrill seeking and unbridled lust. Their constant irritability is punctuated only by severe outbursts of violent rage. They can be callous and habitually blame others for their own failures and sense of frustration. The healthy competitiveness that can be both fun and productive can become an urge to dominate and destroy opposition. Typical preferred occupations of Fire types include sportsman/woman, manager, actor, politician, and priest.

Quintessence

The traditional four elements were unstable and antagonistic to each other, deriving as they did from a single, pure element known as Quintessence. The more perfectly balanced the mix of the four elements, the closer the approximation to this state of purity. Although referred to as the fifth element, Quintessence is probably more accurately described as the first element, or even as the primal substrate from which the four traditional elements arose.

The Q score is designed to reflect the extent to which your scores on the Magic Personality Questionnaire (MPQ) are similar. The smaller the differences between scores, the greater the harmony and balance between different elements. This is reflected in the Q score, which should ideally be as small as possible. The smaller the Q score, the greater the affinity between all the elements. This not only indicates a well-rounded personality, it also indicates greater facility for all aspects of the magical process. The exercises described later are intended to strengthen weaker, relatively undeveloped elements, and consequently reduce the Q score to reflect greater harmony.

The Elements in the Magical Process

Each element is associated with a different stage in the magical process. Magic usually begins and ends in the sphere of Earth. It is the realm of matter that magic is designed to influence, and this is accomplished first by seeking a ritual space into which are brought various ritual tools. These are then manipulated in specific ways in order to bring about the desired changes. Certain considerations of an earthy nature need to be kept in mind. These include realistic expectations, the state of your health, the degree of harmony with the magical environment, and timing.

Ritual performance is simply theater without an appreciation of magical theory. It behooves you to know what you are doing and why, and this is the province of Air. Many occultists are as anti-science as scientists are anti-magic. However, as I hope to have shown earlier in this book, the two may possibly converge, in theory at least. Without an understanding of magical principles, magic will be regarded at best as uninteresting, at worst as impossible. Knowledge supports belief, and without belief you have empty ritual. Air is also the element of conscious intent, and it is at this stage that you combine manipulation of physical tools with active imagination and visualization. The inceptive psychic nature of visualization and carefully chosen incantations connects you via trance with the Otherworld, as if you were opening a door.

If the forgoing constitutes the beginning of the magical process, Fire is magic itself. This is the power that you want to connect with and accumulate before directing it toward your chosen goal. Without this power, the whole process remains theoretical and is doomed to failure. Magical power is represented by a plethora of forces, each of which has a specific nature that fits with your aim. You are acting as a conduit through which the forces that you have contacted may flow.

This accumulated force needs somewhere to go and a path by which to get there. The former is provided by the magical aim, the latter by emotion. This is the sphere of Water. The emotional focus should be intense and specific in order to direct the power effectively. Water is also the element of receptive psychism, the cauldron of rebirth into which the power flows and is transformed. At this stage, spoken language is inappropriate and impossible, as only symbols and associated effects make sense. Symbols are representatives of the powers that swirl behind them, and receptors of the magic power as it charges toward its goal.

These stages are not discrete; indeed they should be as seamless as possible. Each stage naturally incorporates some features of the others. The manipulation of material tools and the physical gestures merge with the verbal and visualization stage. The visualization and invocation stage merges with the accumulation of power through identification. Identification with the forces and the application of will merges with the psychic receptivity and emotional directive stage. Emotional direction merges with the grounding stage where the aim is realized.

You may have noticed various similarities between the temperaments:

Earth and Air types are introverted, verbal, disciplined, methodical, orderly, impressed by facts, objective; they differ in that Earth types dislike theory, fantasy, and change, while Air types embody these same characteristics.

Fire and Water types are extraverted and sociable, intuitive, nonverbal, imaginative, and uncontained; however, Fire types tend to be active, directive, assertive, and impulsive, while Water types are more passive, supportive, self-effacing, and cautious.

Air and Water types are creative, open, and have strong psychic potential; however, Air types are thinkers, originators, inceptive, and objective, while Water types are feeling-based, transforming, receptive, and subjective.

Water and Earth types are cautious, conservative, dependable, passive, and methodical; however, Water types are imaginative, intuitive, and subjective, while Earth types are down-to-earth, hard-nosed, and objective.

You may like to consider other ways in which the temperaments are alike and unalike.

Notes on the Twelve Types

Before going on to read the description of your primary type and its shadow, it is important that you read the following. The first question you may ask about this system is "Does everybody have a type?" This question is answered, in the first place, according to whether you accept a type theory. Many people disagree with the idea of fitting people into a limited number of convenient pigeonholes. In my experience, however, many people do not like personality theories of any description. During my years as a career psychologist, I frequently met people who dismissed psychometrics, psychology, psychotherapy, psychiatry, and anything else that seemed to them to be "ivory-tower nonsense."

It should come as no great surprise that these people tended to be Earth types. Earthy people are notoriously intolerant of theory and of anything that can't be touched, measured, and "proved." Because the whole process of establishing career preferences was based on psychometrics—the "measurement of the mind"—this lack of credibility on their part posed a problem. I overcame the problem by asking a few choice questions that I knew had a high correlation with specific tendencies, identified the person's type from these, and then described them in terms of their (assumed) type. Invariably they were so impressed by the accuracy of the description that all objections to doing the other tests and indicators disappeared. I had first, however, to prove that the system worked. Other clients of a more theoretical inclination (typically Air types in terms of my system) would not only fill in the questionnaires and be very interested in the outcomes, they often wanted to know about the underlying theory and even the relevant statistics!

Generally speaking, people who are interested in the occult will be characteristically open in their attitudes rather than instantly dismissive, and hence more interested in this system and others. Astrology is another type system, the basic twelve signs being enriched by the multitudinous data derived from planetary positions, aspects, and so on. All of this takes astrology far beyond a simple twelvefold system of personality types. The downside to this model is that it takes many years to fully master the art, and the wealth of data can be overwhelming.

Even with an open-minded attitude, each of the four principal types may still find type theories objectionable for different reasons. As we have observed, Earth types are intolerant of pure theory and must be convinced by practical application. Air types need to be thoroughly convinced that the theory is sound even if the system yields practical, verifiable results. Fire types tolerate theory but not the questionnaire method of gathering data. They consider this method to be too divorced from the people involved. They will complain that "you can't tell anything about a person from a few marks made on paper," and will advocate some kind of interactive method instead. Water types are offended by the very idea of categorizing people and will complain that it is clinical and inhuman, even if the system yields highly valid results. As far as they are concerned, a type theory *ought not* to work because human beings are just too complex to be encapsulated by any system.

Let us assume, however, that you bought this book because you are interested in magic, personality, or both, and that you are open to the ideas contained herein. You may still ask the question "Does everybody have a type?" My answer is yes, everybody can be accommodated by this system. As I stated earlier, everybody will express themselves strongly in terms of one, usually two, occasionally three, and rarely all four elements. The (usually) two weaker, less-developed elements are still present and often work at an unconscious level.

You should therefore discover that you are quite clearly a Pegasus with a Wyvern shadow, for example. Sometimes, however, it may be that two elements are tied in first place. In this event you can consider that you have the qualities of both the Pegasus and the Gryphon (for instance). If you study the system you will see that this is true in any case, since the primary elements for both Pegasus and Gryphon are the same but in a different order. Having elements tied in first place simply means that you are neither a pure Air nor Earth type, but express the qualities of both basic types to an equal degree. If you want to identify yourself as either a Pegasus or a Gryphon, consult a friend (friends are often more objective than relatives).

If second or third elements are tied, you will effectively be determining both your primary type and your shadow, depending on which order you give them. Again, get a friend to help, or even have them do the questionnaire for you and see what differences emerge. Follow a similar procedure if the third and fourth elements are tied. In this case you are determining your shadow type, and it is probably of greatest importance to identify this correctly since limitations to practice stem largely from here. If you have a trustworthy horoscope, you can tell from this which elements are best or least well-represented in your chart, and this may be enough to decide the issue.

Although it can be inconvenient to have tied elements it is actually preferable, as long as the scores are above average. This is because ideally we would have a perfect balance among all four elements, and consequently all-round ability. As far as the practice of magic is concerned, this affinity for all the elements equally would mean having a facility for all stages of the magical process and for all possible magical aims. As I have already stated, Jung was of the opinion that weaker temperaments develop naturally over time as the individual matures. Ultimately perfect equilibrium would be reached, although in practice even the oldest, most mature people continue to demonstrate stronger leanings toward particular characteristics at the expense of others.

In the rare event that you do produce four strong element scores, congratulations—you are indeed very well-balanced and have good ability in all areas. Either that or you have not completed the questionnaire properly. It is possible to have four high scores but it is very rare, and even then two of them should still be lower than the other two. Unless this is so, you have no shadow at all. Even the best of us has a darker side, even if it remains hidden except when we are put under pressure and become stressed.

You are more likely to produce four low scores, although even this is fairly unusual. Once again, you should consider whether you have completed the questionnaire properly. If you have, then you are probably not in a good position to make use of the system at present. To produce four low scores means that your primary type has been engulfed by the shadow, and consequently you are expressing entirely shadow qualities. Other than faulty completion of the questionnaire, the most likely explanation for producing a flat profile is that you are under too much stress at present and suffering from too much negative emotion. If you think that this is so, you should forget it for now and come back to it when you are more your usual self. In the meantime you might like to consider why you are so stressed at present and to whom you might talk to about it.

Having identified your type and its corresponding shadow, you should take careful note of the following before reading the type descriptions. Firstly, the primary type is described in terms of the optimal level of functioning for that type. It represents you at your best and points to your potential. The shadow, on the other hand, describes your worst level of functioning—your potential self if you were at your lowest ebb (short of actual psychiatric disorder). These descriptions can therefore seem alarming but they are best and worse scenarios respectively. Most of us are neither paragons of virtue nor crazed neurotics but exhibit characteristics of both, most of the time.

Generally speaking, then, everyone functions well enough overall, their undeveloped elements and their associated defense mechanisms operating to offset the temperamental imbalance and to preserve the integrity of the personality as a whole. During periods when we become very stressed and upset, however, this equilibrium is temporarily lost and our psychological strengths are pared down. The "lost" strengths can then become weaknesses as they descend into the shadow. It is generally at this point that we become difficult to live with, because the usual foibles and quirks characteristic of the shadow are augmented by the negative qualities of the primary type, and everything is much nearer the surface. Hence, someone who has a mild tendency to hypochondria may suddenly become very needy and demanding as his or her personal need for security increases. The somewhat endearing quirk then becomes increasingly irritating to all concerned.

What has all this to do with magic? Well, in the first place, a relatively weak affinity with any given element will undermine your efforts at corresponding stages of the process, and your efforts to bring about change associated with that element. Undeveloped Fire, for instance, means a reduced affinity for the power-raising stage and less chance of succeeding at, say, protection spells. Secondly, the characteristic defense mechanisms can operate to hinder and misdirect you. When can you be absolutely sure that a problem exists "out there" somewhere, rather than in your own makeup? If you are prone to projection, you may be fooling yourself. Similarly, are you truly being contacted by discarnate entities or is this a case of introjection?

These problems of personality and perception can be problematic enough for the solitary practitioner, but they can wreak havoc in joint and group work. On the subject of group working, it can be seen that an understanding of the different strengths and weaknesses of group members can mean the difference between harmonious and difficult operations. It could be argued, in fact, that the most effective group is composed to take account of the elemental makeup of its members. Clearly the advice to "know thyself" is sound. This is good advice whatever you undertake, be it magic or anything else. To be undermined by external forces is bad enough; to be undermined by your own failings is nothing short of tragic.

If you read the descriptions of all the types, you will notice a degree of similarity between some of them. This is to be expected, given that many of them are related by virtue of their shared elemental makeup. In the first place, there are four broad types corresponding to the principle elements. These are:

Earth Centaur, Wodwose, Gryphon

Air Pegasus, Unicorn, Firebird

Fire Dragon, Phoenix, Wyvern

Water Chimera, Mermaid/Merman, Satyr

Each of these elemental types shares the characteristics of the primary element, but each differs from the other according to the nature of the secondary element. For instance, Chimeras have Fire as the secondary element, while Merfolk have Air in second place and Satyrs have Earth. These secondary elements provide the personal qualities that differentiate the primaries.

If the primaries are regarded as siblings, then similar elemental pairings produce cousins. For instance, Unicorns have Air in primary position and Water secondary; Merfolk have Water in primary position and Air secondary. It follows that these types will have common features although they differ in that Unicorns are principally intellectual while Merfolk are principally emotional by nature. There is a corresponding similarity between Firebird and Dragon, Satyr and Centaur, Chimera and Wyvern, Gryphon and Pegasus, Phoenix and Wodwose.

These related types are not necessarily similar, however. Each individual will score slightly differently on each element, producing a unique profile. Two Wyverns with Pegasus shadows will have much in common, but if their scores for each element are very different they will also exhibit striking differences. If one has a very strong Water secondary while the other's Water score is relatively low, then the former will show the associated characteristics of empathy and intuition more spontaneously and more often as a feature of his or her personality. These characteristics will still form part of the other person's personality, but they will be much less evident.

The importance of considering the score differences along with the overall Q score when reading the descriptions should be clear from this example. If you find that the secondary element is relatively weak, then the qualities of that element are less applicable to you and the consequent modification of the functioning of the primary element is less pronounced. In cases where there is a particularly strong primary, the qualities of that element will be expressed more purely. Similar considerations apply to interpretation of the shadow profile. If the tertiary element is relatively well-developed, then obviously its associated characteristics will be less problematic, and the weight of the shadow's limitations will fall on the weakest element.

Two graphic examples are given here. Note in these examples that both individuals are Unicorns with a Wodwose shadow. In example one, however, the secondary Water element is almost as well developed as the primary Air, hence this person will exhibit almost as many watery as airy qualities. His or her Fire and Earth, on the other hand,

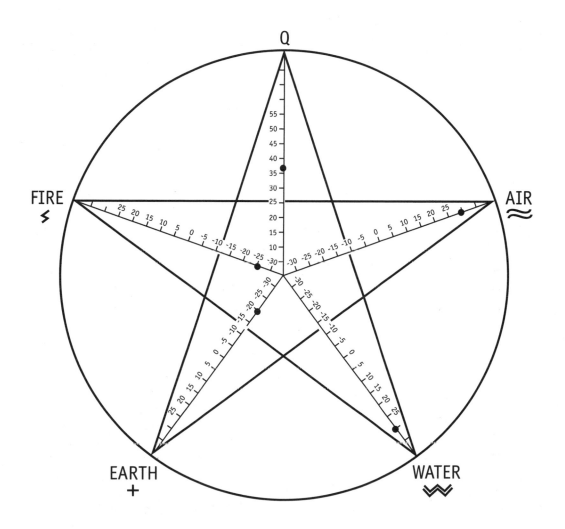

Diagram 4a: Example 1

are very undeveloped and deep in shadow, so these elements will manifest most readily in their negative aspect and unconsciously.

In the second example, the secondary Water is relatively undeveloped, hence this person's watery qualities will be much more muted. His or her Earth element is quite undeveloped and will operate unconsciously and negatively for the most part. The tertiary Fire, however, is relatively well-developed and is in fact almost as well developed as the secondary Water. Hence the fiery qualities of this individual will be far more evident and less problematic, and he or she may even exhibit some of the qualities of the Firebird to some extent.

Thus, although there are just four elements in this system, giving rise to twelve primary types and twelve shadows, the separate scores for each element indicate individual differences among the broad description of types. Moreover, the possibility of type development through the various techniques described later means that the types are dynamic rather than static. If you discover that you have a relative weakness in one function, you can work to develop it.

Although the magical personality types are associated with the astrological signs and houses by virtue of the triplicities, identification of a given type is not calculated from birth data but from the adult personality pattern as revealed through the Magical Personality Questionnaire (MPQ). When I first constructed this system I was struck not only by how well the signs and houses agreed with my descriptions but by how well more modern descriptions of personality types agreed with both.

This should really come as no surprise, however, since as we have seen that modern theories, such as that of Eysenck, began with investigations of the personality descriptions given by the ancients. Jung's typology consisting of four temperaments correlates with the ancient system of four elements. Indeed, much of Jung's thinking, as well as his theory of types, has been adopted by occult circles and New Age enthusiasts.

Jung had an encyclopedic knowledge of symbolism from different times and cultures and he regarded astrology as the "summation of all the psychological knowledge of antiquity." Small wonder, then, that there is a high degree of correspondence between ancient and modern systems. We are, after all, talking about enduring patterns of human relating that remain essentially the same despite differences of time and place.

The interesting thing about astrology as it relates to the magical personality types is that astrology is well known and readily available to anyone in a way that modern

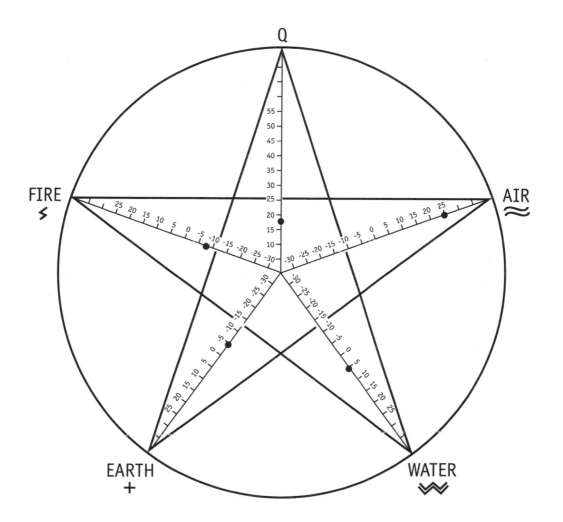

Diagram 4b: Example 2

personality inventories are not. It is also a very rich system that can in some ways enhance and expand the magical personality types. In the first place, you can assess the balance of elements in your natal chart to see to what extent it agrees with your type as identified via the MPQ. You may find that the two systems agree quite well.

Diane's magical personality profile is shown here. As you can see, she is a Mermaid with a Wodwose shadow. However, the balance of triplicities in her horoscope would seem to indicate a Wodwose or Phoenix primary with a Unicorn shadow. The apparent contradiction can be explained by following the reasoning of such astrologers as Arroyo (1975). Essentially this means considering the *quality* of the planetary placements rather than the sheer *quantity* of elements.

Following this technique, we see that Diane's ascendant is in the only Water sign—the caring, nurturing sign of Cancer. The ascendant is one of the four most important indicators of basic chart interpretation and refers to the outward expression of the personality. Air is fairly well-represented in the chart but is given greater emphasis by the fact that the moon, another of the four primary indicators, is in Aquarius along with Mercury. Fire is strong in the chart; indeed, the sun is in Aries. However, the sun is afflicted by three planetary aspects involving Earth signs. This helps to explain the undeveloped Fire in Diane's profile.

Finally, a note on gender. For ease of reading, the masculine pronoun has been used throughout, but this does not mean, for instance, that all Unicorns are male—they are also female, just as Merfolk can be male as well as female, and Satyrs female as well as male. In fact, each type can be male or female because these are characterological descriptions that can apply equally well to either gender, so do not be distracted by the gender of the mythical beast that represents yours, whichever that happens to be.

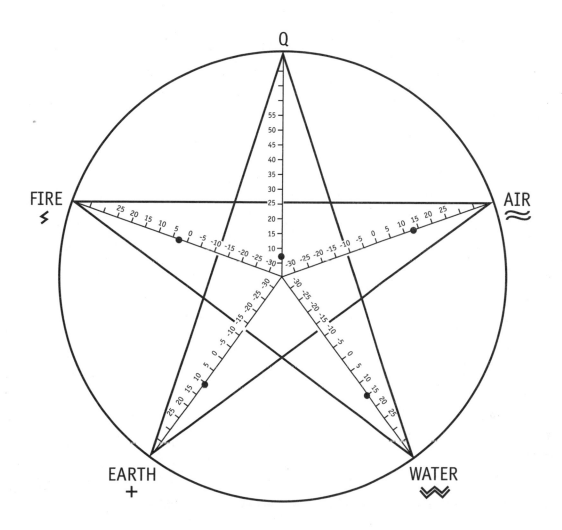

Diagram 5: Diane's profile

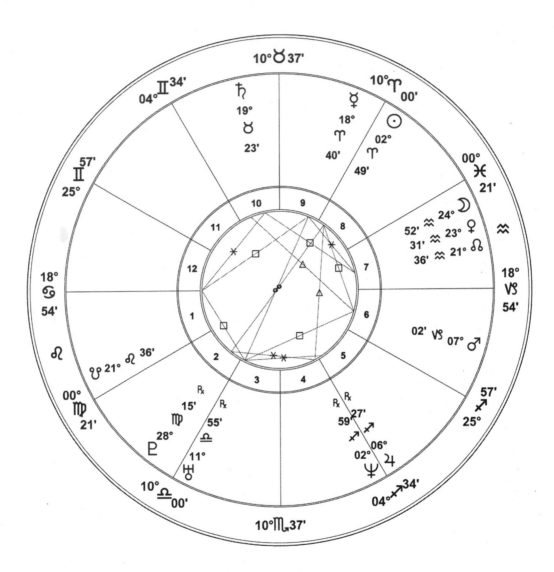

Diagram 6: Diane's horoscope

6

THE TWELVE PRIMARY TYPES

The following descriptions are those of personality factors that are relatively well-developed and conscious. They represent the most salient aspects of the self, as viewed by the self as well as the other.

There is global recognition of the four elements as a means to self-understanding. We are most familiar with the ancient Greek concept of bodily humors, but more recently Native American spirituality has revealed a strikingly similar system. It is generally less well-known that the elements also feature in the spiritual systems of Tibet, India, China, Japan, and Sumeria.

Because the elements concerned are relatively well-developed, the following descriptions are couched in positive terms. However, it is worth noting that strengths can potentially be weaknesses. An overdeveloped or overused elemental quality may mean that the associated characteristics come to dominate the personality. This may not only be at the expense of other elements, but at the expense of an interest in developing other elements.

"Missing" elements may then be sought through relations with others who possess those characteristics that are lacking in the self. Some relationships are symbiotic in nature for this reason, but it may just as easily be the case that such relationships are actually unbalanced and unequal.

This book is about enhancing magical practice via the balancing of the four elements so that the personality is integrated and whole. It follows that to balance the elements as far as possible will have a positive effect on the life of the individual concerned that goes far beyond magic to affect relationships, work, and play.

Please note that some characteristics are shared by different types, and consequently descriptions are the same in some respects. This reflects the fact that different types are comprised of the same elements in different order, e.g., Unicorns are Air and Water, Merfolk are Water and Air. Remember that the emphasis lies with the first element in each case.

Quick Reference Table of Primary Types

Primary Element	Secondary Element	Type	Page
Air	Earth	Pegasus	57–61
Air	Water	Unicorn	62–67
Air	Fire	Firebird	68–72
Fire	Air	Dragon	73–77
Fire	Earth	Phoenix	78–82
Fire	Water	Wyvern	83–87
Water	Fire	Chimera	88–92
Water	Air	Mermaid/Merman	93–98
Water	Earth	Satyr	99–103
Earth	Water	Centaur	104–109
Earth	Fire	Wodwose	110–114
Earth	Air	Gryphon	115–120

Pegasus

Air with Earth

Keywords: Intellectual, rational, curious, radical, imaginative, persistent, achieving, practical, realistic, conventional, restrained, organized, thorough, dependable, perfection, equality, cooperation, shy

Correspondences: Sylph, light yellow, mint, geranium, willow, sapphire, copper, elephant

In myth, Pegasus was born from the blood of the mortal gorgon Medusa in the temple of Athena, goddess of wisdom. Unbridled passion was thus reborn as creative passion. Originally born of earthly material, Pegasus eventually became a stellar constellation. Pegasus therefore symbolizes the need to transcend materialism in favor of the spirit. This symbol of an earthy beast with the ability to fly reflects the Air and Earth combination of this type. The common feature of Air types is their intellect and their facility for communication. The manner of expression of the primary Air element is indicated by the secondary element, in this case Earth. Pegasus is associated with the astrological sign Libra, hence purposeful, unidirectional movement. The intellect is employed especially in matters requiring fairness and justice, and there is a strong interest in social needs. Pegasus is also associated with the seventh house, hence equal partnerships and cooperation.

Typically for an Air sign, Pegasus *theorizes* about love and relationships, and believes that somewhere there is a perfect partner. Likewise, there ought to be perfect balance in relationships. The creation and maintenance of harmony is of central importance, and they hold themselves accountable if this does not happen. Pegasus is a perfectionist and he must get everything right. Only perfection is acceptable, hence the adherence to a notion of an ideal partner. They believe that, in theory at least, there can be fairness and equality for all. They are not always able to see how the world actually is. Consequently they can become disillusioned and either fail to take advantage of "imperfect" opportunities, or they move rapidly from job to job, relationship to relationship, in an attempt to find what they are looking for.

Pegasus does strive to produce order, however, rather than just running away from chaos. The secondary Earth also makes them practical in nature that, combined with the aesthetic sensitivities of Air, gifts them with artistic ability. Pegasus hates ugliness as much as he hates disorder, and he is often excellent at both interior and exterior design, making his home and garden places of inspired beauty. The practicality of Earth combined with the idealism of Air means that Pegasus needs goals, even if these are somewhat lofty and unattainable.

Because of his need to relate well to others, Pegasus has a chronic fear of being disliked. In his attempt to avoid offending anyone, he may seem uncommitted and hence untrustworthy. He is in fact trying to maintain interpersonal harmony and his good standing with other people. Choosing between people and their conflicting opinions is extremely difficult for Pegasus. At the same time, both Earth and Air are the least person-centered of the elements, and Pegasus can come across as cold, clinical, and aloof. This can be an advantage in the world of business and in other relationships where a certain amount of detachment is called for. In these circumstances Pegasus is highly valued for the qualities of impartiality and scrupulous fairness.

Pegasus' excellent organizational ability ensures that they can be trusted to see things through to a successful completion. They have an unusual ability to see both the wood and the trees. They are very independent and will perform extremely well if given free rein and not interfered with. They are often highly original and idiosyncratic in their approach to a job, which can make them seem like rebels or poor team players. Their single-minded search for the truth of the matter can make them appear argumentative, especially if their social skills are poorly developed, and as we have seen this is often the case because the sociable Water and Fire elements are relatively weak. Even the most sociable Pegasus will find the company of others very draining, and will need to be alone for periods of time in order to "recharge."

In common with all the primary Air types, Pegasus is essentially intellectually curious. They are imaginative and artistic, especially in connection to the word, both spoken and written. The strong Earth component, on the other hand, may incline them to a form of visual art such as sculpture, or perhaps song, while their skill with shape and color have already been alluded to. Communication is a central motivation for Air types, but Pegasus tends to be shy and aloof despite his focus on relationships, and he may prefer to express ideas and feelings indirectly to an audience rather than directly to people around him. He may fantasize about grand schemes that are designed to unify society through the power of ideas and the truth as he perceives it.

Alternatively there may be an interest in communicating with beings from other realms, perhaps through channeling or mediumship. He may feel misunderstood and isolated, but at the same time relish being unconventional and even eccentric.

With Earth as the secondary element, Pegasus is more practical than the other Air types. The idealism of Air is tempered by the tough-minded and pragmatic qualities associated with Earth, and indeed they are more likely to produce tangible results from their ideas. However, there is a fundamental conflict between the radical nature of Air and the conservative nature of Earth. This can be resolved if underlying theoretical considerations suggest practical applications, and if the applications can be seen to work in practice. The Air and Earth combination can therefore make Pegasus very productive and original in their chosen fields.

A major limitation that does arise from this elementary pairing is the doubling up of the insularity and potential tactlessness that is a feature of both Air and Earth. A solitary nature combined with poor social skills can produce a person wrapped up in his own world that few are able to penetrate or understand. This is fundamentally at odds with Pegasus' inherent need to relate meaningfully and on an equal footing with others, and a great deal of inner tension can result. Pegasus types might try getting into the habit of demonstrating that they appreciate other people by praising good work or by mentioning their good qualities. Don't assume that other people already know what you think and feel—they like to hear it said.

All three Air types have strong powers of visualization, the importance of which for magical work cannot be overemphasized. Pegasus, as a consequence of the associated Earth element, is generally able to visualize strong, solid images, and by extension to create potent thought-forms. This ability to link the unseen world of spirit with the world of matter is very strong, and there is great potential for successful manifestation of projected aims. Mental images become embodied and durable under the influence of the physical nature of the Earth element, guided with precision by the powerful imagination and laserlike focus conferred by the principle Air element.

The value of this ability in magical work is obvious, not only in ritual, where the ability to visualize clearly opens a gateway to the Otherworld and permits the creation of powerful thought-forms. It also enhances the perception of spirits, possibly by means of clairsentience (because of the strong Earth component), but also via clairvoyance and clairaudience. Pegasus is also potentially skilled in the ability to divine past, present, and future using such diverse techniques as casting runes or scrying, and by other means where the use of physical aids is at a premium.

Like the other Air types, Pegasus tends to be curious and open to novel experiences, but they are unwilling to accept things as given and require a fair measure of objective proof of the validity of their experiences and for the ideas presented to them. Again, because of the Earth component, Pegasus is especially keen that experience and ideas are not accepted blindly. Pegasus in particular is intolerant of ambiguity and uncertainty, preferring that everything is clearly explained and logical. Naturally in occult activities this requirement is sometimes difficult to fulfill, and Pegasus may consequently have some trouble accepting what can happen and what does happen.

Their natural inclination to discipline and order may not always fit well with occult work, but these qualities can definitely be regarded as strengths with respect to magical procedures. Pegasus is not only disciplined and organized, but also imaginative. For these reasons they are able to devise and create effective rituals from scratch, and perform them with great skill. These could easily involve creative, artistic modes of expression, including dance, song, or verse. The facility with language coupled with the characteristic clarity of thought also confers an ability to write precisely defined goals, clear affirmations, and pithy incantations, all of which are a requirement of successful magical working. Their creative urge combined with practicality can also predispose them to making their own ritual tools, such as wands, staves, pentacles, and robes.

The foregoing indicates some of the main areas in which Pegasus is likely to excel magically. These include communication with Otherworld entities, particularly for the purpose of obtaining information about their world and this one, and obtaining information about things past, present, and future. There is also an associated facility for obtaining guides from the unseen realms. In addition, magic related to the Air element promotes success in intellectual work, such as examinations and in learning generally. It can also enhance artistic ability and bring inspiration, especially with regard to the written word.

For Pegasus there are also the magical aims associated with the relatively strong Earth element. Naturally the degree of success with respect to this element will depend on exactly how well-developed it is. The magical aims associated with this element refer to the things of the earth in general, including money, wealth, location of lost items, protection of physical objects and of whole buildings, healing, work and career matters, and work with plants and other growing things.

Unicorn

Air with Water

Keywords: Intellectual, rational, curious, radical, imaginative, persistent, achieving, sensitive, insightful, warm, careful, emotional, supportive, thoughtful, perceptive, altruistic, unconventional

Correspondences: Sylph, yellow, marjoram, lavender, ash, agate, quicksilver, parrot

The unicorn is a composite creature that combines the head and body of a horse with the legs of a deer and the tail of a lion. Its most outstanding feature is its single, spiral horn. Unicorns are usually pure white in color, and it is this along with its horn that associates it with purity. The single horn also indicates the unity behind appearances, and thus it is a symbol of the divine soul. Although Air relates to the conscious mind, the Water secondary links this type with the unconscious and the psychic. The unicorn is therefore symbolic of this type because of the connection between wisdom and altruism, active imagination and unconscious symbolism. The common feature of Air types is their intellect and their facility for communication. The manner of expression of the primary Air element is indicated by the secondary element, in this case Water. Unicorn is associated with the astrological sign Gemini, hence intellectual expansion and movement. There is also a gift for acquiring factual information and using it to generate novel ideas. Unicorn is also associated with the third house, hence the mind, discrimination, communication, relatives, friends, and short journeys to strange places.

As an Air type, the Unicorn is not generally person-centered but the Water secondary ensures that they have a marked sociable streak. Unicorns are therefore more at ease in company than Pegasus and less dominant than Firebirds. Depending on how well-developed the secondary Water element is, they can be quite talkative and witty, especially when in the company of people with whom they feel at ease. This does not mean that they are outgoing by nature—often they are very shy. This is one of the apparent contradictions of the Unicorn, and one of the things that can be confusing for other people. In addition, the volatility of Air allied with the changeable nature of Water can make Unicorns unpredictable.

It is true that they quickly become bored and they typically have many interests that they rapidly move between. To those who do not know them, they can seem superficial because of this, but the reality is that they often possess deep knowledge of numerous complicated subjects. In fact, Unicorns love to develop a broad range of knowledge because they realize that everything connects to everything else. They are consequently easily distracted and not particularly good with details. Although basically good-natured, they possess a cutting wit that is not easily forgotten by those on the receiving end of the Unicorn's rapier tongue.

In common with the other Air types, Unicorns have a gift for writing, especially highly imaginative, creative work. They love to play and are in many ways childlike. They seem to have a good rapport with children for this reason. They regard education as a duty and in any case love to share their vast knowledge, sometimes to the irritation of others, who are just not interested in arcane information. They are socially astute and are often able to discern the motives and problems of other people to an unnerving degree. This could empower them to do a lot of harm were it not for their high ethical standards.

In keeping with the qualities of the mythical beast itself, people of this type are therefore gentle and compassionate, although they can be stubborn. They almost feel obliged to do something for society or even for humanity as a whole. Particularly to this end they constantly have an eye on the future while considering present possibilities. They can often inspire others to follow their lead even though they have a reputation for being dreamers. However, they need to be free to fantasize and it can be both confusing and frustrating for others when Unicorns seem suddenly to lose interest. What has actually happened is that the Unicorn's attention has momentarily shifted elsewhere. This does not mean that they have no intention of continuing where they left off, just that they started something else for the moment. Consequently they are often surrounded by half-finished projects that they will just as suddenly pick up and complete.

Like the other Air types, Unicorns are intellectually inclined and curious about everything, however obscure. Because of the strong Water component, these types are even more volatile, imaginative, and fey than either Pegasus or Firebird types. Communication is equally important to Unicorns as it is to the other Air types, but is more likely to focus on beings from other realms than it is with either of the other Air types. There is the same desire to bring people together through shared aims and ideals, although this desire is likely to remain a pleasant dream for this type because they are so changeable and impractical. Even so, there is a warmth and desire to be of service conveyed through the Water element that serves the Unicorn's social aims and makes them good friends once the initial shyness has been overcome.

Unicorns, then, are logical, rational, and objective, but also unconventional and even eccentric in a way that is more likely to be reflected in their appearance than in the case of either Pegasus or Firebird types. Just as their social and moral reasoning often flies in the face of contemporary mores, so their choice of dress also defies current fashions. They may appear to be odd fish and rather bizarre, but this is not calculated; it is rather a natural consequence of their lack of interest in conforming to social expectations. Unicorns are individualists who please themselves first in matters that are their own concern. They see no reason to conform to the dictates of others unless there is a logical reason or unless it is for the common good. Note that Unicorns are not anticonformist, because this would suggest that they are striking a pose. Unicorns do not much care what society at large has to say about personal choice, because "personal" is exactly what it is and should be.

True to their essentially airy nature, Unicorns base their decisions on available facts rather than on how people feel about it. However, the strong Water component prevents them from being tactless and completely insensitive to how others actually are affected by their decisions. They do not, therefore, tend to fall into the kind of error that Pegasus often does by being too objective, too forthright, and hence unpopular. Their diplomacy is aided in fact by the airy quality of being able to clearly see both sides of an argument, and they do their best to remain scrupulously fair. They can still be let down, however, by their basic mistrust of the subjective and intuitive (even their own), and a potential for intellectual snobbery that can infuriate others. As ever, check your scores on the indicator to see just how strong this component is in your own profile.

The qualities of Air that conflict with those of Water have been alluded to already, namely emotional versus intellectual, objective versus subjective, and rational versus intuitive. Even so, Unicorns find that they themselves embody these conflicting qualities and, as with all the other types, they must find ways to accommodate their own contradictions. Unicorns have an advantage insofar as they have an appreciation of theories that seek to explain these contradictions and the means of dealing with them. If the shadow side is not especially active, then these inner tensions are unlikely to be problematic. Difficulties may arise when the individual is stressed—then the contradictions may come to the forefront.

Unicorns are impressionable and intuitive despite the primary Air qualities, and hence much affected by their surroundings. Their emotional natures require both the focus and containment provided by the rational and constrained Air element to prevent them from being emotionally unrestrained or too wishy-washy. A feature of both Air and Water is a concern with bringing people together—on the one hand with unifying ideas, and on the other by breaking down barriers to harmony. Unicorns are therefore likely to favor if not follow social movements that are intended to bring people together with a common focus and for the good of humanity as a whole.

In their positive mode of interaction, Air freshens Water, and the intellect prevents the emotions from submerging the individual in oversentimentality. At the same time, the empathic nature of Water serves to prevent the intellectual nature of Air from making the subject insensitive. Thus the Unicorn type is able to understand and accept the emotional reactions of other people, and indeed his own reactions. Naturally there has to be an optimal balance for this to work and it can be evident that some Unicorns, although they share the same elemental primaries, will differ in the extent to which this balance is achieved.

Unicorns are somewhat utopian in outlook due to their altruism and desire to be of service to others. However, although they are compassionate and firm believers in cooperation, these urges tend on the whole not to be directed at individuals so much as humanity generally. Even so, they hate conflict, and the airy coolness combined with watery tact mean that they have excellent powers for smoothing over trouble to restore harmony to tense situations. Their diplomatic skills mean that they have a natural ability to act as mediators and negotiators; moreover, all parties can trust them to be fair. They are good listeners, thoughtful, and make excellent confidantes. Due to their strong moral sense, they may go so far as to put the interests of others before their own, especially if this is perceived to be for the common good.

Unicorns and Mermaids are the most psychically gifted of the twelve types because of the combination of the inceptive psychic qualities of the Air element with the receptive and intuitive psychic abilities of Water. As a result both combinations have enhanced psychic potential, but for Unicorns there is a greater clarity and indeed objectivity conferred by the prominence of Air. The greater intellectualism of Unicorns may even lead these types to rationalize psychic experiences or to dismiss them in some other way, especially if these types have already entered into one of the scientific fields of study.

Unicorns are intuitive and have a natural psychic sense due to the influence of Water, but they remain predominantly rational due to Air in the primary position. Depending on the relative strengths of these elements, they can be cautiously accepting of psychic phenomena or completely dismissive of all occult matters, at least consciously. For Unicorns who remain open to psychic experiences and recognize them as such, there can be intense and frequent paranormal experiences related to precognition, clairvoyance, clairaudience, and mediumistic events.

Unicorns may still have to cultivate these powers to some extent, but their critical natures equip them to discern real from imaginary encounters and signs. They are acutely aware of the possibility of self-deception and lapsing into wish fulfillment. Unicorns, because of the empathic qualities inherent in Water coupled with the communicative facility conferred by Air, are often gifted seers and counselors, particularly within a structured system such as astrology. Unicorns may also be gifted in terms of augury, especially in relation to such natural phenomena as the behavior of birds and randomly spoken messages.

As far as the practice of magic is concerned, Unicorns have the same principle advantages of the other Air types, namely the powerful imagination essential to visualization, the portal to the Otherworld. They also have a talent for clarity in formulating clear, realistic goals, appropriate affirmations, and succinct incantations. They have an ability to maintain a laserlike concentration for sustained periods of time that ensures good otherworldly contact, and due to the influence of the Water element this link with the Otherworld and its inhabitants can be greatly empowering. Another positive quality following from the humane nature of Air coupled with the empathy inherent in Water is the desire to help beings from the other side, possibly in the role of medium.

The foregoing indicates some of the main areas in which the Unicorn is likely to excel magically. These include communication with Otherworld entities, particularly for the purpose of obtaining information about their world and this one, and obtaining information about things past, present, and future. There is also an associated facility for obtaining guides from the unseen realms. In addition, magic related to the Air element promotes success in intellectual work, such as examinations and in learning generally. It can also enhance artistic ability and bring inspiration, especially with regard to the written word.

For Unicorns there is also a facility to succeed in aims associated with the relatively strong Water element. Naturally the degree of success achieved will depend on how well-developed this element is. The magical aims associated with Water include healing the emotions, bringing people together in love and harmony, forming and strengthening partnerships, promoting meditation, enhancing otherworldly contact, learning about past lives, and developing psychic ability.

Firebird

Air with Fire

Keywords: Intellectual, rational, curious, radical, imaginative, persistent, achieving, energetic, dominant, enthusiastic, active, impulsive, sociable, detached, unconventional, progressive

Correspondences: Sylph, golden yellow, chives, lemon, hawthorn, amethyst, lead, eagle

The symbol of the firebird reflects the primary Air element in combination with Fire. In myth, the firebird is both human and avian, thereby fusing the qualities of the two. In its avian form, the firebird is a splendid and magical creature that fights evil and helps others. In some respects it is similar to the Native American thunderbird, which is also a powerful sky creature that fights evil. Firebird therefore symbolizes the marriage of human wisdom and divine power. The common feature of Air types is their intellect and their facility for communication. The manner of expression of the primary Air element is expressed through the secondary element, in this case Fire. Firebird is associated with the astrological sign of Aquarius, hence the implication of great potential energy ready to be directed at a target. There is also a strong humanitarian aspect connected to universal principles such as equality. Firebird is also associated with the eleventh house, hence social reform and group activities.

Firebird's intellect is focused on social needs and universal ideals. As an Air sign, he is often fuelled by visions of a scientific utopia in which the brilliance of modern technology and scientific progress are intelligently employed to abolish human want and misery. To him this line of reasoning is obvious, and he is continually frustrated and annoyed by what appears to be the stupidity and short-sightedness of the human race. He displays an abstract love of humanity but is also fiercely supportive of individuals who reveal a similar ethical position. In keeping with the Firebird myth, this type has a great deal of integrity, and they direct their fiery energy to upholding the truth and opposing evil.

Firebirds are both curious and inventive, even ingenious. They see endless possibilities for putting human intelligence to good use for the benefit of all. Once they have produced a sound idea, it becomes a plan and can become a weapon in the crusade against injustice. However, they develop new ideas all the time and frequently fail to follow up on the ones they have already produced, often expecting other people to make them work. Their enthusiasm and drive is such that they can often inspire people to do just that. Their failure to produce something tangible is a constant source of disappointment to them, yet these are quickly replaced by the lure of fresh and exciting challenges. They are impatient to see things develop and are not afraid to take quite big risks rather than watch everything grind to a halt. They are tireless and always active, mentally if not physically. They hate routine of any sort and become stressed by limitation, so they perform best in creative and problem-solving jobs where they have plenty of autonomy.

Their interpersonal style is characterized by a directness that can be mistaken for arrogance or even aggression, when really they are simply expressing themselves with their customary force. They love to engage in passionate discussion, to challenge people's views and to be challenged in order to hammer out the truth of a matter. They can seem inflexible because of their tenacity and urgency in upholding their views, and can even be quite intimidating at times. The primary Air enables them to see the validity of both sides of an argument, however, and they can quite easily argue both sides if they have equal merit.

Despite being person-centered by nature, they are directive and sometimes aloof, and insightful but not giving full weight to the importance of people's emotions. At the same time their essential humanity and sense of justice would cause them to be greatly upset if they discovered that they had unwittingly hurt anyone. Firebirds can hurt others badly and they know exactly where a person's Achilles' heel is located, but as a rule they avoid inflicting pain on anyone.

From a magical perspective, the Air and Fire combination imparts great drive and enthusiasm to these areas of working and an intense ability to focus on the task in hand for sustained periods. However, the power available to Firebirds as a consequence of the secondary Fire element tends to mean that long, drawn-out operations are generally unnecessary. Visualization will be powerful, vivid, and quite potent in affording access to the other realms.

Firebirds are the most volatile and driven of all the Air types, and have a particular need to join with others in the pursuit of common goals. Being Air types, however, Firebirds nevertheless remain somewhat apart from others and do not readily become intimate with people, preferring to work with others as colleagues rather than as close friends. As ever, much depends on the relative strengths of the elemental makeup; it is not a given that Firebirds (any more than Dragons) are stand-offish. Indeed, as Air types, Firebirds are heavily influenced by the need to communicate on as many levels as possible, not only with other people but also with beings from other realms.

Firebirds have a particular interest in working relationships and with bringing together people with shared goals. They tend to play a rather more managerial role in these concerns and can be quite charismatic. An alluring air of mystery can then develop around this person, who is so sure and decisive yet so self-contained and apart. Firebirds are not elitist so much as careful with whom they form close bonds. Despite their wide social contacts, Firebirds are often paradoxically alone. This is because they prefer to engage on an intellectual rather than on an emotional level. Consequently they are often slow to take a relationship into deeper, more personal territory. It can take a lot of persistence to break into the Firebird's personal world, but the effort is usually worth it, for it is then that the full range of his passion and energy is revealed, along with his insatiable curiosity and extraordinary wealth of knowledge. For his part, he will love to engage with someone who can share his breadth of vision and vitality.

Although Firebirds, in common with the other Air types, are logical, rational, and objective, the strong Fire element ensures that they are unconventional and open to radical ideas that fly in the face of established social and moral authority. Air and Fire are the two most radical of the four elements, so Firebirds and their Dragon cousins enjoy upsetting the status quo and confronting what they regard as outworn, outmoded, and obstructive belief-systems as long as there is a rational and viable set of alternatives.

For this same reason they also tend to be zealous and forthright in condemning prevailing social and moral structures, which can make them unpopular with older and more conservative people. These same qualities can make them seem fearless if not reckless, and rather heroic in the eyes of their peers. These are the people who stand up in public and speak for the majority when the time arrives. Their facility with language, in both written and spoken form, can be inspiring. They do not seek change for its own sake, however; Firebirds genuinely want constructive change, and their objectivity allows them to appreciate both sides of an argument. Fire and Air are highly compatible in the right mix. Fire enhances airy idealism. The strong Fire component, on the other hand, can make Firebirds overzealous and rash if it is allowed to flare up uncontrolled by the rationalism of Air.

Fire also imparts optimism, flexibility, and an adventurous spirit that, in combination with the primary Air qualities of curiosity and radicalism, make for a dynamic personality. Fire is the life force as well as the power to transform, and of course magic is all about the power of transformation. However, Fire is also a spiritual power, so there is likely to be a strong religious and moral feature to this type. This aspect of Fire, coupled with the ethical, humanistic, and highly structured qualities associated with the primary Air element, may incline Firebirds toward some kind of organized spiritual activity, such as some form of high magic.

This would probably suit Firebirds' need for structure in a group activity that focuses on the goal rather than the participants. They may even feel unable to work without the companionship of others, who effectively bring the enterprise to life for them. Fire indicates extraversion, hence group activities, but the primary Air indicates introversion, and hence a goal-centered attitude. The essential insularity of the primary Air will normally win out unless the secondary Fire is particularly strong. Even then, the emphasis will be on the goal rather than the people.

The Firebird can be an assertive individual who may stubbornly resist what he perceives to be decisions based on poor logic made by those in authority, and he may even take over the leadership under certain circumstances. They are not natural leaders in the way that Dragons are, but they do have great talent for motivating others. They often require a position of authority, if not a position of power, which is fine if they are supportive rather than tyrannical in this role. There can be problems if there are other members of the group with major Fire components in their personality. In this case, there can be a vying for position that gentler types will wish to avoid. A group can fragment and split up amid acrimony if this conflict cannot be resolved amicably. Firebirds, however, are unlikely to push matters to this extreme because it would not be logical to destroy the group, since this would prevent the goal from being achieved.

The foregoing indicates some of the main areas in which Firebird is likely to excel magically. These include communication with Otherworld entities, particularly for the purpose of obtaining information about their world and this one, and obtaining information about things past, present, and future. There is also an associated facility for obtaining guides from the unseen realms. In addition, magic related to the Air element promotes success in intellectual work such as examinations and in learning generally. It can also enhance artistic ability and bring inspiration, especially with regard to the written word.

For Firebirds there is also a facility to succeed in aims associated with the relatively strong Fire element. Naturally the degree of success achieved will depend on how well-developed this element is. The magical aims associated with Fire include enhancing physical health, success in competitive pursuits including legal actions, spiritual and artistic development, protection of people and property, and sex magic.

Dragon

Fire with Air

Keywords: Energetic, dominant, enthusiastic, extravert, active, impulsive, sociable, achieving, intellectual, rational, curious, radical, imaginative, persistent, assertive, jovial, moral, exploring

Correspondences: Salamander, orange, chervil, sandalwood, oak, topaz, tin, horse

The dragon is one of the most familiar of all mythical beasts and it is found in many different cultures the world over. The dragon stands for the life force and for time itself, including the power of transformation. In the Orient especially it was a benign creature that indicated wisdom and prosperity. In the West it was regarded with fear but it still often guarded great treasures. The symbolism of the dragon as a fiery creature with the ability to fly, used here to represent the combination of Fire and Air, should be obvious.

Of course Water and Earth dragons (wyrms) are also common in folklore, but in general dragons are conceived as having wings and breathing fire.

The common feature of Fire types is their energy and enthusiasm. The manner of expression of the primary Fire element is indicated by the secondary element, in this case Air. Dragon is associated with the astrological sign Sagittarius, hence self-development, personal growth, and kinetic energy that has great power to transform once it has reached its goal. There is also a strong association with religion and moral systems that inform societal values. Dragon is also associated with the ninth house, hence expansion beyond common boundaries, whether geographical or intellectual.

Dragons are essentially dynamic people who thrive on calculated risks. They are the most likely of the types to go out on a limb and take a chance on something. This kind of behavior can make them appear either as bold and fearless or rash and impulsive, depending on the other person's perspective. Being attracted to life's range of adventures, they will readily engage in business partnerships and love affairs but will hate to be constrained by any of them. For Dragons, novelty is what gives life its spice. They are noble and dignified and genuinely expect their partners to share their love of freedom and variety. They are in fact extremely loyal to those they care about, but they also need to respect their own urge for expansion. The complaints from other people regarding their apparent selfishness leaves them mystified, frustrated, and hemmed-in, and their legendary tempers can suddenly flare up into a dramatic fiery display.

Control is a key concern for Dragons. They generally don't want to control others any more than they want to be controlled by others. Dragons like to see people progressing as autonomous, creative individuals like themselves, and everyone together as a socially interwoven whole. They do, however, like to adopt a directive, managerial role if something needs to be done, either at work or socially. They do this because of their natural leadership qualities combined with their gift for logistics. They are confident and convinced that they are doing the right thing, and this alone justifies to them their position as leader. They do not respect indecision or what they perceive as weakness. On the other hand, they expect or even demand that people challenge them, otherwise how will things progress in the right direction? Progress is a social phenomenon and activities demand joint input.

Thus, what often appears to be arrogance can in fact be a robust attitude that is essentially goal-directed and for the good of all. Dragons are as critical of their own shortcomings and failures as they are of others', and usually more so. This critical attitude, combined with their sense of urgency, can make them seem angry and intimidating even if they are neither. The key to understanding Dragons is their love of life's challenges and the exhilaration they feel for being part of life. It is therefore apposite that this type should be symbolized by the dragon, since they regard life as a force to be wrestled with and controlled, otherwise life will control them.

As primarily Fire types, Dragons are impulsive and passionate, energetic and driven to succeed. Their enthusiasm for a chosen project can be boundless and they really can get things done quickly as long as this passion for the work burns bright. On the other hand, their enthusiasm can quickly burn itself out before they manage to achieve their aims unless they are able to cultivate a certain amount of detachment. For this reason they need fuel in the form of new projects, and a containing factor to ensure that both direction and sense of purpose is maintained. For Dragons this second factor is the Air element that feeds the primary Fire and confers clarity of thought and persistence. Fire, for its part, purifies Air and maintains the focus on high ideals. Dragons are the most intellectual of the Fire types.

Dragons are open-minded, flexible in approach, adventurous, open to change, and optimistic. Like Firebirds they are dynamic individuals, but with Fire in primary position Dragons are more so. They look forward to the future with a degree of enthusiasm that may be daunting to others. They themselves are not put off by challenges but see them rather as opportunities to change and progress. They do not view the future as a source of anxiety so much as an exciting plunge into the unknown. They are intrigued by what they regard as a world of limitless possibilities and enjoy fantasizing over the potential of creative projects. They are not concerned much with details, preferring to work with the broad picture and letting others fill in the fine points.

It is at this point that the aforementioned loss of interest may occur, because where Firebirds have ideas in which they invest their energy, Dragons are principally active and energetic and may adopt ideas and causes. Dragons are champions of the underdog. They hate injustice in all its forms and are driven by moral imperatives to help those who can't fight for themselves. This hatred of social injustice is a feature of the Firebird also, but Dragons are less likely to theorize about social reorganization than to leap into action over it.

They are sociable and warm, extraverted, ebullient, the life and soul of the party, but they can sometimes be overbearing. Their interest in others is particularly focused on directive activities, hence they naturally assume roles as leaders. They can be quite charismatic and larger than life. It may even seem to others that they fill the room by sheer force of personality, and they almost inevitably galvanize people into action because of their compulsive drive and optimism. Everything seems possible with a Dragon about. If the secondary Air is particularly well-developed, they can readily back up their plans for action with faultless logic. They positively thrive in the company of others and will tend to feel listless and apathetic if alone for too long. Their faults include a short temper, being too pushy, and acting without due care and attention to possible consequences. Dragons with a strong Air secondary will tend to be more restrained and thoughtful, thus avoiding these problems.

With a strong Air in second place, many of the qualities of Fire are enhanced and burn brighter, so to speak. Thus Dragons are volatile, imaginative, artistic, and even visionary. The Air component imparts an urge to communicate their ideas and opinions, possibly through some form of artistic expression. The passion of Fire combined with the intelligence of Air means that Dragons often have strong powers of oratory. Their dramatic flair and artistic nature mean that they could be performance artists, such as actors or musicians. Unification of people through a shared sense of humanity is a prime focus of Air types, and Fire is a spiritual element, so Dragons will often wish to bring people together under the aegis of combined religious and humanitarian structures.

The Air component makes Dragons logical, rational, objective, and self-disciplined, all qualities that are valuable restraints on their essentially fiery nature. These airy qualities do not, however, detract from the influence of the Fire element, since Air emphasizes the Dragon's unconventional outlook and openness to experience. Air provides the wide range of interests for Fire's enthusiasm to work on, plus an openness to others' ideas. Although Dragons tend to base their decisions on available facts rather than on feelings, they are not usually prone to the tactlessness that sometimes besets the Air types because their warm, sociable nature largely precludes this. Even so, they can be scorching in their direct manner. Few will forget an exchange with an overheated Dragon!

Fire needs fuel to keep it alive, hence the natural desire for those with Fire prominent in their personality to enthusiastically seek out stimulating experiences. Dragons frequently seek out these experiences as means to self-development. Fire is the most spiritual of the elements, and magical activities may serve this end. Fire is also associated with creativity, and this too may serve as a means to self-development as well as self-expression. Fire as a symbol of creativity appears to be paradoxical given the destructive nature of this element. The creative aspect comes from the passionate, dynamic, progressive nature of the element—when we talk about the Fire element, we are not talking about actual combustion in the physical sense, we are talking about a basic quality.

This quality is energy in a broad sense, spiritual energy to be more specific. While actual fire burns things and reduces them to ashes, the Fire element does not destroy things but transforms them. This is the value of Fire in the practice of magic—it provides the transformative power of change that magic is designed to effect. Fire is general rather than specific, which is one reason it needs Air to keep it on track. Like Air, it is also associated with a liking for fantasy and imagination, relativity rather than absolutes. This is why Dragons have such great potential to be powerful magicians.

The foregoing indicates some of the main areas in which Dragon is likely to excel magically. These include enhancing physical health, success in competitive pursuits including legal actions, spiritual and artistic development, protection of people and property, and sex magic.

For Dragons there is also a potential to succeed in aims associated with the relatively strong Air element. Naturally the degree of success achieved will depend on how well-developed this element is. The magical aims associated with Air include communication with Otherworld entities, particularly for the purpose of obtaining information about their world and this one, and obtaining information about things past, present, and future. There is also an associated facility for obtaining guides from the unseen realms. In addition, magic related to the Air element promotes success in intellectual work, such as examinations and in learning generally. It can also enhance artistic ability and bring inspiration, especially with regard to the written word.

Phoenix

Fire with Earth

Keywords: Energetic, dominant, enthusiastic, extravert, active, impulsive, sociable, achieving, practical, realistic, conventional, restrained, organized, thorough, dependable, adaptable, purposeful, transforming

Correspondences: Salamander, red, rosemary, cinnamon, holly, tiger's-eye, gold, lion

As the bird that is consumed by fire and that rises anew from its own ashes, the phoenix is a symbol of transformation. Consequently it is associated with new life and inspiration, the rising sun and continuity through change. The phoenix does not die, because death is final, whereas the cycle of change from one state to another is continuous. Phoenix is about evolution and revolution and is life-affirming. The image of a creature that burns and is reborn from ashes indicates the combination of Fire and Earth.

The common features of the Fire types are energy and enthusiasm. The manner of expression of the primary Fire element is indicated by the secondary element, in this case Earth. Phoenix is associated with the astrological sign of Leo, hence to self-expression, authority, and pride. As a consequence they are strongly associated with leadership and managerial roles. Phoenix is also associated with the fifth house, hence creativity and the use of available resources as a means to self-expression and social development.

The Phoenix exhibits the characteristics of the Fire signs and is therefore energetic, active, confident, and assertive. They are goal-centered, forward-looking achievers who thrive on challenge. They set high standards for themselves and others and display a steady determination in getting things done. Their aims are typically ambitious and sometimes extravagant, and their manner tends to veer toward the theatrical. Whatever they do is done with great style and grandeur. They have a great love of physical beauty and the arts, and enjoy entertaining and putting on a fabulous display.

The secondary Earth component imparts a pragmatism and a realistic attitude that ensures Phoenix is extremely productive in his chosen field of operations. He is able to work long and hard with unflagging enthusiasm in a way that would exhaust most other people. The pragmatism of Earth means that Phoenix is a doer, and the Fire primary means that they like to see immediate results from their efforts. They learn best from doing rather than from books or teaching, and they are quickly bored by routine. They enjoy creative enterprises and crave challenge. Like their Wodwose cousins, they often like to work with tools and their hands. They are indefatigable problem-solvers with a strong analytical tendency based on information derived from their physical senses. With this incisive capability allied with their practicality, they are adept in the process of transforming materials and situations.

Phoenix is extraverted, passionate, and adventurous. The Earth secondary, on the other hand, confers qualities such as caution and conservatism that are somewhat at variance with the essential nature of the primary Fire element. This can result in a certain degree of tension. Where it is in the nature of Fire to push forward, it is in the nature of Earth to pull back. On the face of it, this seems to be an unsatisfactory combination, but the two elements usually work to complement each other. Earth serves to ground Fire, providing necessary boundaries and restraint without which Fire would rage uncontrolled. Fire, on the other hand, informs and stimulates the productive qualities inherent in Earth. It is rather like controlled energy found in the intense, steady heat of a furnace from which the things of the Earth emerge anew.

Phoenix may therefore be particularly attracted to artistic forms such as painting and sculpture. The strong moral aspect conferred by Fire means that they are also attracted to various forms of community service, possibly combining the two to provide community art works, including theater. The association with Leo means that there is often a desire to inspire others through art and especially theater, which may be employed to convey a higher, spiritual message.

In common with the other Fire types, Phoenix is impulsive and passionate, energetic and driven to succeed. As the symbolic beast suggests, he is frequently concerned with transformation of the self but also transformation of others, often in dramatic ways. The passion that they display during these brief but spectacular events is a great force that cannot be prevented from making itself felt. If they are unable, due to circumstances, to go through this regenerative process, they will either change the circumstances to suit their needs or contain the accumulated energy until it can find an even more spectacular release. Change will occur one way or another, whether others like it or not.

It is a common feature of Fire types that their interest in a given project tends to be short-lived. This is less true of the Phoenix than of the other Fire types, because the Earth element's influence fixes the energy of Fire so that direction and purpose are maintained. Phoenix may begin a process of transformation dramatically and then work steadily until the change is achieved, or he may work intensely on something that is then dramatically presented as a fait accompli. This tenacity and endurance is due to the influence of the secondary Earth element acting as a containing factor that maintains the Phoenix's direction and sense of purpose. Phoenix's interests are not, therefore, dissipated in a brief explosion of activity but are steadily maintained up to completion.

The value of a strong Earth for these types cannot be overstated. The principle effect of Earth, not surprisingly, is to ground the Fire so that the spectacular visions that are characteristic of that element can more easily find practical expression in a durable form. Caution, which is not characteristic of Fire, is very much a characteristic of Earth. This caution is one of the reasons that Phoenix's power is able to build up. Earth also confers a consideration for detail that the other Fire types do not usually display, although Phoenix too is more concerned with the big picture than with the finer points.

Yet Earth is typically conventional and conservative by nature, not keen on change for its own sake—but of course Phoenix is not aiming at change for its own sake, but for the good of themselves and others. This change is always connected to a vision of a better future because Phoenix is enthusiastic about radical overhauls. They enjoy fantasy and creativity and are intrigued by the possibilities conjured up by the imagination. Phoenix is therefore a rare creature for many reasons, not least because they live in the future by virtue of their creative vision, and in the present by virtue of their pragmatism.

Achievement is therefore the primary focus for Phoenix, and this cannot be managed with premature action and bad planning. As has already been stated, the Earth element provides the restraint that makes the energy of Fire so effective in this type. It also provides the pragmatism that allows ideas to become reality—without this, the passion of Fire is aimless and does not lead to lasting change. Earth also provides the focus that allows tasks and larger projects to be completed efficiently, rather as an intense flame is directed onto a job in the welding process. In this way Earth serves to rein in Fire's expansive nature by directing it toward specifics in a purposeful rather than haphazard way.

In common with the other Fire types, Phoenix is keen to work with others, but for this type there has to be a specific end in sight. Like the other Fire types, they are independent, assertive, and have good qualities of leadership, but they are more restrained and hence less likely to overwhelm others with their forceful characters. They may, however, be so goal centered that they adopt a utilitarian approach to group members that could make them unpopular and that, in the end, is counterproductive. Nevertheless, they exhibit the characteristic Fire traits of sociability and warmth. They thrive in the company of others, but due to the Earth component they are more able than either Dragons or Wyverns to tolerate periods of seclusion. However, like the other Fire types, they can be short-tempered, pushy, and thoughtless.

For the magician, the benefits of this combination are the energy that derives from Fire coupled with the grounding that derives from Earth. This means that there is great potential to produce lasting, concrete effects. Fire is energy, and this is what the magician is attempting to manipulate. If the magician has Fire (energy) as a primary characteristic, then there is a natural affinity with the agent of change. When coupled with the pull of the Earth element to realize one's aims, the implications are clear. Fire not only provides the raw energy for magic, it provides a strong spiritual, moral, and creative drive too. Earth provides a strong organizing principle as well as a practical, manifesting quality. As the image of the Phoenix implies, this type has great power to transform things from one state of being to another—this is occult power. Of course, the other two elements, Water and Air, have their own magical qualities that are essential to the magical process, and the strength of these also needs to be taken into account (see the appropriate shadow sign for details).

The foregoing indicates some of the main areas in which Phoenix is likely to excel magically. These include enhancing physical health, success in competitive pursuits including legal actions, spiritual and artistic development, protection of people and property, and sex magic.

For Phoenix there are also magical aims associated with the Earth secondary. Naturally the degree of success possible with respect to these aims depends on exactly how well-developed this element is. Magical goals associated with Earth relate to the things of the Earth itself, notably money, all forms of wealth, the physical body and healing thereof, property, the land, growing things, work and career matters, the protection of rooms, buildings, and objects, the discovery of lost objects, and the manifestation of otherworldly entities.

Wyvern

Fire with Water

Keywords: Energetic, dominant, enthusiastic, extraverted, active, impulsive, achieving, sensitive, insightful, sociable, warm, careful, emotional, supportive, thoughtful, urgent, passionate, spontaneous

Correspondences: Salamander, magenta, tarragon, cedarwood, hazel, ruby, iron, ram

The wyvern is similar in appearance to the dragon except that it has just two legs. Wyverns were traditionally harbingers of war, and their ferociousness was legendary. For this reason they were also seen as protectors and powerful, if volatile, companions. The wyvern is used to symbolize this type because it is essentially a fiery creature associated with strong emotional power that links it with Water.

The common feature of Fire types is their energy and drive. The manner of expression of the primary Fire element is indicated by the secondary element, in this case

Water. Wyvern is associated with the astrological sign of Aries, hence to personal development and the growth of the self. Their leadership potential is most frequently directed at initiating new enterprises. Wyvern is also associated with the first house, hence self-awareness, identity, and personal willpower.

Wyvern is courageous and idealistic and likes to ally himself with a cause that expresses his personal interest and passion. He derives a sense of self-esteem and personal satisfaction from upholding the rights of the oppressed. However, where Dragons are interested in helping oppressed groups, Wyverns are interested in fighting for downtrodden individuals. In this way the moral force of Fire is allied to the compassion of Water to produce a personal champion. Wyverns place a high value on friendship and loyalty, and expect other people to reciprocate in kind. They can be as passionate an enemy as they are friends, especially to those they have given their trust. Woe to those who betray a Wyvern!

They have high moral standards, in accordance with the Fire primary, and are not the type to suffer fools gladly. Nevertheless, they are warm-hearted and tolerant as long as their ethical principles are not contravened, and they love friendly competition such as sports, at which they excel. They are socially adept and insightful. They are always active and energetic, like all Fire types, and are extremely gregarious. Along with their close cousin the Chimera, the Wyvern is the most outgoing and sociable of all the types, but because of the Fire primary he is even more dynamic than the Chimera.

Wyvern's activities are therefore focused on interpersonal matters. They not only make people feel needed and valued, they feel their own sense of value from doing so. Hence much of their time is spent in actively encouraging others to either develop their potential or to do their best with the task in hand. They are therefore excellent motivators and are well liked as leaders. They are firm believers in helping others to help themselves. They love social events and are the proverbial life and soul of the party. They are great lovers of display and can be outrageously over the top. They not only work hard and play hard, they have an apparently endless supply of energy with which to do so, and other people often have difficulty keeping up. They typically have a wide circle of friends from diverse backgrounds. Some of their more staid friends can be amazed at the weird and wonderful people that Wyverns suddenly introduce them to.

It follows from this that Wyverns like people-centered, open-ended work and activities in which their natural warmth and bonhomie can be best put to use. They will be crushed by routine, repetitive work—assuming they can be made to do it in the first place. They have a talent for improvisation and need both the challenge and the freedom to be creative on their own terms. The relatively weak Earth means that they are not very practical themselves but they are good at delegating. They may even have difficulty slowing down and relaxing at times, but they can become depressed if not actively engaged in something. They can similarly become depressed and lethargic if they spend too long by themselves. They thrive in the company of others and seem to be energized by interacting with other people.

This is another pairing of apparently antithetical elements that may result in tension if the balance is not right. The urge for self-development can on occasions conflict with the urge to help others, and their need to express themselves can make them seem too overbearing at times. They want other people to develop as well and are not always able to comprehend others' problems and limitations, especially if Air is very undeveloped. When they do understand they are very supportive, however. The two contradictory elements may complement each other in various ways. The dryness of Fire can have the effect of limiting the potential oversentimentality of Water. The caring aspect of Water can damp down the harshness of Fire. The spiritual quality of Fire combined with the nurturing quality of Water can lead these types into social and religious work. Thus, Fire provides the driving force, Water the direction.

As with the other types, the secondary element is of great importance in determining where the energy of the primary element is spent. Water relates to the emotions, to sensitivity, and nurturing. Depending on the relative strength of this secondary element, Wyverns can be intensely active in the service of others. They can also be very sensitive to their surroundings, impressionable, and intuitive. Their emotional natures combined with the predominant Fire can, however, make them feared as well as loved. Both elements are highly volatile, unpredictable, and formless, and Wyverns demonstrate this by suddenly boiling over with fury during which they can be devastating with their vituperative outpourings. They need then to be left alone for a good long time in order to cool down. Fortunately they can also take a long time to reach this fearful state, and timely intervention can remove the threat if others are perceptive enough to notice it.

Wyvern's interest in others is not quite as focused on directing them as it is with the Dragon and Phoenix. However, they can easily assume leadership roles and will secretly enjoy the position, although they may also complain about it. Since both Fire and Water are person-centered elements, Wyverns are very attracted to group work and may even find it impossible to work alone. At the same time, Wyverns are independent creatures and do not as a rule cultivate dependency in others, preferring to encourage similar levels of self-help. They are valuable members of a group for this reason, and because they are both inspiring and achievement oriented they tend to get things done, usually by encouraging others to do things for themselves.

This in fact is one means by which Wyverns reveal their power to transform. They are open-minded, flexible in approach, adventurous, open to change, and optimistic. They enjoy initiating new projects for everyone to work on. They are very imaginative, often artistic, and often benefit society in some way. They are altruistic, sympathetic, and firm believers in cooperation and reciprocation. Despite their fearsome tempers they hate conflict and paradoxically have excellent powers for defusing tense situations.

Due to the Water component they are essentially good-natured, kind, and extremely perceptive. They are less likely to put themselves out for others than their close cousin the Chimera, because they would view this as helping others to be helpless. Consequently they are not easily taken advantage of. They regard the "help others to help themselves" doctrine as a moral necessity. They are thoughtful and good listeners for a time, until they begin to think that you are just talking about your problems rather than overcoming them. If this is the kind of encouragement you are looking for, then Wyverns make excellent confidants, but they will not tolerate helpless whining.

Wyverns have a special interest in mythology, dreams, the occult, and spiritual matters. Water confers a dreamy quality that may make them seem somewhat unfocused and irrational at times. They are essentially forward-looking and intrigued by possibilities, but they can also be a little wistful about the past, although they are unlikely to dwell on it. The combination of Fire and Water makes them very much given to developing a rich fantasy life, the extent of which can astound others. It is from these depths that their creative projects emerge like the fabulous beasts themselves, and often fully formed.

Wyverns hate things to be fixed and known. They much prefer a high level of ambiguity so that they have plenty of room to maneuver. Like the other Fire types they are not overly concerned with details because they prefer the freedom of the broad canvas. Without the dampening power of Water, they can act without due care and attention to the possible consequences of their actions.

Much of the foregoing gives the impression that Wyverns are concerned exclusively with the manifest world of form. Even their rich fantasy lives appear to be geared toward the physical world, and this seems from the above to relate almost entirely to human relationships. While Wyverns do indeed focus very much on the social and interpersonal range of experience, they are also keenly aware of the world beyond this one. As I have implied through reference to religious and occult interests, Wyverns are often engrossed in psychic and spiritual activities because these aid them in their self-definition and self-development. These areas of interest often provide the forum for their interpersonal exchanges and their social lives. Wyverns also have a potential for developing psychic abilities, and their desire to interact with the entities of this world can be rivaled by the desire to contact beings from the other side.

The magical strengths associated with Fire relate especially to the energy used in magical operations—that is, magic itself. Water is intuitive, feeling-based, and receptively psychic, hence Wyverns have great potential as magicians through this combination of the active and passive principles of occult activity. Water confers the ability to cross the boundaries between the worlds, leading to the manifestation stage of the magical process, while Fire represents the energy that is brought to bear on the desired aim. The implication of this combination of Fire and Water for magic is obvious, and further indicates how these two "irreconcilable" elements can complement each other. The limitations of Wyverns in successful magical practice relate more to the relatively undeveloped elements Earth and Air, and as ever the relative strengths of these elements should be assessed.

The foregoing indicates some of the main areas in which the Wyvern is likely to excel magically. These include enhancing physical health, success in competitive pursuits including legal actions, spiritual and artistic development, protection of people and property, and sex magic.

For Wyverns there is also a facility to succeed in aims associated with the relatively strong Water element. Naturally the degree of success achieved will depend on how well-developed this element is. The magical aims associated with Water include healing the emotions, bringing people together in love and harmony, forming and strengthening partnerships, promoting meditation, enhancing otherworldly contact, learning about past lives, and developing psychic ability.

Chimera

Water with Fire

Keywords: Sensitive, insightful, sociable, extravert, careful, emotional, supportive, thoughtful, energetic, dominant, enthusiastic, active, impulsive, achieving, protective, nurturing, intuitive

Correspondences: Undine, violet, lemon verbena, jasmine, vine, moonstone, silver, crab

The chimera is a composite beast of lion, goat, and dragon. For some time it has had a bad reputation as the ravaging monster that was destroyed by Bellerophon, who was mounted on Pegasus, although Graves asserts that this refers in fact to the destruction of the shrine of the triple-moon goddess. Graves also suggests that the chimera was a calendar beast representing Fire and Water and thus sun and moon that together ruled the sky (Graves, 1961). Chimera began life as the divine daughter of the storm god

Typhon and the snake goddess Echidne, and was eventually demonized by later cultures. A chimera in modern parlance has come to mean something wildly fanciful, a product of a fevered imagination.

The common features of Water types are their imagination and empathic natures. The manner of expression of the primary Water element is indicated by the secondary element, in this case Fire. Chimera is associated with the astrological sign of Cancer, hence Water in its dynamic, most volatile aspect. This emotional volatility is most often centered on the home and family. Chimera is also associated with the fourth house, hence with personal security and the domestic base.

Chimeras are emotionally insecure, which explains why they are so protective of their home and family. Emotional and physical security are the twin aims that Chimeras seek to achieve. Like Water types generally they are changeable and moody, but more so as a consequence of their security issues. They have a strong sense of community and a desperate need to belong, not only within their own family but within a surrogate family of their own choosing. This can be a circle of friends, a social organization, or a set of work colleagues. Like Wyverns, they can't stand to be alone, and even short periods of solitude can make them feel drained, depressed, and anxious. This need to have a home among their chosen people makes them extremely sensitive to what others think of them. As a result they are extremely perceptive and insightful. Like Wyverns, they are extremely good at motivating others and seem to know what others want to achieve.

Chimeras display dreamy, imaginative qualities that can be nothing less than inspired. Moreover they have the drive and organization to turn their dreams into reality. They tend to be the most warm, sociable, and well liked of all the types, and they are extremely sensitive to rejection. They can hold a grudge for years and bide their time until the opportunity to exact revenge presents itself. Fortunately they are rarely rejected because they have excellent social skills and a lively sense of humor, so they are good company and popular. Even so, they like to receive praise and affirmation of their value to others. Harmonious relations and surroundings are a prerequisite to relaxation. They make decisions on the basis of how people will feel about things rather than whether their decisions are logical or break any rules.

Chimera is therefore associated with the emotions, especially as they relate to protection and security, not just of the family but of those held to be close. It is apparent from this that while the Wyvern also exhibits a strongly protective stance toward others, in this case it is less personal and more closely linked with notions of fairness and justice. Chimera, on the other hand, is concerned about protecting family and friends.

In some ways, therefore, Chimera is potentially more dangerous an adversary than is the Wyvern, since Chimera's battles are personal. Like the Wyvern, the Chimera is another of the types that is characterized by a combination of apparently irreconcilable elements, here Water and Fire, and indeed there may be tensions in the personality as a result. Water is the most salient element in this type, and this relates to the emotions, to intuition, reflectivity, sensitivity, and psychic ability. Water and Fire can complement each other though; Fire reduces Water's tendency to maudlin sentimentality, while Water takes the potentially damaging heat out of Fire's urgency.

The Fire secondary imparts impulsiveness, passion, energy, enthusiasm, and ambition. It also serves to energize the primary Water element so things get done rather than being left to drift. Chimeras are interested in people, myths, dreams, the occult, and art, not necessarily in that order. These interests follow largely from the principal Water component but the enthusiasm to pursue them comes from Fire, without which they would remain pleasant ideas.

Since both Water and Fire require containment to ensure that the individual stays on track, they generally require external factors to set limits for them. Fortunately one of the main characteristics of Chimeras is their sociability, so they are almost always working with people who can help to keep them on target. Admittedly this can be quite tiring for the other people involved because of the Chimera's tendency to constantly drift, or sometimes race off course. At the same time Chimeras have both a strong moral and social sense and so usually make an effort not to disappoint.

In this way Chimeras are able to achieve their aims, which tend to be socially worthy. They are sociable and warm, and less likely to be overbearing than their cousin, the Wyvern. They can assume a leadership role if necessary but they prefer the role of independent helper. They thrive in the company of others and typically are outgoing, cheerful, and high spirited. Chimeras share the same basic traits as the other Water types: they are emotional, sensitive, impressionable, and extremely intuitive, hence much affected by their surroundings and the moods of other people. The emotional nature of the Chimera requires both focus and containment, much like the Water that symbolizes them, otherwise they can be emotionally unrestrained or too wishy-washy. Fire provides the dynamism and drive without which the Chimera could too easily stagnate for lack of vigor.

Chimeras therefore have the "soft" qualities associated with the Water element, but these are mitigated by Fire in second position. They are person-centered, like Wyverns, but tend more toward helping others as a priority and developing themselves in connection with these activities. For the Chimera, other people tend to come first but only as long as he is not being taken advantage of. If he does sense that he, or indeed others, is being abused in some sense, the savagery of his response is breathtaking. Like Wyverns, Chimeras can boil over suddenly, but they take much longer to provoke—unless their protective instincts are aroused, and then they are fearsome adversaries. On the other hand, they take much longer than Wyverns to cool down, and indeed they may never recover from the upset. This is a consequence of their emotional sensitivity.

Chimeras are principally concerned with bringing people together and breaking down boundaries to harmonious exchange. They are eager to be of service to others but like Wyverns they encourage people to help themselves as far as possible. Chimeras tend to have far more patience and to offer more in the way of sympathetic assistance, although they too will suddenly lose patience with people who do not seem to be making an effort. They are compassionate but also firm believers in cooperation and reciprocation. They hate conflict and will go as far as they can to avoid it. They have excellent powers of diplomacy that can restore peace to tense situations.

Much of the foregoing gives the impression that Chimeras are concerned exclusively with socializing. Even their rich fantasy lives appear to be geared toward this end. While Chimeras do indeed focus very much on the social and interpersonal range of experience, they are also keenly aware of the world beyond this one. It is a feature of Water types especially that they have strong potential for psychic abilities. This is part of the reason why they are so fey and otherworldly—they may well be in contact with entities from the other side without even knowing it. They can have hunches, premonitions, or predictive dreams, especially about family and friends. Chimeras thus have a strong psychic sense and are often engrossed in occult and spiritual activities. As with Wyverns, these areas of interest often provide the forum for their interpersonal exchanges and their social lives.

In magical terms, the Chimera's strengths lie primarily with the qualities inherent in the Water element. These include the psychic link between the worlds that enables the power of magic to be directed toward the Earth plane, where results can manifest. There is also a facility with attracting forces that are in harmony with the work in progress, quite apart from a natural ability to bring harmony and a sense of well-being into the proceedings. In addition, Water confers a methodical attitude and a tendency to carefully considered actions. The addition of Fire is particularly valuable in this regard since it overcomes the natural inclination derived from Water to be too cautious. Fire also provides the very energy of magic itself, plus the optimism that one's aims will succeed. Taken together, this combination of elements makes for a potentially powerful magician, depending to what extent the elements of Earth and Air remain undeveloped.

The foregoing indicates some of the main areas in which Chimera is likely to excel magically. These include goals associated with the primary Water element, such as healing the emotions, bringing people together in love and harmony, forming and strengthening partnerships, promoting meditation, enhancing otherworldly contact, learning about past lives, and developing psychic ability.

For Chimeras there is also a facility to succeed in aims associated with the relatively strong Fire element. Naturally the degree of success achieved will depend on how well-developed this element is. The magical aims associated with Fire include enhancing physical health, success in competitive pursuits including legal actions, spiritual and artistic development, protection of people and property, and sex magic.

Mermaid/Merman

Water with Air

Keywords: Sensitive, insightful, sociable, extraverted, careful, emotional, supportive, thoughtful, intellectual, rational, curious, radical, imaginative, persistent, achieving, impressionable, receptive, subtle

Correspondences: Undine, blue, sage, pine, ivy, pearl, tin, dolphin

The mermaid or merman is just one of the many types of water spirit found the world over. They are one of the more familiar fabulous creatures and are easily recognized for having the upper body of a human and the tail of a fish. In myth, they are mediators between the world of nature and the human world. This creature therefore symbolizes this type because it is primarily of the mysterious Water element, but also has a significant amount of the rational Air in the personality. Thereby a creature is produced that combines the lower with the upper worlds, an essentially feeling type that has the benefit of intellectual qualities usually attributed to the human realm. In this way the primary emotional qualities are to some extent balanced by reason.

This type is more objective than the other two Water types, and also more likely to have psychic ability. Being principally receptive by virtue of the Water primary, they may have potential as mediums and to act as channels for the discarnate beings that wish to contact the living. For the same reason they make good counselors because of their empathic ability allied to an ability to understand, listen, reflect on what is said, and to clarify meanings. Merfolk are also interested in teaching. They are associated with the astrological sign Pisces, which represents Water combined with Air as free-floating vapor. This indicates the strong psychic and intuitive nature of the Mermaid/Merman type, and there is also a marked concern for the environment. Merfolk are also associated with the twelfth house, hence the unconscious, deep understanding of self and others, secrecy, and freedom versus limitation.

Merfolk are more subdued than Chimeras but less insular than Satyrs, and although generally warm and friendly they can seem distant and in a world of their own at times. Much of this is due to their sensitivity to nebulous impressions of the passing moment combined with a sense of the infinite. Being attuned to both the present and to "time-less time" explains their powerful intuitive capabilities. Merfolk are probably the most unworldly of all the types. Sometimes they have such a tenuous link with the physical world that they have an indefinite sense of personal identity, and come close to merging with the Otherworld.

As a consequence, they can seem infuriatingly passive and indecisive. For their own part, they are extremely tolerant of other people because they can see that everything is relative and that there are no absolutes. This is the source of their mystical outlook and their unconventional views and behavior. For the same reason, they have a powerful humanitarian attitude that often combines with strong religious leanings. They consider it to be their duty (and that of everyone) to help others, although their undifferentiated outlook often means that they want to help humanity, indeed the world at large, rather than individuals. They are acutely sensitive to suffering and can feel others' pain as if it were their own. To them all life is sacred, and they do not necessarily value humans more than they value animals or even plants.

Although often regarded by others as strange or even a bit mad, they are also perceived as being wise. The strong Air component imparts a keen intellectual ability, such that they are rarely thought of as stupid. In fact they can even intimidate others with their ability to immediately understand complex problems and swiftly come up with radical and imaginative solutions. The combination of Water and Air gifts them with a boundless imagination and spontaneity that can startle people due to the originality of thought that suggests great depth beneath the moonshine surface. Merfolk refuse to recognize boundaries or limits and are consequently free to entertain bizarre possibilities, then rationally discriminate among them for pertinent answers.

Merfolk and Unicorns are the most psychically gifted of the twelve types because of the combination of the receptive and intuitive qualities of Water with the more direct and inceptive qualities of Air. Both are likely to possess clairvoyant abilities, but for Merfolk there is greater spontaneity and naturalness in keeping with their affinity with the mystical nature of the Water element. While Unicorns usually have to make contact with the hidden realms, Merfolk are already half in the hidden realms. Consequently the inhabitants of the Otherworld readily come to the Mer individual and do not need to be actively contacted. Moreover, they are less likely to dismiss their occult experiences with rationalist explanations, but still retain enough discriminative ability to tell genuine contacts from self-delusion. On the other hand, fear may cause these types to draw back from psychic phenomena or to dismiss them in some way, especially if these types have been discouraged from acknowledging these experiences.

The primary Water element ensures that Merfolk are basically warm, but this quality is to some extent in conflict with the Air secondary. The influence of this element disinclines them from forming close relationships until the other person has become well-known to them. A relational pattern is played out that is the reverse to that of Unicorns; for Unicorns, people are generally kept at arms' length before eventually being claimed virtually as kin. Merfolk tend to confuse people by accepting them readily at first, only to become cool again while they assess them properly. Even so, there is a warmth and desire to be helpful as a feature of the Water element that serves the Merfolk's social aims and makes them good friends once the other person has come to terms with their apparent capriciousness.

Merfolk are intensely curious about the world (and the Otherworld) in general, and also have intellectual leanings that can be at variance with the subjectivity of the primary Water element. Because of the associated Air element, Merfolk are even more changeable, imaginative, and fey than either Chimeras or Satyrs. Communication by different media is important to Merfolk, and it is as likely to be directed toward contacting beings from other realms as it is toward people in this one. Even so, Merfolk are good at relating with people as long as their sense of security isn't compromised. There is a desire to bring people together through shared aims and ideals, as there is with the other Water types. This aim is likely to remain a pleasant dream for Merfolk because they are so volatile and impractical.

Merfolk, then, are unconventional and even eccentric in a way that is more likely to be reflected in their appearance than in the case of either Chimeras or Satyrs. They dress to please themselves rather than to be either conformist or anticonformist. They are true nonconformists, and may appear to be odd fish and rather bizarre as a consequence. Like Unicorns, Merfolk are individualists who please themselves first in matters that they regard as entirely their own concern. They see no reason to conform to the dictates of others unless it is for the common good, plus they have both social grace and sufficient tact to prevent them from upsetting people through insensitivity or selfishness. Most of the time, however, they will simply be unaware of just how eccentric their appearance and behavior makes them seem.

In keeping with their essentially watery nature, Merfolk base their decisions on how they will affect people's feelings, since these are held to be paramount. This does not mean that they are blind to the available facts, however, since the strong Air component ensures that they pay close attention to the logic of the situation. They do not tend to fall into the kind of error that Satyrs sometimes make by being too objective, or that Chimeras sometimes make by being too forthright. Their diplomacy is aided in fact by the airy quality of being able to clearly see both sides of an argument, and they do their best to remain scrupulously fair. They can still be let down by their basic preference for the subjective and intuitive, however, because eventually they have to come down on one side or the other and they hate to disappoint anyone.

The qualities of Air that conflict with those of Water have been alluded to already, namely emotional versus intellectual, objective versus subjective, rational versus intuitive. Even so, Merfolk find that they themselves embody these conflicting qualities and, as with all the other types, they must find ways to accommodate their own contradictions. Merfolk have an advantage insofar as they reject absolutes and regard all things as relative. This means that they are more able to integrate within themselves the apparent contradictions of their composite nature, much like the bizarre notion of a creature that is half human and half fish. Paradox is not an unsettling obstacle to Merfolk, although their contradictory nature can be problematic for those around them.

Despite being opposites in some ways, Air and Water are also complementary. Air keeps Water fresh, and the intellect prevents the emotions from submerging the individual in oversentimentality. At the same time, the empathic nature of Water serves to prevent the intellectual nature of Air from making the subject insensitive. Thus the Mermaid or Merman, like the Unicorn, is able to understand and accept the emotional reactions of other people, and indeed her or his own reactions. Naturally there has to be an optimal balance for this to work, and it can be evident that some Merfolk, although they share the same elemental primaries, will differ in the extent to which this balance is achieved.

Merfolk hate conflict because it upsets their delicate emotional equilibrium. Fortunately their Water-derived tact combined with their airy coolness means that they have excellent powers for smoothing over trouble to restore harmony to tense situations. This is an ability Merfolk share with Unicorns, but where Unicorns' diplomatic skills and reputation of fairness makes them good at sorting out differences of opinion, Merfolk work better with feelings. They are good listeners, thoughtful, and make excellent confidants. They work best on a one-to-one basis, but they can also work with couples or even small groups. Like Unicorns, their strong moral sense may cause them to put the interests of others before their own if this is restore harmony.

Like Unicorns, Merfolk have an excellent potential for divination, especially of the more unstructured, fluid type. Hence scrying—possibly using a pool of liquid in the way Nostradamus is alleged to have done—or noting the action of natural phenomena such as drifting clouds or the movement of birds. Water is the element most closely associated with symbolism because of its direct and nonverbal mode of expression. Thus, Merfolk have a facility for using pictorial methods of divination, such as the tarot, or dream interpretation, or reading the random patterns made by tea leaves. Sometimes messages will simply come to them out of the blue, as if spoken by invisible helpers.

As far as the practice of magic is concerned, Merfolk have the same principal advantages of the other Water types, namely the powerful intuition, psychic receptivity, and emotional depth of expression that permits effective receipt and direction of magical force. By virtue of the strong Air secondary, they also have a talent for powerful and effective visualization that effectively opens the way to the Otherworld. In addition, they may be accomplished in formulating clear goals and appropriate affirmations, depending on how well-developed the Air secondary is. They do not generally need to strive to maintain otherworldly contact since they have good contact ordinarily. Merfolk therefore have great potential for occult work; the extent to which the other elements in the personality are developed will indicate to what extent they can be powerful magicians.

The foregoing indicates some of the main areas in which Merfolk are likely to excel magically. The magical aims associated with the Water element include healing the emotions, bringing people together in love and harmony, forming and strengthening partnerships, promoting meditation, enhancing otherworldly contact, learning about past lives, and developing psychic ability.

For Merfolk there is also a facility to succeed in aims associated with the relatively strong Air element. Naturally the degree of success achieved will depend on how well-developed this element is. Goals associated with Air include communication with Otherworld entities, particularly for the purpose of obtaining information about their world and this one, and obtaining information about things past, present, and future. There is also an associated facility for obtaining guides from the unseen realms. In addition, magic related to the Air element promotes success in intellectual work such as examinations and in learning generally. It can also enhance artistic ability and bring inspiration, especially with regard to the written word.

Satyr

Water with Earth

Keywords: Sensitive, insightful, sociable, extraverted, careful, emotional, supportive, thoughtful, practical, realistic, conventional, restrained, organized, thorough, dependable, penetrating, intense, incisive

Correspondences: Undine, turquoise, basil, myrrh, reed, malachite, iron, snake

The satyr and the gentler faun are nature spirits most closely associated with woodlands and with the god Pan. The image of the satyr is derived from the Mediterranean, but versions of the same creature can be found in Russia and in the British Isles. Shakespeare's Puck is one such being. Satyrs and fauns are notoriously hedonistic and are associated with music, dancing, and the full range of sensual pleasures. These activities, particularly the sexual ones, were held to be natural and enjoyable by the ancients, and it seems that in recent times a similar attitude prevails now that the repressive legacy of the Judeo-Christian heritage is being shaken off. The Satyr is therefore a good symbol for this combination of Water and Earth since it depicts a free-spirited, emotional person who is given over to physical delights.

The common features of the Water types are sensitivity, sociability, and psychic ability. Satyr is associated with the astrological sign of Scorpio, hence vast, unknown depths and the process of death and rebirth. Emotion is focused on the areas of death, union, and the occult. Satyr is also associated with the eighth house, which highlights shared resources and things held in common.

Satyrs, therefore, have greater depth than is immediately obvious. Their close affinity with the hidden Otherworld may be considered as one reason why they are so closely attached to the pleasures of this one. They know, consciously or unconsciously, that this world of which they are a part is transient and illusory, so they are driven to partake of it as far as possible while it lasts. An attachment to the things of the Earth also helps to anchor them in the physical world and distract them from the unknown region that seems so close.

Satyrs are enigmatic and mysterious because they have a hoof in both worlds. Like all Water types, they are deeply sensitive and greatly affected by the environment, both social and physical. They are extremely perceptive and insightful. They are not only aware of their own dark selves, they can recognize the dark side of other people and are consequently aware of our shared humanity. Nor does this recognition of unity end with humans. Satyrs recognize that everything is an expression of the one divine reality, and are thus sympathetic and compassionate to all living things. They are, in keeping with their mythical namesake, very interested in the natural world and its protection, and they love to commune with nature, especially in woods and near water.

In common with other Water types, Satyr is exceedingly sociable, but recognizing the gulf between the worlds he perceives an underlying sense of being alone and therefore needs to relate to others much of the time. At the same time he is careful about with whom he relates on a deep level, and however physically intimate he may be with someone he is nevertheless very discriminating in this important respect. Being emotionally vulnerable creatures, Satyrs exhibit a necessary caution and are as self-defensive as Chimeras are defensive of others. Going beyond the Satyr's façade of hedonism is not easy. Because they like to party and to enjoy themselves, they are often in the company of other pleasure-seekers who are interested only in the present moment. While they are happy to share the moment with others, they are more cynical about their motives if they seem to want more.

Satyrs can therefore appear intolerant of others, which is just one of the many paradoxes inherent in this type. The intolerant, highly sociable pleasure-seeker is one contradiction; the fun-loving hedonist who is self-disciplined and hates laziness is another. The key to this mystery is that Satyrs want control, of themselves and of their environment, in order to feel secure. This can mean having control of others, and since Satyrs are deeply intuitive and seem to know what other people want and need, it is relatively easy for them to gain control of others. Power confers emotional and physical security, and it is on this basis that power is sought. Satyrs can be quite aggressive in this aim but ordinarily they see no need. They are quite capable of using seductive charm and psychological insight to the same end.

Much of the foregoing gives the impression that Satyrs are manipulative and even reprehensible. This is another of the contradictions of the type. Being Water types, they are in fact caring and empathic; they thrive in a harmonious atmosphere and often exude an air of serenity. Far from manipulating others, they prefer to support and encourage others, especially in terms of their emotional and physical health. Satyrs make good counselors because of their ability to delve deep within the psyche, and they make good physical therapists because of the link with the Earth element. A further paradox is that Satyrs yearn to merge with others to achieve union with another like-minded soul.

The Water and Earth combination makes Satyrs both deeply imaginative and highly practical, so they tend to be creative, especially with respect to physical art forms such as dance and sculpture. Their delight in the physical can also make them excellent cooks, while their earthiness can make them keen gardeners. They may combine the two interests and grow their own food or develop an interest in herbalism. Being open-minded and often unconventional, they are frequently attracted to alternative therapies and the more unorthodox spiritual practices such as tantra. There is therefore a strong aesthetic sense such that Satyrs are highly motivated to beautify their homes. They have a good eye for color and form, and know precisely how to influence the mood of a room with lighting and décor. Satyrs may also enjoy making and using their own ritual equipment and aids to divination.

The Earth and Water combination is very compatible. Water provides openness and spontaneity, while Earth makes for a thoroughly grounded, practical individual. Hence, although they may be opposites in some regards, the elements offer mutual support. Earth provides stability for the fluid nature of Water, while Water prevents Earth from being arid and unfeeling. Together they provide the basic conditions for organic growth.

The Earth component makes the Satyr practical, pragmatic, and cautious, and has the benefit of imparting a degree of tough-mindedness. It also emphasizes some of the traits of the primary Water element. Hence the Satyr is often slow at decision-making and can be unfairly regarded by others as indolent, especially considering their characteristic delight in physical indulgence. It can appear that Satyrs are interested in nothing more than their own pleasure, yet as we have seen there is also a melancholy aspect to Satyrs that belies their witty and fun-loving exterior. This may double up with the wistful quality associated with the Water element and make them privately sad. Satyrs are not often gloomy in public, however, since that would not sit well with their social façade, and only their carefully chosen close friends will know about their depressive tendencies. To the rest of the world, Satyrs are characterized by a robust, earthy sense of humor, with shameless flirting and enjoying the physical delights around them, especially music and dancing.

Although Earth imparts realism to this type, fantasy and imagination are not dirty words to Satyrs. They do, however, like to see tangible results for their efforts, and their imaginative abilities are brought into service of practical requirements. The doubling of two conservative elements means that Satyrs are not keen on change, yet they are extremely drawn to self-expression and this inevitably leads to change. The primary Water element means that they are not too eager to work on details, but at the same time the Earth component ensures that what they do is done thoroughly. This makes them dependable up to a point, although their penchant for enjoying things around them (including other people) may slow things down somewhat.

Water types communicate naturally using images and symbols, hence Satyrs will also have a facility for dream interpretation and for methods of divination involving such methods as scrying and the more image-based media such as the tarot. The magical benefits of this type include the psychic receptivity of the Water element manifesting in the physical realm, particularly in terms of clairsentience and openness to occult forces. This latter quality is obviously of particular importance to the practice of magic, where the aim is to make manifest changes in the physical world via occult methods. The strength of the Water/Earth combination in this regard concerns the directing of emotional desire to produce physical change. The Earth component confers practical sense as well as discipline. Thus, the physical paraphernalia of magic and the ritual actions are likely to be scrupulously observed, and the grounding and sealing and other safety precautions followed precisely.

Satyrs are very imaginative, artistic, spiritually inclined, and often have psychic ability. The Water component confers a facility for mediumship, channeling, and a generally enhanced ability to communicate with the invisible realms. Seership and divinatory ability are also highlighted, especially clairvoyance and clairsentience. This type is also likely to embody a number of apparent contradictions; they can be dreamy but logical, intuitive but down-to-earth, and open-minded but skeptical. As a consequence of this, some will find them difficult to understand, and they may infuriate or intrigue others. They are rarely boring.

The foregoing indicates some of the main areas in which Satyrs are likely to excel magically. The magical aims associated with the Water element include healing the emotions, bringing people together in love and harmony, forming and strengthening partnerships, promoting meditation, enhancing otherworldly contact, learning about past lives, and developing psychic ability.

For Satyrs, there are also the magical aims associated with the relatively strong Earth element. Naturally the degree of success with respect to this element will depend on exactly how well-developed it is. The magical aims associated with Earth relate to the things of the earth itself, notably money, all forms of wealth, the physical body and healing thereof, property, the land, growing things, work and career matters, the protection of rooms, buildings, and objects, the discovery of lost objects, and the manifestation of otherworldly entities.

Centaur

Earth with Water

Keywords: Practical, realistic, conventional, restrained, organized, thorough, dependable, sensitive, insightful, sociable, warm, careful, emotional, supportive, thoughtful, analytical, synthesizing, efficient

Correspondences: Gnome, sea green, parsley, rosemary, birch, peridot, quicksilver, cat

The centaur is familiar from Greek myth as being half man, half horse. The most famous of the centaurs was Chiron, who was skilled both as a warrior and as a healer, and who reconciled both conscious and unconscious minds. He was skilled also in music and divination, but is most well-known as the "wounded healer." Chiron is therefore closely linked both to suffering and the relief of suffering, and he is also recognized as one of the guardians of the threshold between the worlds. It seems apposite, therefore, that the Centaur should stand on the solid earth at the edge of the fathomless water and thereby reflect the Earth and Water combination of this type.

The common features of the Earth types are their practicality and their pragmatism. The manner of expression of the primary Earth element is indicated by the secondary element, in this case Water. Centaur is associated with the astrological sign Virgo, hence perfectionism and the pragmatic use of transient resources. Skill is directed toward service to others. Centaur is also associated with the sixth house, indicating community needs and most particularly health matters.

I am aware that Centaur is another name for Sagittarius and that in at least one version of the myth Chiron becomes this constellation. Current astrological thinking therefore associates Centaur with Sagittarius and the ninth house. However, the qualities of Centaur the personality type are closely linked with healing skills, psychic ability, and music, all of which are major characteristics of Chiron. In addition Chiron stands at the threshold between this world and the next, and between consciousness and unconsciousness. The image of the Centaur and of Chiron in particular is more in keeping with the compassionate nature of Water and the pragmatism of Earth than it is to the Fire and Air combination that in my system is represented by Dragon. Furthermore, Reinhart (1989) points out that the planet Chiron is exalted in Virgo and is better integrated in that sign than it is in Sagittarius, the sign of its rulership. Finally, the sixth house is associated with healing, while the ninth house is associated with self-projection. For these reasons, I have associated Centaur with Virgo and the sixth house.

Centaur is an Earth type, and is therefore realistic and pragmatic in outlook. He hates vagueness, and is analytical and able to discriminate among the details that separate apparently similar things to produce order and structure at a fine level. Having successfully categorized everything and produced order out of chaos, he is then able to synthesize compatible ideas and objects so that everything fits together in a harmonious whole. This analytical tendency can make him appear obsessive to others. More discerning people will regard his diversification as subtle and even ingenious. In fact, this type of discriminative analysis is essential to learning about the world; it has to be taken apart to see how it fits together. An example suited to the myth of Chiron would be the medicinal use of herbs. What herb should be used for what illness? Which part of the herb?

In this way Centaur's natural cynicism proves useful. Everything must be tested and proved before its value can be known. He takes a similar line with people, because although he is relatively sociable for an Earth type, Centaur retains his earthy caution. Even so, he is easygoing unless the secondary Water is relatively weak, and demonstrates a strong sense of concern for others, and feels a duty to be of service. In fact Centaur derives much of his personal happiness from being socially useful, and he takes his commitment to duty very seriously. Unlike Satyrs, who are outwardly very sociable yet difficult to know intimately, Centaurs are not confusing in this way. They are friendly and helpful but obviously reserved and do not therefore give out this kind of mixed message. Thus, people are more likely to gently persist rather than be put off by the kind of capriciousness that is typical of the Satyr. Centaur's relationships develop slowly but are usually lifelong.

As an Earth type, Centaur places a high value on the information derived through his five physical senses. These are the basis for his connection with the physical world and the means by which he is able to analyze its constituents. This information is then usefully employed in the service of others in an orderly way, especially in the field of healing. Centaurs love this kind of work and regard it as both fun and personally fulfilling. They are often found working in medical fields as doctors, pharmacists, or as veterinarians.

Centaurs are quiet and reserved (depending on how well-developed the secondary Water is), but always gentle and caring. In fact, they need to be needed and although they are able to spend quite long periods of time alone—and frequently need to in order to recharge—their sense of security comes from knowing that others are easily accessible. Being Earth types they may seem serious at times, but because of the Water secondary they are fascinated by the bizarre and unexplained. Like Satyrs, Centaurs often have an interest in the occult but they typically adopt a practical approach to it. Thus they will explore its various uses and will adopt those methods that appear to be upheld by the evidence of their own eyes. On the other hand, the cynicism inherent in their type may cause them to dismiss such things out of hand rather than risk having their perfectly ordered universe upset by phenomena that are not part of it.

Centaurs will therefore make practical use of "sensible" systems such as herbalism or chiropractic, but will be more wary of apparently dubious therapies such as aromatherapy or homeopathy. This is partly due to a sense of duty with regard to education. Centaurs consider the education and guidance of the young to be of great importance in order that they may be self-caring and caring toward others. Clearly it serves nobody well to use and disseminate a worthless body of knowledge. Chiron was taught all that he knew by Apollo and Artemis, and he in turn taught secret doctrines, medicine, and music to Achilles, Jason, and Hercules. Moreover he was discriminating in what he taught and to whom: Asclepius was educated to be a healer, Jason to be a warrior.

As Earth types, Centaurs can be gloomy, although they are likely to hide themselves away so as not to spoil their good relations with others. Like Chiron, Centaurs often have a strong healing ability that is related to their own inner wound. The moodiness of Water types has been referred to elsewhere, and it is apparent that types such as the Unicorn, Mermaid, Chimera, Wyvern, and Centaur that have strong Water components in their character also have changeable emotions that can be difficult to deal with. The three Water types often take this inherent moodiness to be indicative of their authentic nature, but when this element is not primary it is less easily accommodated. The value of emotional sensitivity is that it facilitates receptivity to contact from otherworldly entities and thus lowers the boundaries leading into the other realm. The difficulty with unruly emotions is that they can be uncomfortable for the individual concerned. Centaurs may therefore find themselves working as counselors or as psychologists.

Centaurs are essentially conventional, conservative, and not keen on change for its own sake. They are, however, tenacious in their efforts to get things done *thoroughly*, which makes them extremely dependable. They like specific answers to their specific questions, and like to see clear, tangible results for their efforts. They may be suspicious of theory and tend to reject what has no obvious practical value. They can be impatient and stubborn, and will often seize upon the first practical solution to a problem.

The Water element confers qualities such as sensitivity, intuition, and receptivity so that they are much affected by the moods of other people and especially by their physical surroundings. It also serves to ameliorate the usual earthy aloofness and insularity. The primary Earth provides both focus and containment for these watery qualities. Consequently Centaurs are not as a rule emotionally unrestrained, and not at all wishy-washy. In contrast to his near cousin the Satyr, Centaur's relations with others tends to be rather more restrained. A feature of Water is that it conveys a desire for harmonizing people via shared goals. Centaurs are also inclined to this aim but they are less likely to be active themselves in the process. They generally prefer to work on a more one-to-one basis as part of the unification process.

Centaurs are sympathetic, compassionate, and eager to be of service to others. They are firm believers in cooperation and reciprocation. They hate conflict and will take whatever steps they can to defuse tense situations or simply withdraw until harmony is restored. They are essentially good-natured, kind, and may go so far as to put the interests of others before their own. The primary Earth component plays an important role in grounding the Water element's more fanciful and impractical tendencies, and allows action to follow desire. There is also a strong organizational capability conferred by Earth that goes hand in hand with the methodical and considered attitude inherent in Water.

There is also a strong aesthetic sense, especially in regard to visual and tactile arts, due to the influence of the primary Earth. Water types tend to communicate in images and symbols, while Earth associates with physical media and music. Centaurs can therefore be imaginative painters or enjoy working with fabrics and wood, and they may enjoy making and using their own ritual equipment and aids to divination. Centaurs will also have a facility for divination, using such methods as runes, the tarot, dream interpretation, and scrying.

The magical benefits of this type include the psychic receptivity of the Water element manifesting in the physical realm in terms of clairsentience and openness to occult forces. This latter quality is obviously of particular importance to the practice of magic, where the aim is to make manifest changes in the physical world via occult methods. The strength of the Earth/Water combination in this regard concerns the directing of emotional desire to produce physical change. The Earth component confers practical sense as well as discipline. Thus, the physical paraphernalia of magic and the ritual actions are likely to be scrupulously observed, and the grounding and sealing and other safety precautions followed precisely.

Centaurs, then, are very imaginative, artistic, spiritually inclined, and often have psychic ability. The Water component confers a facility for mediumship, channeling, and a generally enhanced ability to communicate with the invisible realms. Seership and divinatory ability are also highlighted, especially clairvoyance and clairsentience. Centaurs are also likely to have a facility for psychic healing, dowsing, and psychometry. Geomantic methods of maximizing environmental harmony, such as Feng Shui, and work with the things of the earth, such a crystals, are also highlighted.

The foregoing indicates some of the main areas in which Centaurs are likely to excel magically. The magical aims associated with the Earth element relate to the things of the earth itself, notably money, all forms of wealth, the physical body and healing thereof, property, the land, growing things, work and career matters, the protection of rooms, buildings, and objects, the discovery of lost objects, and the manifestation of otherworldly entities.

For Centaurs there are also the magical aims associated with the relatively strong Water element. Naturally the degree of success with respect to this element will depend on exactly how well-developed it is. The magical aims associated with the Water element include healing the emotions, bringing people together in love and harmony, forming and strengthening partnerships, promoting meditation, enhancing otherworldly contact, learning about past lives, and developing psychic ability.

Wodwose

Earth with Fire

Keywords: Practical, realistic, conventional, restrained, organized, thorough, dependable, energetic, dominant, enthusiastic, warm, active, impulsive, achieving, prudent, disciplined, ambitious

Correspondences: Gnome, green, oregano, cypress, rowan, jet, lead, goat

The wodwose is a woodland spirit that has an association with the Green Man, the divine aspect of nature. He also connects with the human world through the figure of Merlin, who at one time lived in the forest and communicated with animals and trees. Merlin seems to have been a shaman before he was a wizard, and at that time he was sometimes referred to as "the Wild Man of the Woods," which is the other name given to the wodwose. Wodwose therefore combines passion with a close connection to the natural world, and suggests growth, development, unpredictability, and manifestation of the spirit in the world of matter.

The common features of Earth types are their pragmatism and practicality. The manner of expression of the primary Earth element is indicated by the secondary element, in this case Fire. Wodwose is associated with the astrological sign of Capricorn, hence to movement within the physical world. This energy is directed toward the management and organization of vast concerns. Wodwose is also associated with the tenth house: social standing, ambition, and career.

In keeping with his Earth primary, Wodwose is hard working, cautious, materialistic, shrewd, and ambitious. Since what he does is what he is, he needs to succeed, and hence he needs to be highly skilled. Similarly he needs goals to be working toward or he is likely to become depressed and anxious. Because Air is typically undeveloped, he also needs the direction provided by a sound idea. Wodwose are builders and maintainers, but also fiercely protective of things they care about. Unless Fire is well developed, they can be difficult to get to know on a personal level, especially since they have a tendency to suspiciousness. For this reason, they are also self-protective and fiercely individualistic.

They excel in understanding complex technical problems and work tenaciously to overcome them. They therefore place a premium on information derived via their five senses, and are able to translate their observations into enduring external change. They are extremely well-organized and have high standards of excellence that they impose upon themselves more than on others. Hence they can come across as tough-minded, exacting superiors or as highly dependable and loyal coworkers. The primary Earth in their makeup means that they like a lot of structure, whereas the secondary Fire means that they require a lot of autonomy to do things their own way. Earth makes them solid and reliable, Fire makes them gregarious and fun—although fun is never allowed to get in the way of their chosen goals.

As an Earth type, Wodwose is practical, realistic, pragmatic, and concerned with technical know-how. He likes to try things out in practice, to act rather than waste time thinking about things. This feature of the Wodwose is reinforced by the secondary Fire element with its associated dynamism and sense of urgency. Wodwose has much in common with his cousin the Phoenix. Both are impatient to move things ahead, but Wodwose is relatively circumspect and more inclined than the Phoenix to pay attention to details. The secondary Fire element makes Wodwose appear impatient and rash by the standards of either the Satyr or the Gryphon, even if they still seem relatively cautious to the other types. Much depends on the relative strength of the secondary Fire in the profile.

This is another pairing that at first sight seems incongruous. Earth is solid and conservative, while Fire is formless and expansive; moreover Earth is introverted and persistent whereas Fire is extraverted and easily bored. These contradictions may represent tensions in the character of any given individual, again depending on the relative strength of the secondary element. If Fire is relatively undeveloped in the Wodwose's makeup, then there may be an oscillation between careful productivity and impatient forging ahead. Similarly, he can veer between sullen inactivity and furious overwork.

As always, much depends on the nature of the elemental balance and the prevalent circumstances, including presence of other people. On the face of it this seems to be an unsatisfactory combination, but the two elements work to complement each other, Earth providing the boundaries and restraint without which Fire would rage uncontrolled, Fire providing the impetus without which Earth remains static. As with Phoenix, there is a sustained, controlled energy rather like a furnace that slowly but intensely converts material form.

Due to the creative quality of Fire in combination with the sensate quality of Earth, Wodwose may be particularly attracted to artistic forms of expression such as painting and sculpture. The strong moral and outward-looking aspect conferred by Fire means that Wodwose is also attracted to some kind of community service, particularly if it involves conservation and guardianship of the land and its inhabitants. If Fire is very well-developed, he can be actively engaged in public protests and even direct action. The association with Capricorn means that there is often an urge to develop social standing by working in some way for the community, and there can be attempts to inspire others through social activities involving art and spiritual initiatives.

Wodwose can live up to the "Wild Man" image by displaying an impulsiveness associated with an urge to succeed. As the symbol of the Wodwose suggests, he is frequently concerned with transformation of the environment, often in dramatic ways. Wodwose is more likely to pour his energy into evolution rather than revolution because the primary Earth is essentially conservative and cautious by nature. Wodwose does not undertake drastic change without good reason, and his more vigorous efforts are likely to be protective in nature. Ordinarily he works steadily and tirelessly toward a clear goal, and he does not rest from his endeavors until the goal is reached. This can, of course, mean undermining the opposition, and Wodwose can be a severe and immovable thorn in the side of antagonists.

Wodwose therefore presents something of an enigma to others, since Earth is typically conventional and conservative, not keen on change for its own sake. But of course Wodwose is not aiming at change for its own sake but for the general good, rather in the way that the spirit of nature, of which Wodwose is a symbol, engages in slow, occasionally dramatic changes that are ultimately necessary to life generally. These changes are always connected with a vision of a better future because Wodwose is paradoxically cautious and enthusiastic about radical overhauls.

Despite the Earth primary, Wodwose is not dull. On the contrary, he often has an earthy sense of humor and a liking for practical jokes. The Fire secondary ensures that he enjoys fantasy and is intrigued by the possibilities conjured up by the imagination. Achievement of goals is essential for Wodwose, and unless he can conclude his business satisfactorily he will suffer from anxious frustration. Like Phoenix, he is unable to rest properly while things remain undone, although his greater steadiness of purpose means that he is not prone to fretting as long as things remain on course. Like the other Earth types, Wodwose feels that his self-definition and value is derived from what he does. Thus, failure to succeed is devastating for him, and therefore he will do everything in his substantial power to avoid it.

In common with the other Earth types, Wodwose is happy to work with others as long as there is a specific and practical goal in sight. He is more independent than the others, however, and will not tolerate interference. In fact, he makes an effective and popular manager who inspires confidence and respect. This enhanced leadership ability and relative lack of restraint is, of course, derived from the Fire secondary. Depending on the strength of this secondary element, however, Wodwose may be so goal-centered that he adopts a utilitarian approach to group members that makes him unpopular and that, in the end, is counterproductive.

For the magician, the benefits of this combination are the energy that derives from Fire coupled with the grounding that derives from Earth. This means that there is great potential to produce lasting, concrete effects. Fire is energy, and this is what the magician is attempting to manipulate. If the magician has Fire (energy) as a strong secondary characteristic, then there is a natural affinity with the agent of change. When coupled with the pull of the Earth element to realize one's aims, the implications are clear. Fire not only provides the raw energy for magic, it provides a strong spiritual, moral, and creative drive too. Earth provides a strong organizing principle as well as a practical, manifesting quality. This type has great power to transform things from one state of being to another—this is occult power. Of course, the other two elements, Water and Air, have their own magical qualities that are essential to the magical process, and the strength of these needs to be taken into account.

The foregoing indicates some of the main areas in which Wodwose is likely to excel magically. These relate to the things of the Earth itself, notably money, all forms of wealth, the physical body and healing thereof, property, the land, growing things, work and career matters, the protection of rooms, buildings, and objects, the discovery of lost objects, and the manifestation of otherworldly entities.

For Wodwose, there are also magical aims associated with the Fire secondary. Naturally the degree of success possible with respect to these aims depends on exactly how well-developed this element is. Magical goals associated with Fire include enhancing physical health, success in competitive pursuits including legal actions, spiritual and artistic development, protection of people and property, and sex magic.

Gryphon

Earth with Air

Keywords: Intellectual, rational, curious, radical, imaginative, persistent, achieving, practical, realistic, conventional, restrained, organized, thorough, dependable, resourceful, secure, content

Correspondences: Gnome, lime green, thyme, rose, alder, emerald, copper, bull

The gryphon is an eagle from the waist up and a lion from the waist down. It therefore has the qualities of a bird, which is closely linked with spirituality and the divine, and with a mammal, which is associated with regal strength and courage. This beast symbolizes the link between natural forces and spiritual enlightenment. It also serves as a potent guardian for seekers after wisdom. The common feature of the Earth types is their stability, pragmatism, and practicality. The manner of expression of the primary

Earth element is indicated by the secondary element, in this case Air. The Gryphon is associated with the astrological sign of Taurus and refers to the stability and natural rhythm of the Earth element. It also relates to the acquisition and management of wealth. Gryphon is also associated with the second house, hence personal security derived from the things of the Earth.

In common with the other Earth creatures, Gryphons are practical and realistic but tend to be more intellectually inclined than the other two. Unlike empathic Satyrs, Gryphons are likely to adopt a theoretical view of helping others, and especially of helping others to help themselves. This agrees with their essentially conservative outlook, a feature of all the Earth types. Being practical, they will also want to see some evidence that people are actually helping themselves rather than just passively accepting help. They are therefore less likely to give direct help to others than to produce plans and ideas that will help others indirectly, for they believe it's up to people to read the plans and act upon them.

Gryphons want nothing more from life than peace and serenity, both for themselves and for those around them. Their essential earthiness ensures that they exude a calm, placid air that is rooted in a sense of security based on physical well-being and stability. They thrive in stable conditions and hate change for its own sake. In fact, they are not keen on change at all. They are, however, given to the delights of the flesh in its various forms, including art and beauty. They have a particular love of nature and enjoy creating their own oasis of peace and pleasure as much as they enjoy being out in the wilds. They may seem too materialistic to some, but only because they derive a sense of security from wealth. They have a strong need to feel physically secure, hence the focus on physical wealth.

Part of this focus on materialism comes from their realistic outlook. They know that we live in a society based on monetary exchange and they do not split hairs about it. Money is not what they want, though—it's the things that money can buy. And what money buys is freedom from want, from discomfort, from drudgery, from misery. It buys the safe haven within which Gryphons can relax. And it buys the beauty with which they surround themselves. Physical security for Gryphons is nothing less than their continued existence.

It follows from this that Gryphons are hard working and motivated within their chosen career. Work often centers on symbols of financial security, if not the actual bricks and mortar of houses. Gryphons will therefore typically be found in banking, insurance, real estate, and also farming or building. They are logical, systematic, and good organizers, and are consequently often found in management. Being Earth types with Air secondary, they are not very sociable even though they can be very good, reliable friends. This detachment from people means that they are able to make fair and impartial decisions.

The Air secondary, depending on how well-developed it is, will impart an intellectual curiosity that offsets the essential fixed nature of this type and makes them more open to novel ideas and methods. Being naturally pragmatic, they will not be easily convinced by things unless they can be seen to work in practice, but the open-mindedness that is associated with Air will dispose them to try things out. More staid and conservative types will not be interested.

The realism of Earth also combines with the rationalism of Air such that Gryphons are not easily persuaded of the validity of occult phenomena. Again, they have a natural tendency to distrust things that they cannot see or touch, including mystical things. Once again, however, they can be convinced by plausible theory (courtesy of Air) to consider these things, and may accept them if convincing results are forthcoming. They will be even more readily convinced if they get to see or hear otherworldly phenomena, assuming they don't rationalize these things away or simply deny them.

Gryphons are not noted for their outgoing nature but tend instead to be reserved and cautious about starting new relationships. However, they are more fun-loving than immediate first impressions of them suggest. Yet they can become drained of energy after too long spent in the company of others, and will need time alone in their personal haven in which to recover. Similarly, although their view of the world is essentially derived from their five senses, the Air component introduces a healthy openness. Consequently they can surprise people by being more than usually active, spontaneous, and sensual. They can be regarded as unpredictable for this reason.

Being Earth types first and foremost, they like to see tangible results for their efforts. Having Air strongly placed in second place, they are also observant and curious. They can become totally engrossed in their own projects and resent being obliged to do other, less interesting things. They are therefore best employed doing work that gives them a lot of autonomy, with some scope for engaging with others. They like to learn by doing, and they like doing things more than they like social activities. They can therefore appear antisocial to those who do not know them well, and it doesn't help that they favor a small, select band of confidantes because that can make them appear elitist.

For Gryphons, the idealism of Air is tempered by the tough-minded and pragmatic qualities associated with Earth, and indeed they are more likely to produce tangible results from their ideas. However, there is a fundamental conflict between the radical nature of Air and the conservative nature of Earth. This can be resolved if underlying theoretical considerations suggest practical applications, and if the applications can be seen to work in practice. The Air and Earth combination can therefore make Gryphons very productive and original in their chosen fields.

Gryphons have a strong aesthetic sense and they love to surround themselves with the fine things in life. They are also avid collectors and may focus on a particular art form or style. This is particularly likely if the materials can be touched, hence sculpture, jewelry, ceramics; also fabrics and clothes. Gryphons have a keen sense of color and form and love heavy aromas. The Air secondary may induce them to investigate a healing art such as aromatherapy or reflexology, both of which will appeal to the basic earthiness of the primary element. Such activities also have the good effect of allowing Gryphons to interact with other people in a formal, controlled environment.

Communication is a central motivation for all types that have Air as a prominent feature of the personality. Like his cousin the Pegasus, the Gryphon tends on the whole to be shy except in the company of close friends, and may prefer somewhat paradoxically to express ideas and feelings formally to an audience rather than to individuals. Unlike the Pegasus, however, they may not stop at fantasizing about grand schemes designed to unify people, but may actually take practical steps to achieving these lofty aims. Once again their literary and artistic proclivities may be brought into service of these aims, and they will try writing or putting on an exhibition as a means of conveying their ideals and the truth as they perceive it. Alternatively there may be an interest in communicating with beings from other realms through mediumship or channeling, especially if this can be seen to be helping the living in some way.

Because of the Earth/Air combination, like the Pegasus, Gryphons are not the most socially skilled of the types, and because of their shyness and abstraction they may not get the chance to practice these skills. Much depends on life experiences and current circumstances, and the effects of these on the more sociable elements of the shadow, Fire and Water. However, they do possess a strong social sense and some Gryphons can be relatively outgoing, depending on the extent to which the weaker elements are developed and on the kind of work they do. Despite this, however, they are still fundamentally Earth types and consequently will be taken up with either doing or planning practical tasks. This is their natural bent and they are rarely lonely, although at times they may yearn for a like-minded companion with whom to share their love of beautiful things. They do not fit very well into groups, and may have little interest in being part of one. In fact, Gryphons are among the solitary practitioners of the types, and on the whole they prefer it that way.

The combination of Earth and Air can indicate an ability to communicate with the invisible realms through the things of the Earth, as if distant things can be seen and heard as though from a mountain top. Thus, seership and skill with aids to divination such as runes, crystals, and astrology are highlighted. The Earth primary can also indicate an interest in healing, and otherworldly contact may well be felt literally via clairsentience, although clairvoyance and clairaudience are also highlighted. Generally, however, this type is likely to be logical and objective, and hence often disinclined to accept such experiences without question, and may reject them entirely or else rationalize them away. Gryphons are Earth types and hence skeptical about the invisible, while the secondary Air makes them highly rational and to dislike things that do not fit in with accepted theory. This can be a strength though, because Gryphons in particular (along with Pegasus) would not want to fall into the trap of self-deception. They prefer to be convinced by sound reasoning if not by physical proof. Gryphons and Pegasus are the most scientific of all the types.

Gryphons are also very disciplined both physically and mentally. Thus, the physical paraphernalia associated with magic and the necessary ritual actions are scrupulously observed. Similarly, the need for grounding, sealing, and other safety precautions is understood and procedures are followed precisely. Gryphons will have a greater facility for making manifest in the physical world the things of the nonphysical world. The combination of Earth and Air work harmoniously together, as Air stimulates Earth and Earth stabilizes Air.

Thus Gryphons have an enhanced ability for generating both startlingly solid visualizations and powerful thought-forms. As with Pegasus, the ability to link the unseen world of spirit with the world of matter is a valuable consequence of the strong pairing of Earth and Air, and there is great potential for the successful materialization of projected aims. The value of this ability in magical work is obvious, and not only in ritual, where the ability to visualize clearly opens a gateway to the Otherworld. It also enhances the ability to perceive spirits.

There is also likely to be a strong aesthetic sense, especially in regard to visual and tactile arts, although music and poetry may also feature quite prominently in their ritual work. The primary Earth element means that, in common with other Earth types, Gryphons may enjoy making their own ritual equipment such as wands, pentacles, rune stones, and so on. They are imaginative and artistic, especially with regard to the spoken and written word, due to the strong Air element, and naturally this helps greatly with respect to spellcasting. Strong Air promotes ability for precision in deciding magical aims, clear affirmations, and concise incantations with a strong rhythm.

The Earth types tend to be suspicious of theorizing and prefer action to thinking, but the Gryphon is characterized by a strong Air component associated with exactly these usually frowned-upon qualities. Gryphons are therefore the most cerebral of the Earth types. Fantasy and speculation are not dirty words for them as long as the desired goal is always kept firmly in sight and is not perceived to be beyond the realms of possibility. Gryphons remain primarily earthy and pragmatic but the relatively narrow, goal-oriented focus that is typical of the Earth types is greatly ameliorated by the secondary Air element.

The foregoing indicates some of the main areas in which Gryphons are likely to excel magically. The principal Earth element indicates both the most likely areas of interest and the greatest likelihood of success in magical practice. Naturally these relate to the things of the Earth itself, notably money, all forms of wealth, the physical body and healing thereof, property, the land, growing things, work and career matters, the protection of rooms, buildings, and objects, the discovery of lost objects, and the manifestation of otherworldly entities.

The degree of success of magical aims associated with the secondary Air element depends largely on the extent to which this element is developed. Principal among these is the communication with beings from the Otherworld, from which may be discovered secrets about their world and this one. Similarly there can be revelations about the past, present, and future. An affinity with this element can also help in acquiring guides from the Otherworld. Because of the essentially intellectual nature of this element, successful aims include learning and the passing of exams. It also relates to artistic inspiration, especially with respect to the written word.

7

THE TWELVE SHADOWS

The following descriptions of the shadow types refer to those elements that are relatively undeveloped and that consequently exert their effects on an unconscious level. This shows that the type of energy represented by each element is found in everyone even if they don't all find direct, conscious expression.

Each element refers to a different kind of intelligence, perception, and motivation; no element is bad in itself. Each may be viewed as an aspect of the whole, rather like a subpersonality in some ways, and the individual needs to integrate these for optimal functioning.

These descriptions of the shadows are not absolute. The descriptions reflect cases where both elements are very undeveloped. In most cases at least one of the shadow elements will be relatively well-developed, and often both will be fairly well-developed. In a few cases all four elements are relatively well-developed. The point is to modify the descriptions according to your actual profile.

Even in cases where both elements are very undeveloped, it's worth remembering that various external factors, such as significant others, as well as the positive effects of the primary elements, may work to minimize the effects of underdevelopment. However, even in these cases, the undeveloped elements will continue to seek expression and often work quietly and in a subtle way to this end.

The shadow descriptions can appear alarming in some respects, especially in respect to psychological dysfunction. Remember that the personality has ways of preserving the status quo, and this, paradoxically, is the function of the defense mechanisms. These operate in a way designed to reduce stress and to keep the individual on an even keel, albeit at the expense of optimal functioning. It may seem that it would be best to eradicate them, but they preserve the existing level of harmony. The best way to dispel the defenses is to develop the personality so that all four elements find expression in the full light of consciousness, rather than some lurking in the shadow world of the unconscious.

Quick Reference Table of Shadow Types

Tertiary Element	Quaternary Element	Shadow	Page
Air	Earth	Pegasus	123–131
Air	Water	Unicorn	132–140
Air	Fire	Firebird	141–149
Fire	Air	Dragon	150–158
Fire	Earth	Phoenix	159–167
Fire	Water	Wyvern	168–175
Water	Fire	Chimera	176–183
Water	Air	Mermaid/Merman	184–192
Water	Earth	Satyr	193–201
Earth	Water	Centaur	202–209
Earth	Fire	Wodwose	210–218
Earth	Air	Gryphon	219–227

Pegasus Shadow

Air with Earth

Keywords: Superficial, manipulative, neglectful, lazy, confused, irrational, moody, irritable

In this shadow aspect, the bright beast that can fly us to the stars is seen as the nightmare that comes by night from the Underworld to frighten and to challenge. The nightmare is referred to in the legends of various cultures. In Celtic myth she is a terrifying version of the goddess, who appears with her nine fillies in attendance. In Norse myth, Odin defeated her with a charm made from her own hair. In the Bible, Job describes her as dwelling on a rock face where she consumes human blood.

Nightmares usually refer to a source of conflict, and in the case of the Pegasus shadow this is primarily an impossible demand for perfection. Since perfection is not possible, the shadow exhibits the worst aspects of the undeveloped Earth and Air elements and is characteristically critical, judgmental, and fault finding. These individuals are so unrealistic in their demands that inevitably they cannot be pleased. They are so unrealistic in their aims that they verge on the delusional. At one end of the extreme they harbor impossibly grandiose schemes, while at the other they are finicky to the point of obsessive-compulsive tendencies.

At the same time as making unrealistic and unfair demands of others, they are hypocritical, expedient, and follow their own urges. They have difficulty telling the difference between fact and fantasy, so their perspectives frequently change, making them difficult to relate to. At the same time their interpersonal relations are marked by insincerity. They will flatter and charm in an effort to get on to a person's good side but also gossip about him behind his back. They habitually sow seeds of discord among groups in an effort to cause friction and to break up friendships. Even without this feature they are expert at the social faux pas, being tactless and indiscrete.

Much of this behavior is indicative of the shadow's fundamental lack of security and sense of personal inadequacy. Paradoxically he wants to be loved and valued by others but does not recognize that his hidden insecurities are provoking him into acts that will ultimately ensure his rejection. He will therefore engage in competitive relationships, the sole aim of which is to "prove" his personal worth by attracting someone away from their partner or by seducing the object of another's affections. Once this goal has been achieved, he no longer has need of the "target" and becomes cold and rejecting.

He craves the company of others and is superficially charming, pleasant, and good fun. Eventually it becomes evident that he is shallow, capricious, and manipulative. If this were not enough to make him increasingly unpopular, his mounting sense of insecurity in the face of this growing rejection will trigger an escalation of the antisocial behavior that made him unpopular in the first place. These desperate attempts to win back the love that is fast evaporating are frequently coupled with recriminations and spiteful outpourings that only hasten the inevitable, and he will have to seek a new arena, leaving behind him a slew of disturbed relationships.

Various unconscious defense strategies have been identified, and these can be related to the elements. The Pegasus shadow exhibits *denial*, an unconscious refusal to acknowledge external realities because to do so would be too painful; and *somatization*, a preoccupation with physical symptoms that represents a psychological reaction to stressful situations. Denial of the physical self can also be seen among shadows that have a prominent Earth, Pegasus among them.

Since Earth is the least-developed element, this is the one with the greatest potential to cause problems from within the unconscious. The shadow therefore focuses on the physical realm by concentrating on its less-wholesome attractions and by denying the healthy side. Consequently the shadow can appear vain in keeping with his role as seducer while simultaneously feeling that he is physically ugly. He may be sexually voracious while at the same time harboring distaste for his own body and those of others. He may be prone to gender confusion and to idealization of the opposite sex, combined with denigration of his own.

He can be overindulgent or neglectful of his physical well-being by not eating and by not even keeping warm. In some ways his physical body lacks substance for him. Those parts of the physical world that are visible to him will be devalued. Despite the relatively strong Fire component in the primary pair, the shadow may sometimes provoke a sense of apathy and pointlessness that undermines the more optimistic outlook associated with the more developed elements. The shadow may be preoccupied with somatic illness to the extent of being a hypochondriac.

Unconscious defense strategies associated with Air include *fantasy*, the excessive preoccupation with daydreams and the imagination as a means of escaping from life's problems and one's own internal conflicts. This is also known as schizoid or autistic fantasy, because in its most extreme forms this defense mechanism has the effect of removing the person from the social world. *Intellectualization* refers to the overuse of abstract thought in order to avoid psychological discomfort. This is evident from the attempts by some people to split hairs and argue over precise definitions for their behavior as if they can thereby argue that their maladaptive behavior is in fact acceptable.

Rationalization refers to the pathological use of apparently plausible reasons to justify one's behavior. *Projection* is the unconscious rejection of one's own thoughts and character traits. Recognition of these ideas and traits would not fit with the self-concept, and consequently they are ascribed to others. *Repression* is fairly well-known to most people as the exclusion from consciousness of distressing feelings or ideas. It is not the same as *suppression*, which is a deliberate pushing away of unacceptable thoughts and behavior.

As an Air type, this element is especially important, yet here it is undeveloped. This is largely the cause of the previously mentioned perfectionism. According to the shadow's distorted logic, everything is not only possible in theory but also in practice.

Because Air is weak, the individual is prone to confused thinking, hence the inability to decide between fact and fantasy. As a result he may be eccentric in outlook and adopt extreme, sometimes perverse, views.

This inability to think logically exacerbates the weak Earth quality of poor sensory perceptions, which further compromises his ability to make realistic decisions. On top of this his communication skills, especially those pertaining to verbal expression, are typically poor. The inability to articulate his ideas effectively can be the cause of misunderstandings and hence arguments. Not only can he not express himself effectively to others, in order to make himself understood he is limited in self-expression that would enable him to understand himself. He has strong emotions and he knows what he feels but rarely why he feels them. Consequently he can be beset by vague fears and plagued by his own imagination.

He can't cope with his own negative emotions so they are repressed, only to surface as physical illness or as emotional instability, mood swings, or even as psychosis. He often presents himself as irrational to others, and although he deplores intellectual qualities he will readily use pseudo-intellectual reasoning as a means of defense. The defense mechanisms associated with Air may then come into play to uphold the self-destructive behavior attributable to Earth. Inactivity will be rationalized as a need for rest, or even as due to illness. At the same time, genuine illness will be explained away as simple tiredness or as due to the weather, or some such thing. Poor diet and other types of physical self-neglect will be excused on the grounds that they are healthy, as in the claim that they are cutting down on fat or avoiding colds by not keeping warm. Vague references to recent research are often made to back up these claims.

Thus, the negative attributes that characterize the Pegasus shadow are a mixture of the unconscious qualities associated with the undeveloped elements Earth and Air (in that order), plus aspects of the primary elements Fire and Water that are being defended against during periods of stress. Which of these attributes is most salient at any given time depends very much on the learning experiences of the individual coupled with prevailing circumstances. Although the negative qualities of the primary elements are unpleasant when they come to the fore, they are usually transient and will be the focus of guilt feelings later. The effects of the undeveloped Earth and Air are more insidious because they are always unconscious and so work indirectly and constantly to influence feelings, thoughts, and behavior.

The negative qualities associated with Earth and Air tend therefore to be fairly entrenched because they remain unconscious and undeveloped. The defenses listed above exist to safeguard the integrity of the personality as a whole and can be difficult to dislodge. One of the positive features of Earth is to enhance and stabilize the positive features of Air. One of the positive features of Air is to give inspiration and direction to Earth. With both these elements undeveloped, they cannot be mutually supportive in this way. How this disparity affects magical practice will be outlined below.

The less-attractive features associated with the primary elements Water and Fire tend, on the other hand, to be relatively transient and mostly activated at times of extreme tension and stress. Even so, the associated behavior and motivation for acting badly are often unconscious because they are in themselves defense strategies and are consequently characteristics of the shadow. The fact that these behaviors are usually transient can mean that they exert a very damaging effect on interpersonal relations, especially if they are sudden and very much out of character. Of course, some people are chronically stressed and consequently exhibit shadow qualities most of the time. In these cases, it can seem out of character if the usual sources of stress are removed and their behavior becomes less offensive.

While the primary elemental influences found in the shadow are on the whole temporary, traces of these characteristics may be evident all the time. Deformation of personality is not all-or-nothing—it exists as a continuum, ranging from severe to very mild. The patterns that derive from the primary elements manifest in the shadow in the following ways, depending on the primary type.

Wyverns with a Pegasus shadow have Fire as the primary element. Their personal relationships become unstable and the sense of self becomes unclear. Consequently the individual exhibits extreme moodiness and lack of restraint, often related to fear of being abandoned by others. They are therefore highly sensitive to any indication that others do not value them. They themselves veer between idealizing others and denigrating them. They are torn between fiery rage against others and the Water-based need to be accepted and wanted by them. However, manipulative behavior and selfish attention-seeking undermine their essential sociability, and they begin to bring about the very abandonment they are attempting to avoid. With an ever-increasing sense of insecurity, their attempts to elicit care from others become more desperate and they may be prone to vituperative outpourings that further damage relationships. The negative spiral continues until the external pressures are removed, allowing a gradual return to usual functioning.

Chimeras with a Pegasus shadow have Water as the primary element, so emotionalism is more pronounced. Corresponding behaviors that may be emphasized during periods of stress include a compulsive need to be the center of attention, and they may be given to dramatic, over-the-top displays of affection that are essentially exaggerations of their usual behavior. They can become more than usually entertaining and very popular, at least initially. This new behavior can have a slightly manic feel to it, though, and there is an increased tendency to enhance their own popularity at the expense of others, who are the butt of their jokes. As the tension mounts, this aggressiveness becomes more marked and is directed against everyone, eventually including close friends and family. From this point on the individual becomes more openly sarcastic and hurtful, and the popularity falls away to be replaced by dislike, sometimes extreme.

All of this is difficult for the Wyvern or Chimera primary because both are extremely sociable types who like to be liked and appreciated by others. They can't bear to be alone, but at the same time they can be highly unpleasant if the shadow is too powerful in its effects. One aspect of the shadow, however, relates to the primary type, and this relates to pride. Wyverns and Chimeras like to be helpful to others and sometimes arrogantly assume that they can handle any problem that others present them with. This can be dangerous enough if the help being offered falls short of what the other person desperately needs. When the shadow becomes powerful, however, then everyone can suffer.

If the Pegasus shadow emerges during times of stress, or if the character is chronically neurotic, then he can adopt an attitude of superiority and martyrdom. He then becomes intensely irritable and complains constantly about how he is taken for granted by people who offer nothing in return for all the help he gives. He may become increasingly needy himself as he attempts to punish others for using him so badly. At the heart of this neurotic pattern of relating lies the fear of experiencing his own needs. By focusing on the needs of others, he avoids dealing with his own "weaknesses," for implicit in his attitude is that to give is to be strong and to receive is to be weak. This further implies that he despises those he helps for being failures, while his helping them is a sign that he is a success. Under certain circumstances, therefore, he becomes vengeful and vindictive.

All of these weaknesses can represent powerful limitations to successful magical outcomes. Since Earth is the weakest element in this shadow, it exerts the strongest negative influence. The most important of these for the Pegasus shadow is the most limiting of all—failure in the final stage of the process to produce the manifest changes that magic is designed to achieve. The sphere of the Earth element is the beginning and the end of magical activity. The magician brings into a carefully chosen, specifically designed working area ritually significant aspects of the physical world, like the wand and the athame, and manipulates them using sounds and gestures to effect desired changes in the physical world. This starting point is also the end point. Recall what was said about performing magic as if it was already accomplished. You stand in the Earth sphere at the beginning and the end of the process simultaneously.

The problem with the weak Earth now becomes apparent: poor organization, disregard for ritual procedures, lack of connection with the forces of Earth, or alternatively being too bogged down in technique. Disregard for ritual procedures often includes a disregard for the postoperative grounding and sealing, and consequently being left open to the disruptive effects of incomplete connection from the Otherworld.

Of course, the biggest problem produced by a negative Earth is the very earthiness of the element. Earth is characteristically skeptical, pragmatic, hard-nosed, and literally too down-to-earth to believe in magic in the first place, and this skeptical attitude can work unconsciously to undermine your efforts. If you can't suspend disbelief for a while and open yourself up to the possibilities, then naturally you will have major difficulty progressing to the final stage and succeeding in your aims. Without conviction that you will bring about your desired aims, your performance is literally empty ritual. The paradox here is that in order to work effectively with earthy forces, you need to transcend them.

More insidious than these considerations are the unconscious beliefs that you don't actually deserve the things you aim for, or that it's wrong to be self-indulgent, selfish, and so on. Or a common underlying belief for people from a Judeo-Christian background is the fear of tampering with nature, or offending God, or doing deals with Satan. Some people simply fear success and the responsibility and other changes it brings. For these people, to succeed at what they want would be worse than to fail constantly, so they are unconsciously motivated to undermine their own attempts and to bring about their own failure. Constant failure despite your best efforts is frustrating, but at least you can avoid change. These are some of the reasons why an undeveloped Earth can spell failure for the magical enterprise. You will have others that are personal to yourself, but their effects are the same.

From the preceding paragraphs it is apparent that attitude is of central importance, and here we see the connection with Air. Air shares with Earth an attitude of skepticism. In the Pegasus shadow, the skepticism of both elements is working unconsciously to undermine your efforts, which is why the pre-ritual baths and other preliminaries are necessary. These procedures are designed to cancel out the limiting factors of your own personality. Other limitations associated with undeveloped Air are poor skills of visualization, poor focus, and imprecise statements in the form of goals, affirmations, and incantations. These amount to a block in your capacity for communication with the occult forces that successful magic depends on. By the same token, it means inhibition of divinatory abilities.

This last is in itself a major limiting factor, since it refers directly to psychic power. Even if you are not going to make much use of divination (and what occultist doesn't?), you will want oracular guidance in formulating goals and uncovering barriers to success. In this event, a reduced capacity for seership is a serious handicap that means having to work blind. Finally, there is the question of ethics, or lack thereof. Undeveloped Air can mean that the magician believes that he knows what's best for everyone else, and as a consequence does not hesitate to work magic for or even against others "for their own good." Needless to say, this should be resisted, which is why the magician should fully understand the motivational basis of his own actions.

Additional unconscious factors associated with Air are likely to be more insidious and limiting. The very rationalism and logic that Air symbolizes militates against the very notion of magic. Since the inception of the Age of Enlightenment, when superstition was swept away and rationalism became our creed, the mechanical, clockwork universe replaced the occult universe that had preceded it. As we have seen, modern science now cleaves more to an apparently irrational model, with which ordinary people are still not entirely familiar. We have all grown up imbued with rationalist principles and the scientific endeavor. This lifetime of obeisance to rationalism can be difficult to dismiss entirely, no matter how fully you may disregard it on a conscious level. At the back of your mind there lurks a man in a white coat, shaking his head at magic—and you believe he is right.

These elemental shortcomings and preoccupations may reveal themselves in dreams and fantasies involving inertia, of being trapped, buried alive, unable to move, or of strange beasts that lurk within the earth waiting to reach up and devour you. You may even dream that you are such a beast. Alternatively there can be dreams about earthquakes, unstable houses, volcanoes, and landslides. Similarly there can be dreams and fantasies involving air, particularly of falling from a great height or of desperately trying to fly. You may dream of being attacked by giant birds or even of the nightmare herself taking you up to her nest in the cliff.

Unicorn Shadow

Air with Water

Keywords: Confused, capricious, unemotional, cold, unstable, irrational, paranoid

The unicorn is usually portrayed as a benevolent creature and it was even adopted by medieval Christians as a symbol of spiritual purity. Like all the other fabulous beasts, however, it had its dark side. The unicorn is also associated with the Crone aspect of the triple moon goddess, and hence with transformation through destruction. Unicorns were held by the ancients to be extremely dangerous. Only a virgin could capture a unicorn because the animal would willingly submit to her as a symbol of wisdom and spiritual integrity.

What this indicates about the Unicorn shadow is this type's lack of wisdom and feeling. There is a particular tension in this type, as there is in his close cousin the Mermaid or Merman shadow, between the undeveloped Water and Air. Water is most closely linked with the unconscious and the emotions, while Air is most closely linked with the conscious mind and the intellect. In both these shadow types, these elements are undeveloped, thus producing a peculiar set of conflicts. It's as if the single, spiral horn itself is composed of two mutually antagonistic elements.

Unicorn shadows are therefore characteristically unpredictable and capricious creatures that are constantly being influenced by opposing forces. Small wonder, then, that they have great difficulty staying focused and are easily distracted. They also appear shallow and superficial, both in terms of reasoning and feelings. They are prone to moodiness but have a poor understanding of their emotional states and have difficulty expressing their feelings anyway. As a result of the self-alienation resulting from the conflict between opposites, they are uncertain of their own motives or rationale for doing anything.

Their relationships are usually limited and lacking in intimacy. This shadow engages with others on a shallow, transient level and usually flits from person to person according to need rather than on the basis of friendship. He can be autocratic and even aggressive as he deflects his internal discomfort toward others. He can therefore be quite cruel and cutting, which naturally makes him disliked and unwelcome, thereby further exacerbating the initial problem of social transience. Thus a self-fulfilling prophesy is activated in which he alienates people who then genuinely dislike him. He then becomes paranoid about them, spreading rumors and gossiping.

He can be as deceitful to others as he is with himself, and evasive partly because he doesn't trust other people, partly because he is genuinely uncertain about his own thoughts and feelings. Since he doesn't recognize or understand his own motivations, he can't trust those of others. Because he feels cut off from others, he doesn't see the need to respect common boundaries or obey social rules. At the same time, he often exhibits an attitude of entitlement and does not hesitate to sponge off others. He does not feel beholden and is expedient.

None of this should be too surprising when his essential inner split is considered. The dissociation between Water and Air means that his rational mind is constantly at odds with his intuition, and his conscious mind is constantly interfered with by the unconscious. This poor integration of conflicting elements (in contrast with the Unicorn primary) inevitably leads to role confusion stemming from a poor sense of identity that may include gender confusion. No wonder that he tends toward brooding and morbid speculation.

Various unconscious defense strategies have been identified, and these can be related to the elements. The psychological defense mechanisms that relate to Water include *devaluation*, which refers to the demeaning of one's self or others by exaggerating negative attributes, ridiculing competence, and generally destroying the sense of self-worth. *Introjection* refers to the incorporation of the values or traits of others in order to prevent conflict with them or reduce the sense of threat from them. Introjection also serves to defend against loss, usually following a death. In this event, a living person begins to express qualities belonging to the dead person. Doubtless some cases of possession are actually instances of introjection.

Reaction-formation is a means of preventing the expression or even the experience of unacceptable desires by exaggerating the very opposite desire. A disgust of all things sexual that is frequently and powerfully expressed may in fact conceal a sexually voracious appetite. The stereotype of the uptight librarian who suddenly becomes sexually unrestrained following a little bit of encouragement is a good example of this. *Regression* to more infantile modes of behavior is a common means of avoiding stress and of forcing others to adopt a caring role. *Isolation of affect* refers to the separation of painful emotions from associated events. An example would be the distress felt by soldiers when they have to kill. *Repression* is the exclusion from consciousness of distressing feelings or ideas. It is not the same as *suppression*, which refers to deliberate avoidance of disallowed thoughts and behavior.

The main limitation for the Unicorn shadow derives from the undeveloped element of Water. Water refers principally to the world of the emotions, and where this element is weak, as it is here, the individual's insight into the world of emotions can be very limited and limiting. He has difficulty recognizing the emotional needs and motives of others, and in fact he has very little understanding of his own feelings. His prevailing fear is that these powerful forces will overwhelm him, so he represses them. The empathic qualities of Water are typically lacking, and so the individual appears cold and even callous. He may adopt an instrumental attitude toward other people, and because the ethical impulse derived from Air is also relatively weak, he may even make a habit of transgressing formal laws as well as social prohibitions.

Consequently he is deceptive and self-deceptive, as well as emotionally illiterate. Having an incomplete sense of self, he projects his fears onto others. People are a mystery to him, and he becomes paranoid. He can't trust what he doesn't know, and he doesn't know about feelings, which means that he doesn't know about relationships. Yet the Fire primary drives him to seek others, and he does so—but only to manipulate and control them. These strange beings with their loyalties and emotional needs are fair game to him, and he will use them as tools to get what he wants.

The shadow can serve the primary Earth's desire for gain and the primary Fire's desire for power by gaining control over them through lies and half-truths, and by teasing their darkest secrets from them and then holding them to ransom. Intelligent shadows know how to mimic friendship and can be very charming, but their aim is often to dominate, or to split groups and couples for their own ends. The only alternative is to yield to the asocial qualities of Air and become isolated and embittered. A strong Fire primary makes this unlikely, however, and it may be used to burn rather than help others.

Unconscious defense strategies associated with Air include *fantasy*, the excessive preoccupation with daydreams and the imagination as a means of escaping from life's problems and one's own internal conflicts. This is also known as schizoid or autistic fantasy because, in its most extreme forms, this defense mechanism has the effect of removing the person from the social world. *Intellectualization* refers to the overuse of abstract thought in order to avoid psychological discomfort. This is evident from the attempts by some people to split hairs and argue over precise definitions for their behavior, as if they can thereby argue that their maladaptive behavior is in fact acceptable. *Rationalization* refers to the pathological use of apparently plausible reasons to justify your behavior. *Projection* is the unconscious rejection of your own thoughts and character traits. Recognition of these ideas and traits would not fit with the self-concept, and consequently they are ascribed to others.

The negative effects of the undeveloped Air can exacerbate the problems associated with the undeveloped Water by reducing the degree of insight. Without the cool understanding conferred by Air, the shadow is irrational and unpredictable, perhaps even psychotic. Air relates to the intellect and so this shadow type is limited with respect to logical thought and verbal communication skills. They will therefore appear inarticulate when trying to discuss things rationally, and will use bizarre and specious theories in an attempt to justify their outlook. The inability to make themselves properly understood leads to misunderstandings, and if the Fire primary is strong this will in turn lead to fierce arguments.

The negative attributes that characterize the Unicorn shadow are therefore a mixture of the unconscious qualities associated with the undeveloped elements Water and Air (in that order), plus aspects of the primary elements that are being defended against during periods of stress. Which of these attributes is most salient depends very much on the learning experiences of the individual coupled with prevailing circumstances. Although the negative qualities of the primary elements are unpleasant when they come to the fore, they are usually transient and will be the focus of guilt feelings later. The effects of the undeveloped Water and Air are more insidious because they are unconscious, and so work indirectly and constantly to influence feelings, thoughts, and behavior.

The negative qualities associated with Water and Air tend, therefore, to be fairly entrenched because they remain unconscious and undeveloped. The defenses listed above exist to safeguard the integrity of the personality as a whole and can be difficult to dislodge. One of the positive features of Water is to enhance the positive features of Air through understanding of the emotions. One of the positive features of Air is to impart rationalism to Water. With both these elements undeveloped, they cannot be mutually supportive in this way. How this disparity affects magical practice will be outlined below.

The less-attractive features associated with the primary elements Earth and Fire tend, on the other hand, to be relatively transient and mostly activated at times of extreme tension and stress. Even so, the associated behavior and motivation for acting badly are often unconscious because they are in themselves defense strategies, and are consequently characteristics of the shadow. The fact that these behaviors are usually transient can mean that they exert a very damaging effect on interpersonal relations, especially if they are sudden and very much out of character. Of course, some people are chronically stressed and consequently exhibit shadow qualities most of the time. In these cases it can seem out of character if the usual sources of stress are removed and their behavior becomes less offensive.

While the primary elemental influences found in the shadow are on the whole temporary, traces of these characteristics may be evident all the time. Deformation of personality is not all-or-nothing—it exists as a continuum, ranging from severe to very mild. The patterns that derive from the primary elements manifest in the shadow in the following ways, depending on the primary type.

The Wodwose with a Unicorn shadow does not believe that he has intrinsic personal worth; he believes that his value lies in what he owns. To have nothing is therefore the worst possible fate, while the means to getting things is of paramount importance. The threat to his moral and ethical sense is clear. He believes that his failure to succeed in material terms and to acquire prestige from this success reveals his superficiality and the very worthlessness he believes himself to embody. He therefore displays an intense need for recognition through material gain, and his drive to succeed in this as a means of bolstering his sense of security amounts to a compulsion.

Believing at heart that he is inferior to everyone else, he overcompensates by attempting to do more than anyone else. This attempt to do too much allows him to think that he has greater worth than others, and he consequently displays contempt for "lesser" mortals who do far less. He may appear cold and overbearing or merely patronizing, or have a deadly charm that masks sociopathic tendencies. Either way, he is demonstrating his superiority over others. This is why Phoenix and Wodwose types are often given to extravagant display—the Unicorn shadow is pushing for admiration in order to bolster self-esteem.

The Phoenix with a Unicorn shadow differs from the Wodwose sub-type in being less trusting of others. This reflects the influence of Fire as the primary element. Ordinarily Fire is energetic and sociable, offering leadership ability combined with openness and bonhomie. When stressed, however, the ordinarily happy-go-lucky aspect of this element sours and is replaced by a suspicious, overprotected outlook in which the good intentions of others are misinterpreted as malevolent. All kinds of unsupportable slights and damages are referred to and the individual may even attack others suddenly and without warning. Where the Wodwose attempts to prove his superior worth by doing more and having more, the Phoenix proves his greater worth by being directly combative and by subduing people around him. Thus, the socially constructive aspect of Fire may turn antisocial and destructive, even as far as physical aggression.

The paranoia associated with the weak Air feeds this defensive aggression to produce a negative spiral of accusation and recrimination. Because Earth is also strong in this sub-type, the imagined injuries may often center on claims of damage or theft, and consequently the individual concerned will be particularly protective and jealous of personal possessions. Alternatively they may feel that their physical health is being adversely affected by other people's selfish demands, and they may begin to entertain morbid fears. Or they may display mood swings as powerful, unrecognized emotion alternates between sadness and elation. Neither the individual nor those around him will be able to explain or understand this disturbing behavior, and consequent interpersonal disturbances will only serve to make the picture worse.

All of this is difficult for the Phoenix or Wodwose primary because both are sociable types who like to be admired and appreciated by others, but at the same time they can be highly unpleasant if the shadow is too powerful in its effects. Both these types display an aggressive need for power that is tempered by ethical and social considerations when they are functioning well, but during times of extreme stress they can simply be aggressive and confrontational. At these times they trample over others' feelings in an effort to avoid facing their own vulnerability or pain. Unable to face a loss of power over the environment or themselves, they mask their feelings of inadequacy with aggressive displays of strength and recklessness. They can't afford to be defeated by anyone or anything. Strength equals safety, control equals security. Power is good, might is right.

This is explicable in terms of the primary Fire/Earth combination of each type that resides within the shadow. Fire refers to power, Earth to possession. In its shadow aspect, Fire is antisocial and destructive. In its shadow aspect, Earth is grasping and without soul. Thus, the Unicorn shadow indicates the worst features of both primary elements. Unicorns are mystical and otherworldly; Unicorn shadows are cynical and base. The difference in presentation obviously depends on the nature of the primary type. The Unicorn shadow itself is composed of two fundamental opposites, each vying for expression. Consequently, when this shadow emerges, he can exist as a split personality, possibly even as several personalities at different times. The unity symbolized by the unicorn's single horn is therefore lost in the shadow due to poor personal integration.

Any of the psychological qualities referred to above can serve to work against your magical ambitions. From a specifically magical viewpoint, the limitations associated with Unicorn shadows relate mainly to overcoming difficulties of both inceptive and receptive psychic links between this world and the Otherworld. This is a particular problem for Unicorn shadows (as it is for Mer shadows), given that both Air and Water afford access to the other realms and here both are relatively underdeveloped and unconscious.

Thus, not only is there a weakness in the intuitive link, there is also a weakness in the creative link. For the Unicorn variant (as opposed to the Mermaid), the difficulty is associated principally with Water's receptive aspect and with emotional limitation. Emotion is the power that drives intention, so limitations in this regard will manifest as dissipation of power due to being emotionally subdued, or to losing the psychic link at the crucial point of exchange. Basically, shadow Unicorns are at risk of being cut off from the very otherworldly forces that magic is designed to influence, both at the initial contact stage and at the direction stage.

Each individual has the potential to sabotage his or her own efforts, and the greatest potential for this depends on the undeveloped elements. Water is the least developed, most unconsciously active element in the case of the Unicorn shadow. Thus, the emotional focus that should lead toward the goal can be unconsciously directed away from the desired end for various reasons. The main reason is fear. In the first place, the emotions are fearful forces to the owner of the shadow, and he will be defending against their expression and application.

Secondly, there is a fear of magic. That a magician should fear magic sounds odd at first, but remember that we should all be wary of it and cultivate a healthy respect. Further than this, however, is the deep-rooted moral admonition against "playing God." A lifetime of conditioning has to be overcome before this particular limitation can be uprooted. Another lifetime of conditioning concerns the fear of the Otherworld, of ghosts, demons, and all the other occult things that fall outside the sphere of the "good." If you intend to practice magic, you have presumably made a conscious decision that it is not of itself evil, and that you will not be pursued and destroyed by devils. Unconsciously, however, you may continue to believe these things and will therefore want to fail in order to maintain your sense of security.

As mentioned, this problem is exacerbated by the undeveloped Air element (although a low Q score reflects lesser difficulties). Where Water provides the intuitive, nonverbal link with psychic forces and the emotional strength and maturity for the magical enterprise, the Air element provides the verbal, more direct communication and the necessary focus. Air confers a particular ability to state goals with precision, formulate appropriate affirmations, and use powerful incantations. It also predisposes you to a skill with visualization that is essential to successful practice, since this effectively opens the door to the

Otherworld. All these skills and abilities are compromised by the shadow facets of Water and Air.

Additional unconscious factors associated with Air are likely to be more insidious and limiting. The very rationalism and logic that Air symbolizes militates against the very notion of magic. Since the inception of the Age of Enlightenment, when superstition was swept away and rationalism became our creed, the mechanical, clockwork universe replaced the occult universe that had preceded it. As we have seen, modern science now cleaves more to an apparently irrational model with which ordinary people are still not entirely familiar. We have all grown up imbued with rationalist principles and the scientific endeavor. This lifetime of obeisance to rationalism can be difficult to dismiss entirely, no matter how fully you may disregard it on a conscious level. At the back of your mind there lurks a man in a white coat, shaking his head at magic—and you believe he is right.

These elemental shortcomings and preoccupations may reveal themselves in dreams and fantasies involving water, particularly drowning, but also of thirst, and often as mysterious creatures from the hidden depths. You may dream of being on a sinking ship or of being unable to swim. Similarly there can be dreams and obsessions with falling, choking, being lost, or of huge birds and other powerful entities that come from the sky. There may also be dreams or waking preoccupations about other people, especially fighting with them. Dreams of crowds or of isolation may also be prominent.

Firebird Shadow

Air with Fire

Keywords: Intolerant, multiple personality, cowardly,
apathetic, unmotivated, irrational, paranoid

The firebird is a benevolent creature that guards against evil. Where the Firebird primary is bright and soars upward toward the sun, the Firebird shadow is an ill omen that swoops down from the sky as a bird of prey. This creature is malevolent and harbors ill will toward people. It is even resentful of being helped and will seek revenge for imagined injuries. Where the Firebird is a symbol of creativity, the Firebird shadow is a symbol of destruction.

It should be clear from the above that the Firebird shadow is neither tolerant nor forgiving of human failings. The strong primary Water belies the unconscious influence of the undeveloped Fire coupled with the undeveloped Air. Consequently the emotions are not informed and tempered by Air's rationalism, and misinterpretation of people's motives is a frequent result. The quiet, smoldering Fire hidden in the back of the mind then burns on, fed by imagined slights. Moreover, this type does not have sufficient personal insight to know why they are upset and will therefore be prone to rapidly shifting affects that can make them difficult to understand.

Paradoxically he is embarrassed by emotions while simultaneously giving free vent to the full range of affective response. His emotional states are all-or-nothing affairs that betray the lack of Air as a moderating factor. Without a sufficiently strong intellectual component, this shadow virtually becomes a different person according to which emotion holds sway at any given moment. Not only that, these states are so compartmentalized that they can even seem to be autonomous. Without his emotional personae, this shadow will feel that he does not exist, and if he is extolled to be less emotional he would react as if his whole identity were being stolen from him, so total does each of these transient states seem.

What this amounts to is a lack of a properly integrated personal self. The constant oscillation between states and between personalities, depending on the company and the situation, means that he is constantly confused about what he should be feeling—indeed, who he should be—and what he actually does feel. To be on the safe side, he will usually take on the mood and character of his surroundings. As a result, this overtly sociable and fun-loving person actually lacks spontaneity and tends to be extremely conventional despite a rebellious attitude.

This indicates that the Firebird shadow is someone who not only is different people at different times but also wants to be all the people he sees around him. Who he wants to be at any given time will depend on prevailing circumstances, but resentment and jealousy are the twin bases that keep the desire constant and universal. Usually this wish to have those qualities observed in others centers on intellectual skills or physical power and authority. He is not gifted with an acute intellect of the academic type even if he is actually highly intelligent. Consequently he resents it in others and regards it as a personal slur. He will also try to bolster his self-esteem by reference to spurious logic and incredible theories, then become angry and sulk if these are refuted. On other occasions he will arrogantly dismiss well-thought-out arguments as pretentious garbage. The next day will find him stating the same things from a position of assumed authority.

Authority is what this type wants and feels he does not have. He may in fact be gifted with a sound practical sense by virtue of the strong primary Earth, or have great powers of empathy by virtue of the strong Water primary. Still he will believe that he lacks all the qualities that will give him self-worth, and these qualities are those belonging to other people. It's as if his precious attributes were stolen from him and given away, when the fact of the matter is that he simply does not possess them and never did. What it comes down to is an inability to accept himself for what he is.

Various unconscious defense strategies have been identified, and these can be related to the elements. Psychological defense mechanisms that stem from Fire include *acting out*, the direct expression of feelings such as rage without reflection, guilt, or regard for consequences. Like the other defense strategies, this is a means of coping with stress and inner conflict. Deliberate self-harm in its various forms, including drug abuse and self-mutilation, can be recognized as essentially acts of aggression against the self in order to affect others in some way. *Displacement* is easier to understand. This involves directing pent-up rage onto others who are weaker and hence less dangerous than yourself. Kicking the cat would be an example. *Splitting* is an alternation between idealization and devaluation. Here the other person is seen as either all good or all bad. *Devaluation* involves demeaning oneself or another by exaggerating perceived negative attributes, ridiculing competence, and so on. *Idealization* involves exaggerating your own virtues or more commonly those of another in order to avoid recognizing bad aspects of yourself.

Identification is similar to idealization, and the two may coexist. Identification refers to the unconscious modeling of another person's attributes in order to increase one's own sense of self-worth. Identification with an aggressor is a common method of reducing one's fear of him or her. The belief here is that the potential threat will diminish if the aggressor recognizes the similarities. *Introjection* is similar in that it involves incorporation of another's values or personal traits in order to prevent conflict with or threat from them, but it does not have to uphold self-esteem. It is seen following loss, however, when the characteristics of the departed person (most commonly the case) are expressed by a living person as a defense against the loss.

Authority also comes from having strength and physical power. Control is of fundamental importance to this shadow, since he does not want to be under the control—

and hence at the mercy—of others. Far better that he should be in a position of control so that he can have a sense of security. From this position he can arrogantly set about changing everyone according to how they "ought" to be. This is, of course, a projection of his own wish to change, but since he cannot, he tries to make others do so. As far as this goes, he is hypocritical and does not practice what he preaches, keeping one rule for himself and another for everyone else.

Fire is undeveloped in this shadow, however, and his aggression is submerged and smoldering. Attempts to control or to dominate others will therefore most likely be passive-aggressive in nature, although there can be spectacular displays of more direct aggression at times. Being inactive, forgetful, late, neglectful of detail, and so on are common means of being aggressive without being openly confrontational. The neurotic defense mechanisms characteristic of Air, such as rationalization, are then employed in order to justify the failure to arrive on time, or for having done things in the wrong order, or whatever, and to avoid blame. Direct aggression will usually be reserved for those who are weaker and therefore unable to fight back. This shadow is desperate to fit in and be accepted and to be well-thought-of by others. This tends to mean others with whom he would like to fit in. Established relationships, such as family, are often taken for granted until there are signs that he has gone too far.

Firebird shadows exhibit the negative aspects of Fire in an unconscious, uncontrolled way and may lack the positive qualities in everyday behavior. Accordingly, there is a lack of energy, drive, passion; the power to project himself effectively and to make his presence felt is diminished, and belief in his ability to effect change is reduced. Clearly this is a great handicap in any venture and amounts to a failure of ambition, a problem that can be characteristic of the Firebird shadow's life generally. Without the urge to succeed, this type will be prone to vacillation and to years of aimless drifting, sometimes for years, perhaps always, unless the individual concerned determines to take charge of his life and takes steps to combat the problem. Given the prospect of a lifetime of aimlessness, it can actually be to this type's advantage to be shaken up by some kind of apparent disaster that provides the impetus for overhaul.

Unconscious defense strategies associated with Air include *fantasy*, the excessive preoccupation with daydreams and the imagination as a means of escaping from life's problems and one's own internal conflicts. This is also known as schizoid or autistic fantasy because in its most extreme forms this defense mechanism has the effect of removing the person from the social world. *Intellectualization* refers to the overuse of abstract thought in order to avoid psychological discomfort. This is evident from the attempts by some people to split hairs and argue over precise definitions for their behavior, as if they can thereby argue that their maladaptive behavior is in fact acceptable. *Rationalization* refers to the pathological use of apparently plausible reasons to justify behavior. *Projection* is the unconscious rejection of one's own thoughts and character traits. Recognition of these ideas and traits would not fit with the self-concept, and consequently they are ascribed to others. *Repression* is fairly well-known to most people as the exclusion from consciousness of distressing feelings or ideas. Note that it is not the same as *suppression*, which is a deliberate pushing away of unacceptable thoughts and behavior.

Stress such as this can stir up emotions and all the various personae so that he doesn't know what to do or who to be. Overwhelmed by this confusing flood of competing voices, he can suffer transient psychotic episodes. This is one of the most threatening of all the qualities of the undeveloped Air, since without rationality we are unable to tell what's real from what isn't, and therefore we can't function as autonomous individuals. It is at this point that the shadow begins his paranoid recriminations and accusations, many of them stored up since childhood. People who know the Firebird shadow well will often suspect that he is a little paranoid. At these times of crisis there is no doubt.

The negative attributes that characterize the Firebird shadow are therefore a mixture of the unconscious qualities associated with the undeveloped elements Fire and Air (in that order), plus aspects of the primary elements that are being defended against during periods of stress. Which of these attributes is most salient depends very much on the learning experiences of the individual coupled with prevailing circumstances. Although the negative qualities of the primary elements are unpleasant when they come to the fore, they are usually transient and will be the focus of guilt feelings later. The effects of the undeveloped Fire and Air are more insidious because they are unconscious and so work indirectly and constantly to influence feelings, thoughts, and behavior.

The negative qualities associated with Fire and Air tend, therefore, to be fairly entrenched because they remain unconscious and undeveloped. The defenses listed above exist to safeguard the integrity of the personality as a whole and can be difficult to dislodge. One of the positive features of Fire is to enhance the positive features of Air through spiritual nourishment of ideals. One of the positive features of Air is to feed and give direction to Fire. With both these elements undeveloped, they cannot be mutually supportive in this way. How this disparity affects magical practice will be outlined below.

The less-attractive features associated with the primary elements Earth and Water tend, on the other hand, to be relatively transient and mostly activated at times of extreme tension and stress. Even so, the associated behavior and motivation for acting badly are often unconscious because they are in themselves defense strategies and are consequently characteristics of the shadow. The fact that these behaviors are usually transient can mean that they exert a very damaging effect on interpersonal relations, especially if they are sudden and very much out of character. Of course, some people are chronically stressed and consequently exhibit shadow qualities most of the time. In these cases it can seem out of character if the usual sources of stress are removed and their behavior becomes less offensive.

While the primary elemental influences found in the shadow are on the whole temporary, traces of these characteristics may be evident all the time. Deformation of personality is not all-or-nothing—it exists as a continuum, ranging from severe to very mild. The patterns that derive from the primary elements manifest in the shadow in the following ways, depending on the primary type.

The Centaur with Firebird shadow has Earth as the primary element. Consequently, behavior that may become prominent during times of stress includes a sense of apathy and pointlessness to the point of physical self-neglect. A particular danger for Firebird shadows, therefore, is the undeveloped Fire element that represents lack of motivation. Coupled with the inertia inherent in the Earth element, there is great potential to produce a very sluggish, depressed individual. Because the influence is unconscious, the cause of this depression will often be unknown; indeed, the depression itself may go unrecognized and manifest as physical weakness, lack of appetite, and so on, such that a physical illness is suspected.

The alternative response is to overindulge as a means of numbing the discomfort and reducing the anxious distress. At these times he may drink too much, take drugs, or engage in indiscriminate sexual encounters. Since it is in the nature of the primary Earth to be restrained and cautious, this kind of behavior is decidedly out of character, even if the Water secondary is quite strong. Following these binges, after the crisis period has ended, he will usually be overcome with remorse and shame at having behaved in this way.

The Satyr with Firebird shadow has Water in primary position. This makes it unlikely that the individual will become socially isolated. However, during times of stress and tension, the less-attractive features associated with this element emerge as part of the shadow. These include a compulsive tendency to engage in competitive relationships and sexual conquests. The motivation for this kind of behavior is to boost a flagging self-esteem and to counter insecurity. The target for these endeavors will often be someone who is already attached, because what better to prove your own worth than stealing someone else's partner? In order to accomplish this aim the shadow will use anything and everything, from charm and flattery to the most outrageous flirting, to achieve their aim.

They are outrageous flirts but have no real interest in the target, and as soon as they get the necessary response they lose interest. The response can be as little as a knowing smile, but they will pursue more difficult quarry as far as having an affair with them, only to drop them suddenly and without a hint of guilt. Mission accomplished, they become as cold and rejecting as they had been warm and inviting. Of course the shadow finds negative emotions such as jealousy difficult to deal with and may repress all knowledge of them. Yet they will continue to manifest, often in disguised form, possibly as depression, often as physical illness.

Another common manifestation of temporary stress, however, is the reverse of this picture. This involves an excessive need to be taken care of such that the individual concerned becomes clingy and desperate in the face of imagined separation and loss. Consequently the person concerned will appear helpless and needy but no more accepting of reassurance than they are able to make decisions. Their sense of personal security is delegated entirely to those whose affection they are so unsure of. They are therefore submissive and manipulative in the attempt to satisfy their emotional insecurity.

All of these weaknesses can represent powerful limitations to successful magical outcomes. Since Fire is the weakest element in the Firebird shadow, the magician consequently loses the source of energy that magic depends on. Fire refers to the actual energy we call magic. This is the drive, the passion, and the very power that you want to direct. It goes without saying that in the absence of this passion and drive, the enterprise is doomed to failure. This energy is stirred up by the application of the will at the point in the process during which the magician attempts to petition the entities that have hopefully been contacted already. If because of the makeup of his or her personality the magician has a poor affinity with this element, the associated magical qualities will not be readily available. A limited disposition toward Fire can be very limiting indeed, not least because success depends in part on the conviction that the goal is already attained. Fire provides this conviction, the desire, and the will.

There can also be unconscious self-sabotage at work. Fire relates to morals and religious feeling, so the underlying belief that magic is an affront to God or just plain wrong can be a major factor leading to failure. Among the contradictions of Western society is the urge to succeed coupled with admonition for being successful. The socioeconomic system encourages pursuit of worldly success, while the Church condemns it. We grow up trying to reconcile the elements of this paradox and cannot assume that it does not continue to exert an unconscious effect even if we consciously reject it.

The undeveloped Air of the Firebird shadow makes for a weakness in the creative, inceptive link with the forces of the Otherworld. Firebird shadows are at risk of being cut off from the very otherworldly forces that magic is designed to influence. This is because an affinity for the Air element provides the verbal, more direct communication and focus required in magic. As stated elsewhere in this book, Air confers a particular ability to state goals with precision, formulate appropriate affirmations, and use powerful incantations. It also predisposes you to a skill with visualization that is essential to successful practice, since this acts to open the door to the Otherworld through which the magician hails the invisible entities with which he hopes to associate. This initial contact—and with it, the magical intention—are compromised by the undeveloped Air of the shadow.

Additional unconscious factors associated with Air are likely to be more insidious and limiting. The very rationalism and logic that Air symbolizes militates against the very notion of magic. Since the inception of the Age of Enlightenment, when superstition was swept away and rationalism became our creed, the mechanical, clockwork universe replaced the occult universe that had preceded it. As we have seen, modern science now cleaves more to an apparently irrational model with which ordinary people are still not entirely familiar. We have all grown up imbued with rationalist principles and the scientific endeavor. This lifetime of obeisance to rationalism can be difficult to dismiss entirely, no matter how fully you may disregard it on a conscious level. At the back of your mind there lurks a man in a white coat, shaking his head at magic—and you believe he is right.

These elemental shortcomings and preoccupations may reveal themselves in dreams and fantasies involving symbols of Fire principally, particularly the threat of being burned or of wandering in deserts, but also of being very cold and in need of warmth. There may often be dreams of fierce animals such as lions and tigers that are associated with the sun and hot countries. Similarly there can be dreams and obsessions with falling, choking, being lost, or of huge birds and other powerful entities that come from the sky. There may also be dreams or waking preoccupations about other people, especially of feeling threatened by them.

Dragon Shadow

Fire with Air

Keywords: Shallow, destructive, irrational,
paranoid, bizarre, cowardly, apathetic

Dragons represent the powers of Nature in all her manifestations, but in the West the dragon has acquired an enduring sinister aspect associated with malignancy and brute force. Since the dragon represents the very essence of nature, it also stands for the destructive, devouring effects of time and of the Earth itself. The dragon in its negative aspect thus represents the inevitability of old age and death, and the eventual triumph of the forces of the Underworld over the questing hero.

The Dragon shadow has the same capacity to destroy as the primary Dragon does to create. When nature's equilibrium is undisturbed, these forces of creation and destruction are in harmony, and life proceeds as a consequence of the dynamic interplay between opposites. Here, of course, we are faced with only one-half of the equation in the realm of personal and interpersonal relations, and magic.

Probably the most outstanding feature of the Dragon shadow is his shallowness. Everything is show and calculated to produce an effect that is entirely for the moment to impress others. And the people he wants to impress are important in some way, because he will only mix with the best. This is because he believes that he is the best, and so must associate with his own. Hence he is conceited and arrogant, a supreme snob. He is infuriatingly superior and an incurable name-dropper, always emphasizing his own superiority by alluding to his illustrious contacts and acquaintances and your lesser status by implication.

He will therefore work hard to make these connections between himself and the famous and wealthy, and will contrive to be at all the right places and social events in order to rub shoulders with them. If he can have them come to him, then so much the better. This places him one step closer to having these people as his personal friends. This would be his dream come true, because then he would be one of them and in his rightful place among the crème de la crème.

For this reason, and as far as his means will allow, he will be extremely ostentatious as well as opportunistic. The whole point of dressing extremely well and hosting fabulous parties is to set traps into which the great and good can be lured like moths to a flame. Once there, the Dragon shadow can begin the task of ingratiating himself in earnest. It's the same even if the primary element is Earth. This just means that the shadow will home in on particular people and work more steadily and unobtrusively, making less blatant plays for their attention and hosting smaller, more intimate affairs.

If Water is the primary element, however, the shadow is more likely to be indiscriminate in his choice of targets, caring only that they are high profile. Satyr primaries are also more likely to attend and host bigger parties where they can be in the presence of more people, and hopefully more famous people. He is also more likely to indulge in indiscriminate sexual encounters as far as opportunity permits. The Centaur variant is more likely to home in on certain people. It doesn't matter if the shadow does not live in a neighborhood teeming with celebrities. There are always local dignitaries who can be the focus for social climbing, and there is always the possibility of moving on from here to richer ground.

None of this sounds very commendable, but then it doesn't sound very destructive either. The destructive aspect tends to manifest over a period of time, although particular events can be particularly damaging. In the first place the shadow can grow stronger over time with increased success. As he moves up and on within the world of the glorious, he can become increasingly insensitive and superior to the other people around him. This inevitably means that he offends more people, more and more of whom are themselves in positions of power, and inevitably makes more enemies. Eventually he can be hung by his own petard and suffer a spectacular fall from grace, much to the satisfaction of those he has injured.

This would be a tragedy for this shadow, because it would reveal his own basic sense of worthlessness. Worse, it would humiliate him before the very people he wishes to impress. Dragon shadows are no more likely than the rest of us to have the means to keep up a showy display, and so they tend on the whole to be utterly dependent on those with whom they would be allied. There comes a point, therefore, when they are trapped, having maneuvered themselves into a position from which they are unable to escape or progress. By now, of course, their dignity is compromised because they will have to be more obvious toadies in order to maintain their privileged position. These shadows are surprisingly easy to trap in this way because they are as gullible when their benefactors make promises as they are astute in their social climbing.

The other destructive potential relates to their treatment of people who have outlived their usefulness as rungs in the ladder to the stars. These people can suddenly find themselves snubbed and discarded and the targets of the shadow's contempt once he has surpassed them in his climb. These people can then become the enemies that engineer the shadow's downfall at a later date.

Various unconscious defense strategies have been identified, and these can be related to the elements. Psychological defense mechanisms that stem from Fire include *acting out*, the direct expression of feelings such as rage without reflection, guilt, or regard for consequences. Like the other defense strategies, this is a means of coping with stress and inner conflict. Deliberate self-harm in its various forms, including drug abuse and self-mutilation, can be recognized as essentially acts of aggression against the self in order to affect others in some way.

Displacement is easier to understand. This involves directing pent-up rage onto others who are weaker and hence less dangerous than yourself. Kicking the cat would be an example. *Splitting* is an alternation between idealization and devaluation. Here the other person is seen as either all good or all bad. *Devaluation* involves demeaning oneself or another by exaggerating perceived negative attributes, ridiculing competence, and so on. *Idealization* involves exaggerating your own virtues or more commonly those of another in order to avoid recognizing bad aspects of yourself.

Identification is similar to idealization, and the two may coexist. Identification refers to the unconscious modeling of another person's attributes in order to increase one's own sense of self-worth. Identification with an aggressor is a common method of reducing one's fear of him or her. The belief here is that the potential threat will diminish if the aggressor recognizes the similarities. *Introjection* is similar in that it involves incorporation of another's values or personal traits in order to prevent conflict with or threat from them, but it does not have to uphold self-esteem. It is seen following loss, however, when the characteristics of the departed person (most commonly the case) are expressed by a living person as a defense against the loss.

The shameless dropping of friends betrays the shadow's rashness. His desire to be among the best can make him impulsive, and this is a feature of the undeveloped Fire. This relatively weak element can also incline the shadow to passive-aggressive strategies such as being late, losing things, and making mistakes as a means of attacking people. Thus, they "forget" to meet you, or they "lost" your number (despite having it for years). They are also unreliable, promising much and delivering little. The shadow's Fire can also flare up unpredictably, typically when he is acting defensively for having betrayed someone, but more frequently it will be directed at those who are lower down the pecking order. On these occasions he can be blistering in his attack on the unfortunate recipient, after which he will act the injured party as a way of smothering a sense of guilt.

Dragon shadows exhibit the negative aspects of Fire in an unconscious, uncontrolled way and tend to lack the positive qualities associated with this element. Since Fire relates to energy and drive, the shadow may feel listless and unmotivated except in the pursuit of the all-important goal of vicarious success. He does not believe in his own ability to succeed, and therefore does his best to bathe in reflected glory as a substitute. Lack of ambition is a great handicap in any venture, and so it is in magic, since success depends in part on the conviction that the goal is already attained. This problem can be characteristic of the Dragon shadow's life generally. Without the urge to succeed by their own efforts, this type faces the prospect of a lifetime of aimlessness and drifting, hence the concentration on other people's success. At heart, however, the Dragon shadow regards all worldly success to be futile, including that of others.

Unconscious defense strategies associated with Air include *fantasy*, the excessive preoccupation with daydreams and the imagination as a means of escaping from life's problems and one's own internal conflicts. This is also known as schizoid or autistic fantasy because in its most extreme forms this defense mechanism has the effect of removing the person from the social world. *Intellectualization* refers to the overuse of abstract thought in order to avoid psychological discomfort. This is evident from the attempts by some people to split hairs and argue over precise definitions for their behavior, as if they can thereby argue that their maladaptive behavior is in fact acceptable.

Rationalization refers to the pathological use of apparently plausible reasons to justify behavior. *Projection* is the unconscious rejection of one's own thoughts and character traits. Recognition of these ideas and traits would not fit with the self-concept, and consequently they are ascribed to others. *Repression* is fairly well-known to most people as the exclusion from consciousness of distressing feelings or ideas. Note that it is not the same as *suppression*, which is a deliberate pushing away of unacceptable thoughts and behavior.

The undeveloped Air also means that they do not have the qualities of good judgement and foresight to see the truth in the old maxim "Be careful who you tread on as you go up, you may meet them again on the way down." They place great faith in chance and in their destiny as successful people. They can be rather unconventional at the best of times, but increased stress can make them quite bizarre, even to the point of psychosis and paranoia. All kinds of specious reasoning will be employed to justify their actions and, more importantly, to fool themselves and avoid having to face up to reality.

This last point is the main key to understanding the motives of the Dragon shadow. It was pointed out above that in its negative aspect the dragon symbolizes the triumph of old age and death. This is the unpalatable reality that the Dragon shadow unconsciously and assiduously attempts to avoid by frantically chasing after the trappings of worldly success. The Dragon shadow believes in death absolutely, and life therefore becomes a futile struggle to postpone the inevitable. The constant distraction provided by the facile world of local or even international celebrity is a focus to avoid realization of this ultimate horror. The Dragon shadow is afraid of failure, and death is the greatest of all.

The negative attributes that characterize the Dragon shadow are therefore a mixture of the unconscious qualities associated with the undeveloped elements Air and Fire (in that order), plus aspects of the primary elements that are being defended against during periods of stress. Which of these attributes is most salient depends very much on the learning experiences of the individual, coupled with prevailing circumstances. Although the negative qualities of the primary elements are unpleasant when they come to the fore, they are usually transient and will be the focus of guilt feelings later. The effects of the undeveloped Air and Fire are more insidious because they are unconscious, and so work indirectly and constantly to influence feelings, thoughts, and behavior.

The negative qualities associated with Air and Fire tend therefore to be fairly entrenched because they remain unconscious and undeveloped. The defenses listed above exist to safeguard the integrity of the personality as a whole and can be difficult to dislodge. One of the positive features of Fire is to enhance the positive features of Air through spiritual nourishment of ideals. One of the positive features of Air is to feed and give direction to Fire. With both these elements undeveloped, they cannot be mutually supportive in this way. How this disparity affects magical practice will be outlined below.

The less-attractive features associated with the primary elements Earth and Water tend, on the other hand, to be relatively transient and mostly activated at times of extreme tension and stress. Even so, the associated behavior and motivation for acting badly are often unconscious because they are in themselves defense strategies and are consequently characteristics of the shadow. The fact that these behaviors are usually transient can mean that they exert a very damaging effect on interpersonal relations, especially if they are sudden and very much out of character. Of course, some people are chronically stressed and consequently exhibit shadow qualities most of the time. In these cases it can seem out of character if the usual sources of stress are removed and their behavior becomes less offensive.

While the primary elemental influences found in the shadow are on the whole temporary, traces of these characteristics may be evident all the time. Deformation of personality is not all-or-nothing—it exists as a continuum, ranging from severe to very mild. The patterns that derive from the primary elements manifest in the shadow in the following ways, depending on the primary type.

The Centaur with Dragon shadow has Earth as the primary element. Consequently, behavior that may become prominent during times of stress includes a sense of apathy and pointlessness to the point of physical self-neglect. A particular danger for Firebird shadows, therefore, is the undeveloped Fire element that represents lack of motivation. Coupled with the inertia inherent in the Earth element, there is great potential to produce a very sluggish, depressed individual. Because the influence is unconscious, the cause of this depression will often be unknown; indeed, the depression itself may go unrecognized and manifest as physical weakness, lack of appetite, and so on, such that a physical illness is suspected.

The alternative response is to overindulge as a means of numbing the discomfort and reducing the anxious distress. At these times he may drink too much, take drugs, or engage in indiscriminate sexual encounters. Since it is in the nature of the primary Earth to be restrained and cautious, this kind of behavior is decidedly out of character, even if the Water secondary is quite strong. Following these binges, after the crisis period has ended, he will usually be overcome with remorse and shame at having behaved in this way.

The Satyr with Dragon shadow has Water in primary position. This makes it unlikely that the individual will become socially isolated. However, during times of stress and tension, the less-attractive features associated with this element emerge as part of the shadow. These include a compulsive tendency to engage in competitive relationships and sexual conquests. The motivation for this kind of behavior is to boost a flagging self-esteem and counter insecurity. The target for these endeavors will often be someone who is already attached, because what better to prove your own worth than stealing someone else's partner? In order to accomplish this aim, the shadow will use anything and everything, from charm and flattery to the most outrageous flirting, to achieve his or her aim.

They are outrageous flirts but have no real interest in the target, and as soon as they get the necessary response they lose interest. The response can be as little as a knowing smile, but they will pursue more difficult quarry as far as having an affair with them, only to drop them suddenly and without a hint of guilt. Mission accomplished, they become as cold and rejecting as they had been warm and inviting. Of course the shadow finds negative emotions such as jealousy difficult to deal with, and may repress all knowledge of them. Yet they will continue to manifest, often in disguised form, possibly as depression, often as physical illness.

Another common manifestation of temporary stress, however, is the reverse of this picture. This involves an excessive need to be taken care of such that the individual concerned becomes clingy and desperate in the face of imagined separation and loss. Consequently the person concerned will appear helpless and needy but no more accepting of reassurance than they are able to make decisions. Their sense of personal security is delegated entirely to those whose affection they are so unsure of. They are therefore submissive and manipulative in the attempt to satisfy their emotional insecurity.

All of these weaknesses can represent powerful limitations to successful magical outcomes. Since Air is the weakest element in the Dragon shadow, there is a particular weakness in the creative, inceptive link with the forces of the Otherworld. Dragon shadows are at risk of being cut off from the very otherworldly forces that magic is designed to influence. This is because an affinity for the Air element provides the verbal, more direct communication and focus required in magic. As stated elsewhere, Air confers a particular ability to state goals with precision, formulate appropriate affirmations, and use powerful incantations. It also predisposes you to a skill with visualization that is essential to successful practice, since this acts to open the door to the Otherworld through which the magician hails the invisible entities with which he hopes to associate. This initial contact—and with it, the magical intention—are compromised by the undeveloped Air of the shadow.

Additional unconscious factors associated with Air are likely to be more insidious and limiting. The very rationalism and logic that Air symbolizes militates against the very notion of magic. Since the inception of the Age of Enlightenment, when superstition was swept away and rationalism became our creed, the mechanical, clockwork universe replaced the occult universe that had preceded it. As we have seen, modern science now cleaves more to an apparently irrational model with which ordinary people are still not entirely familiar. We have all grown up imbued with rationalist principles and the scientific endeavor. This lifetime of obeisance to rationalism can be difficult to dismiss entirely no matter how fully you may disregard it on a conscious level. At the back of your mind there lurks a man in a white coat, shaking his head at magic—and you believe he is right.

With a weak affinity for the undeveloped Fire of the shadow, the magician loses the source of energy that magic depends on. Fire refers to the actual energy we call magic. This is the drive, the passion, and the very power that you want to direct. It goes without saying that in the absence of this passion and drive, the enterprise is doomed to failure. This energy is stirred up by the application of the will at the point in the process during which the magician attempts to petition the entities that have hopefully been contacted already. If, because of the makeup of his personality, the magician has a poor affinity with this element, the associated magical qualities will not be readily available. A limited disposition toward Fire can be very limiting indeed, not least because success depends in part on the conviction that the goal is already attained. Fire provides this conviction, the desire, and the will.

There can also be unconscious self-sabotage at work. Fire relates to morals and religious feeling, so the underlying belief that magic is an affront to God or just plain wrong can be a major factor leading to failure. Among the contradictions of Western society is the urge to succeed coupled with admonition for being successful. The socioeconomic system encourages pursuit of worldly success, while the Church condemns it. We grow up trying to reconcile the elements of this paradox and, even if we consciously reject it, cannot assume that it does not continue to exert an unconscious effect.

These elemental shortcomings and preoccupations may reveal themselves in dreams and fantasies involving symbols of Air principally, particularly dreams and obsessions with falling, choking, being lost, or of huge birds and other powerful entities that come from the sky. Similarly, there can be preoccupations with and dreams about fire, symbolized as the threat of being burned or of wandering in deserts, but also of being very cold and in need of warmth. There may often be dreams of fierce animals such as lions and tigers that are associated with the sun and hot countries. There may also be dreams or waking preoccupations about other people, especially of feeling threatened by them.

Phoenix Shadow

Fire with Earth

Keywords: Pessimistic, disillusioned, lethargic, lazy,
neglectful, apathetic, cowardly, unmotivated

In myth, the phoenix symbolizes regeneration and rebirth, continuity through change, and the power of the divine. The phoenix in its negative aspect, therefore, symbolizes the failure of this process. It refers to stagnation and loss of hope. Since the phoenix is also a symbol of the rising sun reborn at the start of the new day, it is also a symbol of the resurrection of the god. It is no surprise that the Christians appropriated this mythical beast to represent Christ. The cold, dark phoenix, therefore, represents nothing less than the failure of the divine spirit.

In personal terms, the Phoenix shadow refers to personal stagnation. This type combines the worst features of undeveloped Earth with those of undeveloped Fire, hence laziness and lack of motivation. At the heart of the Phoenix shadow's dilemma is disillusionment. He does not believe that things will or can change for the better, and he believes that he cannot develop either. There is a fundamental lack of confidence in this type that can be difficult to overcome. This is associated with a quest for self-definition, a need to establish a clear identity. Until this is achieved, lack of self-confidence allied with intense self-consciousness places a limitation on his potential. In short, he needs to be transformed.

Until this quest for self is finalized, the shadow will engage in distractions that over-compensate for the sense of failure. With Water in first position, he may be exhibition-istic as a means of establishing his presence. He may be self-centered and take people for granted. He may be imperious and autocratic, full of a sense of his own importance that is, of course, born of a deep-seated sense of futility. He considers himself to be of special importance and may even show signs of megalomania. At the same time, other people are regarded as lacking distinction. Indeed, he may go so far as to gloss over individual differences entirely, as if the people around him were little more than num-bered sheep.

This failure to recognize people as individuals in their own right may cause him to appropriate their ideas and innovations and to genuinely think that they originated with him. He may even accuse the person who had the idea of stealing it from him! It is impossible for him to imagine that someone else can do something special and unique, because that's what he does. He regards himself as the shining one, God's gift—and perhaps God, in fact, for all anyone knows.

This grandiosity and insensitivity masks a lack of self-esteem and an intense need to be valued by other people. On the other hand, he can't meet people as equals because to do so would be to admit that he is not unique. The fact that everyone is unique makes everyone equal, and he cannot feel valued unless he is special. He must stand out from the crowd or be subsumed within the mass of undifferentiated humanity, hence the neurotic drive to be outstanding.

This assumption of being special means that he does not have to obey the same social rules as the rest of us. Thus he frequently flouts the rules of common courtesy by not saying thanks, or ignores the law of the land by driving the wrong way along one-way streets, and so on. He can be sincerely amazed if he is reprimanded for any of this behavior because for one thing, he can do as he likes, and secondly, no one has the authority to tell him not to. In many ways, he is the law as he sees it.

Yet he knows that he is no more special than anyone else, even if he has a special talent that makes him shine. Somewhere within his unconscious is the knowledge that we are all divine and that worldly acclaim is transient and peripheral. The inability to accommodate this within the normal run of things presents a problem, and he attempts to distract himself from this by concentrating on display, either of himself or things. Hence he is much given to extravagance and spending sprees, whether or not he has the means, and he can run up breathtaking levels of debt in the process.

Various unconscious defense strategies have been identified, and these can be related to the elements. Defense strategies related to Earth include *projection*, the unconscious rejection of unwanted thoughts and personal traits by ascribing them to others. The Phoenix shadow also exhibits *denial*, an unconscious refusal to acknowledge external realities because to do so would be too painful; and *somatization*, a preoccupation with physical symptoms that represents a psychological reaction to stressful situations. Denial of the physical self can also be seen among shadows that have a prominent Earth, Phoenix among them.

Much of this is also sheer laziness due to the undeveloped Earth. The undeveloped Earth also makes this shadow unrealistic in his aims, and this in turn is exacerbated by the undeveloped Fire's lack of ambition. Similar problems beset other shadow types with weak Fire, but the problem is greatest for Phoenix and Wodwose shadows because of the associated drag of the undeveloped Earth. Without the urge to succeed, this type will be prone to vacillation and to a lifetime of aimless drifting. His attempt to succeed on the backs of others is his only real ambition, but this vicarious success is only a poor substitute for the real thing. Of course the problem is his sense of futility. He does not believe he can change anything, including himself.

Another consequence of the undeveloped Earth is that the things of the earth are disregarded and devalued, including the body itself. There are two possible patterns of behavior connected with this. One is that Phoenix shadows are neglectful of their physical needs entirely, and don't eat properly or even dress to keep warm when necessary. They may deny that they have genuine physical illnesses that are obvious to other people. This pattern can be evident even when the individual is apparently functioning well. He may rationalize his poor nutrition in terms of special diets and deny illness as simple tiredness. Tiredness is something he genuinely feels much of the time, but he will deny this, too. In private he may be listless and inactive, having poured his energy into interpersonal interactions that are essential to his social ambitions.

The other pattern involves overindulgence in unhealthy foods, mainly for convenience and as comforters. Thus, chocolate and other sweet things may be consumed avidly as a substitute for proper food. There can be a concern with imaginary illnesses of the life-threatening variety, which reveals an underlying sense of insecurity. In addition to the poor sense of identity, this type is often convinced that he is ugly despite reassurance to the contrary. He may also partake of excessive drink or drugs to help numb the unpleasant sense of physical reality. These two patterns can alternate or even coexist, causing much confusion for both other people and for the shadow himself.

Psychological defense mechanisms that stem from Fire include *acting out*, the direct expression of feelings such as rage without reflection, guilt, or regard for consequences. Like the other defense strategies, this is a means of coping with stress and inner conflict. Deliberate self-harm in its various forms, including drug abuse and self-mutilation, can be recognized as essentially acts of aggression against the self in order to affect others in some way. *Displacement* is easier to understand. This involves directing pent-up rage onto others who are weaker and hence less dangerous than yourself. Kicking the cat would be an example. *Splitting* is an alternation between idealization and devaluation. Here the other person is seen as either all good or all bad. *Devaluation* involves demeaning oneself or another by exaggerating perceived negative attributes, ridiculing competence, and so on. *Idealization* involves exaggerating one's own virtues or more commonly those of another in order to avoid recognizing bad aspects of oneself.

Identification is similar to idealization, and the two may coexist. Identification refers to the unconscious modeling of another person's attributes in order to increase your own sense of self-worth. Identification with an aggressor is a common method of reducing your fear of him or her. The belief here is that the potential threat will diminish if the aggressor recognizes the similarities. *Introjection* is similar in that it involves incorporation of another's values or personal traits in order to prevent conflict with or threat from them, but it does not have to uphold self-esteem. It is seen following loss, however, when the characteristics of the departed person (most commonly the case) are expressed by a living person as a defense against the loss.

One of the consequences of undeveloped Fire for this type is his inability to cope with his own negative emotions. Emotions like anger and jealousy are disowned and repressed, only for them to resurface in another form as physical illness. He is too cowardly and too upset by his own anger to face up to people directly, and typically adopts passive-aggressive strategies as a way of hindering and punishing them. People who are weaker than him may be targets of open bullying. Almost everyone is at risk from his barbed wit, and his aggression can be most effectively unleashed through a few carefully chosen words. The depression associated with the undeveloped Earth may alternate with the repressed passion and irritability of the undeveloped Fire to appear as emotional instability and mood swings.

The negative attributes that characterize the Phoenix shadow are therefore a mixture of the unconscious qualities associated with the undeveloped elements Earth and Fire (in that order), plus aspects of the primary elements that are being defended against during periods of stress. Which of these attributes is most salient depends very much on the learning experiences of the individual coupled with prevailing circumstances. Although the negative qualities of the primary elements are unpleasant when they come to the fore, they are usually transient and will be the focus of guilt feelings later. The effects of the undeveloped Earth and Fire are more insidious because they are unconscious and so work indirectly and constantly to influence feelings, thoughts, and behavior.

The negative qualities associated with Earth and Fire tend, therefore, to be fairly entrenched because they remain unconscious and undeveloped. The defenses listed above exist to safeguard the integrity of the personality as a whole, and can be difficult to dislodge. One of the positive features of Fire is to enhance the positive features of Earth by galvanizing the potential qualities into action and by inspiring the individual. One of the positive features of Earth is to direct Fire's energy toward practical ends. With both these elements undeveloped, they cannot be mutually supportive in this way. How this disparity affects magical practice will be outlined below.

The less-attractive features associated with the primary elements Air and Water tend, on the other hand, to be relatively transient and mostly activated at times of extreme tension and stress. Even so, the associated behavior and motivation for acting badly are often unconscious because they are in themselves defense strategies and are consequently characteristics of the shadow. The fact that these behaviors are usually transient can mean that they exert a very damaging effect on interpersonal relations, especially if they are sudden and very much out of character. Of course, some people are chronically stressed and consequently exhibit shadow qualities most of the time. In these cases it can seem out of character if the usual sources of stress are removed and their behavior becomes less offensive.

While the primary elemental influences found in the shadow are on the whole temporary, traces of these characteristics may be evident all the time. Deformation of personality is not all-or-nothing—it exists as a continuum, ranging from severe to very mild. The patterns that derive from the primary elements manifest in the shadow in the following ways, depending on the primary type.

The Unicorn with a Phoenix shadow has Air as the primary element. Consequently, behavior that may become prominent during times of stress relates to distortion of the rationalism that is so much a feature of this element. Hence, the individual may begin to behave in an increasingly eccentric, even bizarre manner as the integrity of the intellectual and cognitive functions becomes compromised. They may become vague in their speech and unable to concentrate. At the same time they can become focused on insubstantial matters as though they were of major importance. They can become paranoid and lose touch with reality, thereby exacerbating the problems associated with the weak elements of the Phoenix shadow. They will be less and less inclined to be with other people, and be increasingly withdrawn as pressure mounts. The saving grace of the Air primary is the high degree of personal insight afforded by this element, such that the individual is able to recognize the need to break off and recuperate and thus stall the negative spiral before it goes too far.

The Mermaid with a Phoenix shadow has Water in primary position. This makes it unlikely that the individual will become socially isolated. However, during times of stress and tension, the less-attractive features associated with this element emerge as part of the shadow. In many ways these qualities represent a worsening of the basic pattern of the shadow, and are mostly evident when the individual's hard-won social position is under threat. Hence he can become increasingly grandiose and boastful, full of a sense of his own importance. This outrageous conceit and snobbery is, however, usually based on nothing more than wish fulfillment. He does not pay attention to the facts but is guided entirely by the theme of his own grandeur and self-importance.

Interpersonally, he becomes increasingly obnoxious and aggressive. He is self-assured, self-centered, increasingly dominant and overbearing. He becomes more and more demanding of attention and admiration, and less and less patient and relenting. Other people are merely vassals to serve his ego. He feigns concern and interest in others only in order to exploit them, and is otherwise utterly disdainful of everyone. It is evident that the distortion of reality that is involved here follows the subsuming of the secondary Air element within the shadow. The individual concerned is both insensitive to others and hypersensitive regarding himself. Any attempt at contradiction of his inflexible and mistaken views is regarded as a personal attack and is rewarded with explosive rage.

All of these weaknesses can represent powerful limitations to successful magical outcomes. Since Earth is the weakest element in this shadow, it exerts the strongest negative influence. The most important of these for the Phoenix shadow is the most limiting of all: failure in the final stage of the process to produce the manifest changes that magic is designed to achieve. The sphere of the Earth element is the beginning and the end of magical activity. The magician brings into a carefully chosen, specifically designed working area ritually significant aspects of the physical world, like the wand and the athame, and manipulates them using sounds and gestures to effect desired changes in the physical world. This starting point is also the end point. Recall what was said about performing magic as if it was already accomplished. You stand in the Earth sphere at the beginning and the end of the process simultaneously.

The problems with the weak Earth now become apparent: poor organization, disregard for ritual procedures, lack of connection with the forces of Earth, or alternatively being too bogged down in technique. Disregard for ritual procedures often includes a disregard for the postoperative grounding and sealing, and consequently being left open to the disruptive effects of incomplete connection from the Otherworld.

Of course, the biggest problem produced by a negative Earth is the very earthiness of the element. Earth is characteristically skeptical, pragmatic, hard-nosed, and literally too down-to-earth to believe in magic in the first place, and this skeptical attitude can work unconsciously to undermine your efforts. If you can't suspend disbelief for a while and open yourself up to the possibilities, then naturally you will have major difficulty progressing to the final stage and succeeding in your aims. Without conviction that you will bring about your desired aims, your performance is literally empty ritual. The paradox here is that in order to work effectively with earthy forces, you need to transcend them.

More insidious than these considerations are the unconscious beliefs that you don't actually deserve the things you aim for, or that it's wrong to be self-indulgent, selfish, and so on. Or a common underlying belief for people from a Judeo-Christian background is the fear of tampering with nature, or offending God, or doing deals with Satan. Some people simply fear success and the responsibility and other changes it brings. For these people, to succeed at what they want would be worse than to fail constantly, so they are unconsciously motivated to undermine their own attempts and to bring about their own failure. Constant failure despite your best efforts is frustrating, but at least you can avoid change. These are some of the reasons why an undeveloped Earth can spell failure for the magical enterprise. You will have others that are personal to yourself, but their effects are the same.

With a weak affinity for the undeveloped Fire of the shadow, the magician loses the source of energy that magic depends on. Fire refers to the actual energy we call magic. This is the drive, the passion, and the very power that you want to direct. It goes without saying that in the absence of this passion and drive, the enterprise is doomed to failure. This energy is stirred up by the application of the will at the point in the process during which the magician attempts to petition the entities that have hopefully been contacted already. If, because of the makeup of his personality, the magician has a poor affinity with this element, the associated magical qualities will not be readily available. A limited disposition toward Fire can be very limiting indeed, not least because success depends in part on the conviction that the goal is already attained. Fire provides this conviction, the desire, and the will.

There can also be unconscious self-sabotage at work. Fire relates to morals and religious feeling, so the underlying belief that magic is an affront to God or just plain wrong can be a major factor leading to failure. Among the contradictions of Western society is the urge to succeed coupled with admonition for being successful. The socioeconomic system encourages pursuit of worldly success, while the Church condemns it. We grow up trying to reconcile the elements of this paradox and cannot assume that it does not continue to exert an unconscious effect even if we consciously reject it.

These elemental shortcomings and preoccupations may reveal themselves in dreams and fantasies involving symbols of Earth such as a sense of inertia, of being trapped, buried alive, unable to move, or of strange beasts that lurk within the earth waiting to reach out and devour you. Alternatively there can be dreams about earthquakes, unstable houses, volcanoes, and landslides. Similarly there can be preoccupations with and dreams about fire, symbolized as the threat of being burned or of wandering in deserts, but also of being very cold and in need of warmth. There may often be dreams of fierce animals such as lions and tigers that are associated with the sun and hot countries. There may also be dreams or waking preoccupations about other people, especially of feeling threatened by them.

Wyvern Shadow

Fire with Water

Keywords: Spiteful, gullible, unsociable, insensitive, hypersensitive, apathetic, unmotivated

Dragons were said to develop in the sea, beginning as snakelike wyrms that evolved into winged wyverns before finally becoming the four-legged, winged, fire-breathing creatures with which we are most familiar. Wyverns therefore stand at the midpoint between the depths of the oceanic unconscious and the fiery realms of spirit. In its negative aspect, the Wyvern has neither the sense of connection with other life forms nor the ability to discriminate accurately between self and other. The Wyvern therefore symbolizes unconscious, uncontrolled emotion emerging as hypersensitivity and angry spite. In medieval times, the wyvern was held to be even more ferocious than the dragon, and was a signal for war and destruction.

Fire and Water are the two social elements, and the two most closely connected with the emotions. In this shadow they are undeveloped and unconscious, so the associated qualities tend to be negatively and unconsciously expressed. It follows that the Wyvern shadow, along with his cousin the Chimera shadow, will be assailed by constant, uncomfortable emotions that influence behavior uncertainly and without reason. If the primary Air element is well developed, there can be a good level of personal insight into the causes of these unpleasant emotional states, otherwise they will adversely affect interpersonal relations and make the owner the victim of disquiet.

Since Water is weakest in this shadow, the negative qualities of this element will be most evident. The emotions are powerful forces, like unknown monsters that roam the vast depths of the sea. They are therefore frightening and unpredictable. The individual cannot know what they are or when they will suddenly surface to engulf him. His emotional responses are therefore primitive, like the wyrms themselves, hence he has an immature side despite the very adult face of the primary type. He can be quite childish and sulky. Like the child who is yet to decentralize, he regards himself emotionally as the center of the universe, and does not consider other people's feelings to be as important as his own.

Because of this, he is both hypersensitive with regard to his own feelings and extremely insensitive toward others. It is therefore not unusual for him to hurt someone badly and be crushed and resentful following a gentle rebuke, as if he were the injured party. It is, however, true that his emotional lack of sophistication leaves him wide open to abuse. He has a childlike expectation that he will receive the consideration he deserves. This gullibility makes him a poor judge of character, and he is prone to being taken advantage of by people who are more worldly and unscrupulous than he is. When he is able to discern peoples' faults, he is unable to tolerate them because he is no more able to face their emotional shortcomings than he is his own. The foregoing means that he is prone to disillusionment and bitterness.

The psychological defense mechanisms that relate to Water include *devaluation*, which refers to the demeaning of one's self or others by exaggerating negative attributes, ridiculing competence, and generally destroying the sense of self-worth. *Introjection* refers to the incorporation of the values or traits of others in order to prevent conflict with them or reduce the sense of threat from them. Introjection also serves to defend against loss, usually following a death. In this event a living person begins to express qualities belonging to the dead person. Doubtless some cases of possession are actually instances of introjection.

Reaction-formation is a means of preventing the expression or even the experience of unacceptable desires by exaggerating the very opposite desire. A disgust of all things sexual that is frequently and powerfully expressed may in fact conceal a sexually voracious appetite. The stereotype of the uptight librarian who suddenly becomes sexually unrestrained following a little bit of encouragement is a good example of this. *Regression* to more infantile modes of behavior is a common means of avoiding stress and of forcing others to adopt a caring role. *Isolation of affect* refers to the separation of painful emotions from associated events. An example would be the distress felt by soldiers when they have to kill. *Repression* is the exclusion from consciousness of distressing feelings or ideas. It is not the same as *suppression*, which refers to deliberate avoidance of disallowed thoughts and behavior.

The undeveloped Water of the Wyvern shadow can make him appear shallow and superficial as well as emotionally illiterate. His insight into the world of emotions is limited and limiting. He has as much difficulty recognizing the emotional needs and motives of others as he does his own feelings. He knows that he feels troubled by something, but doesn't know by what. Because emotion gives shape to the personality, he typically suffers from identity confusion because of this inability to recognize feelings. Since he doesn't know about feelings, he is ill equipped to master the complexity of social relationships. Much of his time will therefore be spent on solitary activities that do not involve others.

Psychological defense mechanisms that stem from Fire include *acting out,* the direct expression of feelings such as rage without reflection, guilt, or regard for consequences. Like the other defense strategies, this is a means of coping with stress and inner conflict. Deliberate self-harm in its various forms, including drug abuse and self-mutilation, can be recognized as essentially acts of aggression against the self in order to affect others in some way. *Displacement* is easier to understand. This involves directing pent-up rage onto others who are weaker and hence less dangerous than yourself. Kicking the cat would be an example. *Splitting* is an alternation between idealization and devaluation. Here the other person is seen as either all good or all bad. *Devaluation* involves demeaning oneself or another by exaggerating perceived negative attributes, ridiculing competence, and so on. *Idealization* involves exaggerating your own virtues, or more commonly those of another, in order to avoid recognizing bad aspects of yourself.

Identification is similar to idealization and the two may coexist. Identification refers to the unconscious modeling of another person's attributes in order to increase one's own sense of self-worth. Identification with an aggressor is a common method of reducing one's fear of him or her. The belief here is that the potential threat will diminish if the aggressor recognizes the similarities. *Introjection* is similar in that it involves incorporation of another's values or personal traits in order to prevent conflict with or threat from them, but it does not have to uphold self-esteem. It is seen following loss, however, when the characteristics of the departed person (most commonly the case) are expressed by a living person as a defense against the loss.

Wyvern shadows exhibit the negative aspects of Fire in an unconscious, uncontrolled way and may lack the positive qualities in everyday behavior. Accordingly, there is a lack of energy, drive, and passion. As in all cases where Fire is weak, the power to project himself effectively and to make his presence felt is diminished, along with belief in his ability to effect change, specifically in the interpersonal world.

There is a characteristic lack of ambition and motivation. The primary Gryphon or Pegasus may fantasize over grand schemes that could have practical application, but without the urge to succeed conferred by Fire, these ideas remain pipe dreams. This state of affairs will continue until the individual concerned develops his fiery qualities and decides to take charge of his life. Given the prospect of a lifetime of drifting, it can actually be to this type's advantage to be shaken up by some kind of apparent disaster that provides the impetus for a necessary personal review.

The other negative qualities of Fire that exert an unconscious effect, and which are usually less welcome to other people, are the aggressive and domineering ones. Again, low self-esteem and insecurity is often the motivation for such behavior. Because Fire is undeveloped and unconscious, these aggressive behaviors are likely to be quiet and indirect. There is therefore a quiet, smoldering quality to this shadow that is not always detectable by others because he often appears emotionless. Even a persistent irritability can be mistaken for crotchety lack of social grace rather than angry brooding. He can therefore be very destructive because he is not even suspected of being aggressive, and he can take people very much by surprise with sudden outbursts and tantrums followed by sulking.

Despite the primary Earth, he can also be impatient and occasionally rash and care-less. There is an anxious edge to him that originates with the submerged Fire and Water that makes him feel uneasy about his work. He may feel that he is not doing well enough, that he is open to criticism from himself, if not others. He is therefore impatient to have things finished but does not possess the drive to do more than fret about things. He won't do routine work, in any case, because it is beneath him, and he is quite happy to let other people do whatever strikes him as menial or dull. Thus, his impatience and intolerance combine to make him demanding and critical of others' efforts.

In this way, he can be quite the bully. A feeling of entitlement and an arrogant belief that he is above the common herd makes him indolent and persnickety. A frosty silence followed by an unexpected thunderclap of rage results if he is frustrated in his expectations. Other people can find themselves walking on eggshells for fear of upsetting the ice king. He can be utterly imperious, uncompromising, and thereby domineering. In order to maintain his position of power, he may deliberately provoke conflict among people as a strategy of divide and conquer. The Wyvern shadow can hold people to ransom emotionally for years because he can't recognize or own his negative emotions.

The negative attributes that characterize the Wyvern shadow are therefore a mixture of the unconscious qualities associated with the undeveloped elements Water and Fire (in that order), plus aspects of the primary elements that are being defended against during periods of stress. Which of these attributes is most salient depends very much on the learning experiences of the individual coupled with prevailing circumstances. Although the negative qualities of the primary elements are unpleasant when they come to the fore, they are usually transient and will be the focus of guilt feelings later. The effects of the undeveloped Water and Fire are more insidious because they are unconscious and so work indirectly and constantly to influence feelings, thoughts, and behavior.

The negative qualities associated with Water and Fire tend, therefore, to be fairly entrenched because they remain unconscious and undeveloped. The defenses listed above exist to safeguard the integrity of the personality as a whole, and can be difficult to dislodge. One of the positive features of Fire is to enhance the positive features of Water by providing inspiration and direction for Water's social, caring potential. One of the positive features of Water is to cool Fire's ardor and reduce its ability to scorch. Both these elements are social in nature—Fire in a managerial, directive sense; Water in a nurturing, supportive sense. With both these elements undeveloped, they cannot be mutually supportive in this way and the social sense of both is lacking. How this disparity affects magical practice will be outlined below.

The less-attractive features associated with the primary elements Air and Earth tend, on the other hand, to be relatively transient and mostly activated at times of extreme tension and stress. Even so, the associated behavior and motivation for acting badly are often unconscious because they are in themselves defense strategies and are consequently characteristics of the shadow. The fact that these behaviors are usually transient can mean that they exert a very damaging effect on interpersonal relations, especially if they are sudden and very much out of character. Of course, some people are chronically stressed and consequently exhibit shadow qualities most of the time. In these cases it can seem out of character if the usual sources of stress are removed and their behavior becomes less offensive.

While the primary elemental influences found in the shadow are on the whole temporary, traces of these characteristics may be evident all the time. Deformation of personality is not all-or-nothing—it exists as a continuum, ranging from severe to very mild. The patterns that derive from the primary elements manifest in the shadow in the following ways, depending on the primary type.

The Pegasus with a Wyvern shadow has Air as the primary element. When the elements of the primary type submerge into the shadow, the vibrancy even of Air is lost and the individual becomes ever more lethargic. Whatever social interest he had has now vanished and he is completely isolated. The quick wit and spontaneity associated with Air is lost and even his speech is monotonous. If he was not thought of as a cold fish before, he is now. His thought processes are no longer sharp, and he is prone instead to poor concentration and indecisiveness. His wide range of interests and thirst for knowledge gives way to disinterest and he seems preoccupied with irrelevancies. It's as if he has switched off, which is effectively what he has done as a means of defense, and he will not switch back on until the prevailing stress abates.

The Gryphon with a Wyvern shadow has Earth in primary position. When the elements of this primary type submerge within the shadow, the individual retains interest in other people but regards them as a threat. The control that is a feature of Earth comes defensively into play, such that he feels constantly awkward and unsure of himself. Consequently, he attempts to control every word and action for fear of criticism, and loses whatever spontaneity he may have had. He will not trust anyone without testing them first to see if they represent a threat to his precarious sense of security.

His surroundings, physical and social, are perceived as a source of danger. He may fear that he will lose the material possessions, such as his home, from which he derives much of his sense of being grounded. He may even be plagued by irrational fears of his home being burned down. Similarly, he fears theft and burglary. He may have groundless fears about his health or the health of significant others as another potential source of loss. He may at times have the uncomfortable experience of being somehow unreal. All these peculiarities will ease as the stressful situation is resolved.

All of these weaknesses can represent powerful limitations to successful magical outcomes. Since Water is the weakest element in this shadow, it exerts the strongest negative influence. The most important of these for the Wyvern shadow is associated principally with Water's receptive aspect and with emotional limitation. Emotion is the power that drives intention, so limitations in this regard will manifest as dissipation of power due to being emotionally subdued, or to losing the psychic link at the crucial point of exchange. Basically, the Wyvern shadow is at risk of being cut off at the initial contact stage from the very otherworldly forces that magic is designed to influence.

Each individual has the potential to sabotage his own efforts, and the greatest potential for this depends on the undeveloped elements. Water is the least developed, most unconsciously active element in the case of the Wyvern shadow. Thus, the emotional focus that should lead toward the goal can be unconsciously directed away from the desired end for various reasons. The main reason is fear. In the first place, the emotions are fearful forces to the owner of the shadow, and he will be defending against their expression and application.

Secondly, there is a fear of magic. That a magician should fear magic sounds odd at first, but remember that we should all be wary of it and cultivate a healthy respect. Further than this, however, is the deep-rooted moral admonition against "playing God." A lifetime of conditioning has to be overcome before this particular limitation can be uprooted. Another lifetime of conditioning concerns the fear of the Otherworld, of ghosts, demons, and all the other occult things that fall outside the sphere of the "good." If you intend to practice magic, you have presumably made a conscious decision that it is not of itself evil, and that you will not be pursued and destroyed by devils. Unconsciously, however, you may continue to believe these things and will therefore want to fail in order to maintain your sense of security.

With a weak affinity for the undeveloped Fire of the shadow, the magician loses the source of energy that magic depends on. Fire refers to the actual energy we call magic. This is the drive, the passion, and the very power that you want to direct. It goes without saying that in the absence of this passion and drive, the enterprise is doomed to failure. This energy is stirred up by the application of the will at the point in the process during which the magician attempts to petition the entities that have hopefully been contacted already. If, because of the makeup of his personality, the magician has a poor affinity with this element, the associated magical qualities will not be readily available. A limited disposition toward Fire can be very limiting indeed, not least because success depends in part on the conviction that the goal is already attained. Fire provides this conviction, the desire, and the will.

There can also be unconscious self-sabotage at work. Fire relates to morals and religious feeling, so the underlying belief that magic is an affront to God or just plain wrong can be a major factor leading to failure. Among the contradictions of Western society is the urge to succeed coupled with the admonition for being successful. The socioeconomic system encourages pursuit of worldly success, while the Church condemns it. We grow up trying to reconcile the elements of this paradox and cannot assume that it does not continue to exert an unconscious effect, even if we consciously reject it.

These elemental shortcomings and preoccupations may reveal themselves in dreams and fantasies involving symbols of water, particularly drowning, but also of thirst, and often as mysterious creatures from the hidden depths. You may dream of being on a sinking ship or of being unable to swim. Similarly there can be preoccupations with and dreams about fire, symbolized as the threat of being burned or of wandering in deserts, but also of being very cold and in need of warmth. There may often be dreams of fierce animals such as lions and tigers that are associated with the sun and hot countries. There may also be dreams or waking preoccupations about other people, especially of feeling threatened by them.

Chimera Shadow

Water with Fire

Keywords: Insecure, deceitful, lethargic, unmotivated,
unsociable, insensitive, hypersensitive

The chimera started out as a goddess and became a nightmarish creature that was destroyed by Bellerophon. Chimera was a fire-breathing monster that brought terror to the Mediterranean. Today the term is used to refer to a mental aberration, a grotesque illusion produced by a fevered imagination. In psychological terms, the chimera refers to someone who hides behind various personae and who is rarely known for who they are. It therefore indicates someone who hides and misleads out of fear, and who instills fear in those around them.

The key to understanding the Chimera shadow is emotional insecurity. He harbors a deep longing for relatedness and belonging, and feels emotionally adrift and unsafe without this sense of stability. The Chimera shadow is essentially insecure and desperately needs the safe, familiar nest that he left behind years ago. His search is for another warm bosom that he can snuggle up to and feel safe. He is therefore very much rooted in the past. This past varies, sometimes wistfully idyllic and recalled with a tear in the corner of his eye, sometimes full of injustices that he angrily relates as if they are happening right now.

The Chimera shadow is therefore ambivalent about the past. On the one hand, he wishes he could go back; on the other, he exhibits the "burnt child syndrome" suggestive of damaging experiences. This attitude is carried into the present and into the future. He has great difficulty trusting other people, yet he yearns to be accepted by everyone. He is therefore extremely self-protective and especially vulnerable to people's opinions of him. He is oversensitive and terrified of ridicule and humiliation because these inevitably mean rejection and confirmation of his underlying sense of worthlessness. All his pain seems to happen in the present, no matter how long ago the event occurred. He feels things as acutely as if they are happening right now—and as far as he is concerned, they are.

Unfortunately, most of these damaging events are the fault of his distorted perceptions based on hypersensitivity. He expects to be rejected and therefore sees ridicule and rejection where none is intended. Other people can be mystified as to why he gives them the cold shoulder when they have genuinely done nothing to deserve it. The slightest hint of ridicule is enough to convince him that you have engineered his fall from grace and that he has become a laughing stock. Anything will suffice—a friendly joke, a nod, a wink, more especially if you smile at someone else, because that means you're both laughing at him, and by extension so is everyone else.

The undeveloped Water is the origin of his oversensitivity, groundless imaginings, and vague fears. One of the negative qualities of Water is dreaminess that borders on nightmares, and it is ironic that this type should be plagued by chimeras of his own creation. Because Water is weak, he doesn't recognize or understand his own emotional reactions, even more so since they are like an unsettled sea. His constantly changing moods, desires, and fears confuse everyone, not least himself. This constantly shifting affect is rather like possession by a host of disparate entities. As a result, he has many faces and identities, depending on where and with whom he is. At the same time he reveals his true self to a very few, and he may not know this self at all.

Because he frequently doesn't understand his own motives, he is deceitful to himself and others. He is quite disingenuous and manipulative in his attempts to curry favor, and he will readily play the martyr when he feels threatened by what he regards as abandonment. He is extremely possessive as a consequence of his basic emotional insecurity, and is not above using emotional blackmail to keep people from slipping away. He can be quite tenacious in the use of these strategies, but they are ultimately self-defeating because they only engender resentment on the part of those he wants to keep near. Finally, therefore, he achieves the very opposite of what he most ardently desires. Instead of being accepted, loved, and secure, he finds himself rejected and disliked. He responds to this by storing up another set of resentments, becoming sulky and withdrawn, and resolving once again to trust no one.

Psychological defense mechanisms that stem from Fire include *acting out*, the direct expression of feelings such as rage without reflection, guilt, or regard for consequences. Like the other defense strategies, this is a means of coping with stress and inner conflict. Deliberate self-harm in its various forms, including drug abuse and self-mutilation, can be recognized as essentially acts of aggression against the self in order to affect others in some way. *Displacement* is easier to understand. This involves directing pent-up rage onto others who are weaker and hence less dangerous than yourself. Kicking the cat would be an example. *Splitting* is an alternation between idealization and devaluation. Here the other person is seen as either all good or all bad. *Devaluation* involves demeaning oneself or another by exaggerating perceived negative attributes, ridiculing competence, and so on. *Idealization* involves exaggerating your own virtues, or more commonly those of another, in order to avoid recognizing bad aspects of yourself.

Identification is similar to idealization, and the two may coexist. Identification refers to the unconscious modeling of another person's attributes in order to increase one's own sense of self-worth. Identification with an aggressor is a common method of reducing one's fear of him or her. The belief here is that the potential threat will diminish if the aggressor recognizes the similarities. *Introjection* is similar in that it involves incorporation of another's values or personal traits in order to prevent conflict with or threat from them, but it does not have to uphold self-esteem. It is seen following loss, however, when the characteristics of the departed person (most commonly the case) are expressed by a living person as a defense against the loss.

The undeveloped Fire contributes to his frequent bouts of depression and lethargy. Since this element is weak, the usual qualities of energy and drive that are associated with it are also weak. This type will also be fearful of offending anyone or of standing up to them directly. Passive aggression is far safer and less obvious, and is in keeping with his secretive nature. In addition, he is jealous and vengeful, and will engage in character assassination and gossip in an effort to improve his own stock while simultaneously destroying what he regards as the opposition. This sniping can be habitual rather than reactionary, however, because he actually resents needing others and therefore attacks people indiscriminately. This is the greatest problem that the Chimera shadow has to face: resentment at having to obey his need to merge.

The psychological defense mechanisms that relate to Water include *devaluation*, which refers to the demeaning of one's self or others by exaggerating negative attributes, ridiculing competence, and generally destroying the sense of self-worth. *Introjection* refers to the incorporation of the values or traits of others in order to prevent conflict with them or reduce the sense of threat from them. Introjection also serves to defend against loss, usually following a death. In this event a living person begins to express qualities belonging to the dead person. Doubtless some cases of possession are actually instances of introjection.

Reaction-formation is a means of preventing the expression or even the experience of unacceptable desires by exaggerating the very opposite desire. A disgust of all things sexual that is frequently and powerfully expressed may in fact conceal a sexually voracious appetite. The stereotype of the uptight librarian who suddenly becomes sexually unrestrained following a little bit of encouragement is a good example of this. *Regression* to more infantile modes of behavior is a common means of avoiding stress and of forcing others to adopt a caring role. *Isolation of affect* refers to the separation of painful emotions from associated events. An example would be the distress felt by soldiers when they have to kill. *Repression* is the exclusion from consciousness of distressing feelings or ideas. It is not the same as *suppression*, which refers to deliberate avoidance of disallowed thoughts and behavior.

The Chimera shadow can make the owner appear shallow and superficial as well as emotionally illiterate. He is especially unable to recognize and own negative emotions, such as anger. His great fear is that these frightening, hidden forces will overwhelm him, so he represses them. Since he doesn't fully understand feelings, he is ill equipped to master the complexity of social relationships. People often regard him as needy and demanding, or paradoxically as cold and rejecting. His behavior is therefore highly inconsistent as he attempts to satisfy mutually exclusive needs and desires. Much of his time will be spent on solitary activities that do not involve others, yet his emotional yearning means that he frequently needs to be near people—small wonder that he often seems tense and confused.

The negative attributes that characterize the Chimera shadow are a mixture of the unconscious qualities associated with the undeveloped elements Fire and Water (in that order), plus aspects of the primary elements that are being defended against during periods of stress. Which of these attributes is most salient depends very much on the learning experiences of the individual coupled with prevailing circumstances. Although the negative qualities of the primary elements are unpleasant when they come to the fore, they are usually transient and will be the focus of guilt feelings later. The effects of the undeveloped Fire and Water are more insidious because they are unconscious and so work indirectly and constantly to influence feelings, thoughts, and behavior.

The negative qualities associated with Fire and Water tend, therefore, to be fairly entrenched because they remain unconscious and undeveloped. The defenses listed above exist to safeguard the integrity of the personality as a whole and can be difficult to dislodge. One of the positive features of Fire is to enhance the positive features of Water by providing inspiration and direction for Water's social, caring potential. One of the positive features of Water is to cool Fire's ardor and reduce its ability to scorch. Both these elements are social in nature—Fire in a managerial, directive sense; Water in a nurturing, supportive sense. With both these elements undeveloped, they cannot be mutually supportive in this way, and the social sense of both is lacking. How this disparity affects magical practice will be outlined below.

The less-attractive features associated with the primary elements Air and Earth tend, on the other hand, to be relatively transient and mostly activated at times of extreme tension and stress. Even so, the associated behavior and motivation for acting badly are often unconscious because they are in themselves defense strategies and are consequently characteristics of the shadow. The fact that these behaviors are usually transient can mean that they exert a very damaging effect on interpersonal relations, especially if they are sudden and very much out of character. Of course, some people are chronically stressed and consequently exhibit shadow qualities most of the time. In these cases it can seem out of character if the usual sources of stress are removed and their behavior becomes less offensive.

While the primary elemental influences found in the shadow are on the whole temporary, traces of these characteristics may be evident all the time. Deformation of personality is not all-or-nothing—it exists as a continuum, ranging from severe to very mild. The patterns that derive from the primary elements manifest in the shadow in the following ways, depending on the primary type.

The Pegasus with a Chimera shadow has Air as the primary element. When the elements of the primary type submerge into the shadow, the vibrancy even of Air is lost and the individual becomes ever more lethargic. Whatever social interest he had has now vanished, and he is completely isolated. The quick wit and spontaneity associated with Air is lost, and even his speech is monotonous. If he was not thought of as a cold fish before, he is now. His thought processes are no longer sharp and he is prone instead to poor concentration and indecisiveness. His wide range of interests and thirst for knowledge gives way to disinterest, and he seems preoccupied with irrelevancies. It's as if he has switched off, which is effectively what he has done as a means of defense, and he will not switch back on until the prevailing stress abates.

The Gryphon with a Chimera shadow has Earth in primary position. When the elements of this primary type submerge within the shadow, the individual retains interest in other people but regards them as a threat. The control that is a feature of Earth comes defensively into play such that he feels constantly awkward and unsure of himself. Consequently he attempts to control every word and action for fear of criticism, and loses whatever spontaneity he may have had. He will not trust anyone without testing them first to see if they represent a threat to his precarious sense of security.

His surroundings, physical and social, are perceived as a source of danger. He may fear that he will lose the material possessions, such as his home, from which he derives much of his sense of being grounded. He may even be plagued by irrational fears of his home being burned down. Similarly, he fears theft and burglary. He may have groundless fears about his health or the health of significant others as another potential source of loss. He may at times have the uncomfortable experience of being somehow unreal. All these strange behaviors will disappear as the stressful situation is resolved.

All of these weaknesses can represent powerful limitations to successful magical outcomes. Since Water is the weakest element in this shadow, it exerts the strongest negative influence. The most important of these for the Chimera shadow is a weak affinity for the undeveloped Fire. The magician thereby loses the source of energy that magic depends on. Fire refers to the actual energy we call magic. This is the drive, the passion, and the very power that you want to direct. It goes without saying that in the absence of this passion and drive, the enterprise is doomed to failure. This energy is stirred up by the application of the will at the point in the process during which the magician attempts to petition the entities that have hopefully been contacted already. If, because of the makeup of his personality, the magician has a poor affinity with this element, the associated magical qualities will not be readily available. A limited disposition toward Fire can be very limiting indeed, not least because success depends in part on the conviction that the goal is already attained. Fire provides this conviction, the desire, and the will.

There can also be unconscious self-sabotage at work. Fire relates to morals and religious feeling, so the underlying belief that magic is an affront to God or just plain wrong can be a major factor leading to failure. Among the contradictions of Western society is the urge to succeed coupled with the admonition for being successful. The socioeconomic system encourages pursuit of worldly success, while the Church condemns it. We grow up trying to reconcile the elements of this paradox and cannot assume that it does not continue to exert an unconscious effect, even if we consciously reject it.

The undeveloped Water means that the magician has less affinity with the receptive aspect of that element and is more limited with respect to the emotional charge. Lack of emotion is less of a problem for Chimera shadows than chaotic emotions. Emotion is the power that drives intention, so limitations in this regard will manifest as dissipation of power due to being emotionally subdued, or to losing the psychic link at the crucial point of exchange. Basically, as with the Wyvern shadow, the Chimera shadow is at risk of being cut off at the initial contact stage from the very otherworldly forces that magic is designed to influence.

Each individual has the potential to sabotage his own efforts, and the greatest potential for this depends on the undeveloped elements. In the case of the Chimera shadow, Water is the least developed and most unconsciously active element. Thus, the emotional focus that should lead toward the goal can be unconsciously directed away from the desired end for various reasons. The main reason is fear. In the first place, the emotions are fearful forces to the owner of the shadow, and he will be defending against their expression and application.

Secondly, there is a fear of magic. That a magician should fear magic sounds odd at first, but remember that we should all be wary of it and cultivate a healthy respect. Further than this, however, is the deep-rooted moral admonition against "playing God." A lifetime of conditioning has to be overcome before this particular limitation can be uprooted. Another lifetime of conditioning concerns the fear of the Otherworld, of ghosts, demons, and all the other occult things that fall outside the sphere of the "good." If you intend to practice magic, you have presumably made a conscious decision that it is not of itself evil, and that you will not be pursued and destroyed by devils. Unconsciously, however, you may continue to believe these things and will therefore want to fail in order to maintain your sense of security.

These elemental shortcomings and preoccupations may reveal themselves in dreams and fantasies involving symbols of fire, particularly the threat of being burned or of wandering in deserts, but also of being very cold and in need of warmth. There may often be dreams of fierce animals such as lions and tigers that are associated with the sun and hot countries. Similarly there can be preoccupations with and dreams about water, particularly drowning, but also of thirst, and often as mysterious creatures from the hidden depths. You may dream of being on a sinking ship or of being unable to swim. There may also be dreams or waking preoccupations about other people, especially of feeling threatened by them.

Mermaid/Merman Shadow

Water with Air

Keywords: Excess, cruel, megalomania, irrational,
paranoid, bizarre, unstable, cold

The negative side of the mermaid/merman is described in myths about the German Lorelei and the Greek Sirens. In these and other comparable myths from around the world, these water beings are dangerous, typically luring sailors onto the rocks or raising storms that cause shipwrecks. They also have the power to lose their fish tails temporarily and to develop legs, so that they can come ashore to seduce humans before disappearing back into the sea and leaving their lovers bereft or drowning as they attempt to follow.

The Mer shadow, therefore, inhabits deep water that can spell disaster for anyone who is drawn into the whirlpool of confusion. Like the Unicorn shadow, the Mer shadow combines the undeveloped qualities of Water with the undeveloped qualities of Air, hence emotion conflicts with reason, the unconscious interferes with the conscious, and neither is completely free of the other. Mer shadows are therefore understandably confused and confusing, unpredictable, capricious, and extremely changeable, rather like unknown waters.

This type also lacks a definite sense of self, and he consequently adopts the qualities and characteristics of the people he is with at any given time, rather like a social chameleon. As a result he is an unknown quantity both to himself and to others, so nebulous that his true self never emerges. Friends with alternate perceptions may find themselves talking about him as if he is several different people. He can be very outgoing if the primary Fire is well developed, but nevertheless remains strangely aloof. His socializing will tend to involve a high level of overindulgence, of both alcohol and drugs, and sex. He lacks discrimination and restraint and can get involved in all kinds of excess, and may fall foul of the law, the underworld, or both.

Excess is less noticeable if Earth is the stronger of the primaries, but this does not mean that overindulgence will not take place secretly. Earth is, after all, less sociable than Fire, although both can produce similar behavior if for different reasons—Earth for sheer pleasure, Fire for stimulation. Earth is also more passive, and this shadow may manage to dominate others through playing the martyr or via passive aggression. In some ways, this is worse than if Fire predominates in the primary, since with a more directly aggressive bully at least you know where you are with him. Passive aggression, by contrast, can actually be more destructive and frustrating because the recipient often doesn't know what's happening or when.

Various unconscious defense strategies have been identified, and these can be related to the elements. The psychological defense mechanisms that relate to Water include *devaluation*, which refers to the demeaning of one's self or others by exaggerating negative attributes, ridiculing competence, and generally destroying the sense of self-worth. *Introjection* refers to the incorporation of the values or traits of others in order to prevent conflict with them or reduce the sense of threat from them. Introjection also serves to defend against loss, usually following a death. In this event, a living person begins to express qualities belonging to the dead person. Doubtless some cases of possession are actually instances of introjection.

Reaction-formation is a means of preventing the expression or even the experience of unacceptable desires by exaggerating the very opposite desire. A disgust of all things sexual that is frequently and powerfully expressed may in fact conceal a sexually vora-cious appetite. The stereotype of the uptight librarian who suddenly becomes sexually unrestrained following a little bit of encouragement is a good example of this. *Regression* to more infantile modes of behavior is a common means of avoiding stress and of forcing others to adopt a caring role. *Isolation of affect* refers to the separation of painful emotions from associated events. An example would be the distress felt by soldiers when they have to kill. *Repression* is the exclusion from consciousness of distressing feelings or ideas. It is not the same as *suppression*, which refers to deliberate avoidance of disallowed thoughts and behavior.

There is in fact a sadomasochistic quality to this type, both in the sexual sense and more generally. He can be directly and indirectly aggressive and even cruel, but he is also open to abuse from others due to his poor sense of self, combined with his indis-criminate social behavior and love of excess. Control is very much the key here. He wants the security that comes from having control because a clear role of whatever sort has the effect of sharpening the outlines of his blurred self-image. Being controlled has the same effect, but neither strategy can work for more than a short time. The Mer shadow is actually indifferent to people except insofar as they can provide this kind of self-definition. His emotional transience does not permit deep, abiding relationships, except with a few.

Quite apart from that, the Mer shadow can't stand being limited, and so can't bear being controlled too long or having the responsibility of control over others. As a result, he will be quite intense for a short time and then suddenly lose interest, much to the mystification of the other people concerned. The undeveloped Air and Water combina-tion effectively makes him morally lax and selfish. He not only does not respect social or personal boundaries, he doesn't see why he should restrict himself to rules that he didn't agree to. Even the person with a relatively weak shadow will come across as something of a maverick, amoral if not immoral.

Unconscious defense strategies associated with Air include *fantasy*, the excessive pre-occupation with daydreams and the imagination as a means of escaping from life's problems and one's own internal conflicts. This is also known as schizoid or autistic fantasy, because in its most extreme forms this defense mechanism has the effect of removing the person from the social world.

Intellectualization refers to the overuse of abstract thought in order to avoid psychological discomfort. This is evident from the attempts by some people to split hairs and argue over precise definitions for their behavior, as if they can thereby argue that their maladaptive behavior is in fact acceptable. *Rationalization* refers to the pathological use of apparently plausible reasons to justify behavior. *Projection* is the unconscious rejection of one's own thoughts and character traits. Recognition of these ideas and traits would not fit with the self-concept, and consequently they are ascribed to others.

The other aspect of this shadow's lack of a sense of limits concerns his ambitions. The effect of the unconscious Water and Air elements makes this type grandiose to the point of megalomania, his surreal aims being driven on by the indefatigable power of the primary Fire but without the realism of the undeveloped Air. Indeed, this is even the case despite an obvious lack of talent in the chosen field.

The undeveloped Air means that he lacks personal insight. He will simply press on, regardless of failure, fueled by a passionate intensity that is rooted in fantasy. The feeling that he is meant for greatness lurks in the back of his mind somewhere but cannot be fully recognized or rationally assessed, merely expressed. He is unable to face the harsh realities of life and adopts escapism as a means to avoid them. In an extreme case, there can be psychotic symptoms or evidence of emotional disorder. Eventually, of course, it becomes apparent that his goals will not be reached, and he typically blames others for his failure, becoming bitter and disillusioned.

The negative attributes that characterize the Mer shadow are therefore a mixture of the unconscious qualities associated with the undeveloped elements Air and Water (in that order), plus aspects of the primary elements that are being defended against during periods of stress. Which of these attributes is most salient depends very much on the learning experiences of the individual, coupled with prevailing circumstances. Although the negative qualities of the primary elements are unpleasant when they come to the fore, they are usually transient and will be the focus of guilt feelings later. The effects of the undeveloped Air and Water are more insidious because they are unconscious, and so work indirectly and constantly to influence feelings, thoughts, and behavior.

The negative qualities associated with Water and Air tend, therefore, to be fairly entrenched because they remain unconscious and undeveloped. The defenses listed above exist to safeguard the integrity of the personality as a whole, and can be difficult to dislodge. One of the positive features of Water is to enhance the positive features of Air through understanding the emotions. One of the positive features of Air is to impart rationalism to Water. With both these elements undeveloped, they cannot be mutually supportive in this way. How this disparity affects magical practice will be outlined below.

The less-attractive features associated with the primary elements Earth and Fire tend, on the other hand, to be relatively transient and mostly activated at times of extreme tension and stress. Even so, the associated behavior and motivation for acting badly are often unconscious because they are in themselves defense strategies and are consequently characteristics of the shadow. The fact that these behaviors are usually transient can mean that they exert a very damaging effect on interpersonal relations, especially if they are sudden and very much out of character. Of course, some people are chronically stressed and consequently exhibit shadow qualities most of the time. In these cases it can seem out of character if the usual sources of stress are removed and their behavior becomes less offensive.

While the primary elemental influences found in the shadow are on the whole temporary, traces of these characteristics may be evident all the time. Deformation of personality is not all-or-nothing—it exists as a continuum, ranging from severe to very mild. The patterns that derive from the primary elements manifest in the shadow in the following ways, depending on the primary type.

The Wodwose with a Mer shadow does not believe that he has intrinsic personal worth; he believes that his value lies in what he owns. To have nothing is, therefore, the worst possible fate, while the means to getting things is of paramount importance. The threat to his moral and ethical sense is clear. He believes that his failure to succeed in material terms, and to acquire prestige from this success, reveals his superficiality and the very worthlessness he believes himself to embody. He therefore displays an intense need for recognition through material gain, and his drive to succeed in this as a means of bolstering his sense of security amounts to a compulsion.

Believing at heart that he is inferior to everyone else, he overcompensates by attempting to do more than anyone else. This attempt to do too much allows him to think that he has greater worth than others, and he consequently displays contempt for "lesser" mortals who do far less. He may appear cold and overbearing or merely patronizing, or have a deadly charm that masks sociopathic tendencies. Either way he is demonstrating his superiority over others. This is why Phoenix and Wodwose types are often given to extravagant display—the Unicorn shadow is pushing for admiration in order to bolster his self-esteem.

The Phoenix with a Mer shadow differs from the Wodwose sub-type in being less trusting of others. This reflects the influence of Fire as the primary element. Ordinarily Fire is energetic and sociable, offering leadership ability combined with openness and bonhomie. When stressed, however, the ordinarily happy-go-lucky aspect of this element sours and is replaced by a suspicious, overprotected outlook in which the good intentions of others are misinterpreted as malevolent. All kinds of unsupportable slights and damages are referred to, and the individual may even attack others suddenly and without warning. Where the Wodwose attempts to prove his superior worth by doing more and having more, the Phoenix proves his greater worth by being directly combative and by subduing people around him. Thus, the socially constructive aspect of Fire may turn antisocial and destructive, even as far as physical aggression.

The paranoia associated with the weak Air feeds this defensive aggression to produce a negative spiral of accusation and recrimination. Because Earth is also strong in this sub-type, the imagined injuries may often center on claims of damage or theft, and consequently the individual concerned will be particularly protective and jealous of personal possessions. Alternatively he may feel that his physical health is being adversely affected by other people's selfish demands, and he may begin to entertain morbid fears. Or he may display mood swings as powerful, unrecognized emotion alternates between sadness and elation. Neither the individual nor those around him will be able to explain or understand this disturbing behavior, and consequent interpersonal disturbances will only serve to make the picture worse.

All of this is difficult for the Phoenix or Wodwose primary because both are sociable types who like to be admired and appreciated by others, but at the same time they can be highly unpleasant if the shadow is too powerful in its effects. Both these types display an aggressive need for power that is tempered by ethical and social considerations when they are functioning well, but during times of extreme stress they can simply be aggressive and confrontational. At these times they trample over others' feelings in an effort to avoid facing their own vulnerability or pain. Unable to face a loss of power over the environment or themselves, they mask their feelings of inadequacy with aggressive displays of strength and recklessness. They can't afford to be defeated by anyone or anything. Strength equals safety, control equals security. Power is good, might is right.

This is explicable in terms of the primary Fire/Earth combination of each type that resides within the shadow. Fire refers to power, Earth to possession. In its shadow aspect, Fire is antisocial and destructive. In its shadow aspect, Earth is grasping and without soul. Thus, the Mer shadow incorporates the worst features of both primary elements. Merfolk are emotional and intuitive; Merfolk shadows are cold and lack insight. The particular shadow that is encountered may therefore either be an alluring but ultimately cold fish or a dangerous animal that swims in dark water where is shouldn't be followed. The difference in presentation obviously depends on the nature of the primary type.

Any of the psychological qualities referred to above can serve to work against your magical ambitions. From a specifically magical viewpoint, the limitations associated with Mer shadows relate mainly to overcoming difficulties of both inceptive and receptive psychic links between this world and the Otherworld. This is a particular problem for Mer shadows (as it is for Unicorn shadows), given that both Air and Water afford access to the other realms, and here both are relatively underdeveloped and unconscious.

Thus, not only is there a weakness in the intuitive link, there is also a weakness in the creative link. For the Merfolk variant (as opposed to the Unicorn), the difficulty is associated principally with the inceptive aspect and with creative limitation. Creativity, primarily in the form of visualization, opens the portal to the Otherworld and establishes contact with the entities that reside there, so limitations in this regard mean that the invocation of these spirits and gaining their attention is not so easily accomplished. Basically, Merfolk shadows are at risk of being cut off from the very otherworldly forces that magic is designed to influence, both at the initial contact stage and at the direction stage.

Undeveloped Water further exacerbates the difficulties of the undeveloped Air. If Air provides the direct, verbal exchange between the worlds in the form of affirmations and incantations, Water provides the intuitive, nonverbal link with psychic forces, and the emotional strength and maturity for the magical enterprise. All these skills and abilities are compromised by the shadow facets of Water and Air.

Each individual has the potential to sabotage his own efforts, and the greatest potential for this depends on the undeveloped elements. Air is the least developed, most unconsciously active element in the case of the Mer shadow. Thus, the intellectual force that should guide you toward the chosen goal can actually serve to undermine your efforts for various reasons. The main reason is cynicism. Unless Air is swayed by a sound argument, in the absence of actual proof the whole enterprise is rejected.

The very rationalism and logic that Air symbolizes militates against the very notion of magic. Since the inception of the Age of Enlightenment, when superstition was swept away and rationalism became our creed, the mechanical, clockwork universe replaced the occult universe that had preceded it. As we have seen, modern science now cleaves more to an apparently irrational model with which ordinary people are still not entirely familiar. We have all grown up imbued with rationalist principles and the scientific endeavor. This lifetime of obeisance to rationalism can be difficult to dismiss entirely, no matter how fully you may disregard it on a conscious level. At the back of your mind there lurks a man in a white coat, shaking his head at magic—and you believe he is right.

The unconscious effect of the undeveloped Water also goes beyond poor affinity with the magical qualities of that element to include unconscious self-sabotage. In the first place, the emotional realm is submerged in this type and the emotions are guarded against such powerful, upsetting forces. It follows that an activity such as magic, which makes special use of emotion, is difficult to engage in. Thus the first problem is fear of the emotions, one of the central tools of the magician's art.

Secondly, there is a fear of magic itself. That a magician should fear magic sounds odd at first, but remember that we should all be wary of it and cultivate a healthy respect. Further than this, however, is the deep-rooted moral admonition against "playing God." A lifetime of conditioning has to be overcome before this particular limitation can be uprooted. Another lifetime of conditioning concerns the fear of the Otherworld, of ghosts, demons, and all the other occult things that fall outside the sphere of the "good." If you intend to practice magic, you have presumably made a conscious decision that it is not of itself evil, and that you will not be pursued and destroyed by devils. Unconsciously, however, you may continue to believe these things and will therefore want to fail in order to maintain your sense of security.

These elemental shortcomings and preoccupations may reveal themselves in dreams and fantasies involving symbols of the undeveloped elements. The weak Air can manifest as fear or dreams of falling, choking, suffocating, being lost, or of huge birds and other powerful entities that come from the sky. Dreams and preoccupations with water will also be common, symbolized particularly by drowning, but also by thirst, and often as dangerous, mysterious creatures from the hidden depths, possibly in the form of Sirens trying to lure you to your death on the rocks. Similarly there can be dreams and obsessions about other people, especially fighting with them. Dreams of crowds or of isolation may also be prominent.

Satyr Shadow

Water with Earth

Keywords: Controlling, aggressive, rapacious, lazy,
neglectful, hypersensitive, unstable, cold

The dark side of the satyr is characterized by lechery, rape, fear, and uncontrolled aggression. This is nature red in tooth and claw, and the bestial side of human beings. In Greek myth, Pan is the god of nightmares and the mere sight of him produced terror (hence "panic"). He was also believed to be responsible for epilepsy.

The Satyr shadow, therefore, refers to underlying, uncontrolled excess. Power is a key theme in this shadow's motivations. He can be extremely controlling, particularly since both Air and Fire primaries are expansive in nature, but more especially since Fire is dominant and overpowering. Here Water is undeveloped and so does not have the same cooling effect on Fire's more scorching nature. In addition the sensitivity and empathic qualities of Water are also less in evidence. Satyr shadows focus on control and dominance of situations and of other people issues. They are driven to acquire power, not only to control others but simply for its own sake. Because of the strength of the primary Fire they are driven, and frequently ruthless, in achieving this end.

They are as controlling of themselves as they are of everything else. The weak Earth means that they are self-disciplined with respect to physical matters, including those of the flesh, but in a negative way. Hence, they can be severely ascetic in both outlook and practice, denying themselves and those over whom they have control everything except the necessary basics for physical survival, and they may even deny those if Earth is particularly weak. The primary Fire may incline them toward demanding exercise regimes as well as self-imposed dietary restrictions that can become intensely unhealthy.

Various unconscious defense strategies have been identified, and these can be related to the elements. Defense strategies related to Earth include *projection*, the unconscious rejection of unwanted thoughts and personal traits by ascribing them to others. The Phoenix shadow also exhibits *denial*, an unconscious refusal to acknowledge external realities because to do so would be too painful; and *somatization*, a preoccupation with physical symptoms that represents a psychological reaction to stressful situations. Denial of the physical self can also be seen among shadows that have a prominent Earth, Phoenix among them.

The effect of the weak Earth is to devalue and even ignore the needs of the physical, and to make a virtue out of self-denial. The body is treated like a temple to a severe god of self-immolation. Otherwise it is treated like one of the hidden temples of southern India that is entirely covered in explicit depictions of sexual abandon. Sexual power can be a big problem for the Satyr shadow. The primary Fire makes this type highly charged and in need of expression and dominance. At the same time, the undeveloped Earth negates the physical.

There are a number of ways in which this conflict can be resolved, none of them especially healthy. The primary Air can come into play to provide an alternative channel for the energy that would otherwise be directed toward sex. An obvious example would be the excessive prude who spends an inordinate amount of time fulminating against sex as if it is the primary evil in the world. Or the primary Air can lead the individual to work on sex intellectually or artistically without actually indulging in the forbidden fruit. Freud believed that sex and work were the two most important things in a person's life. As we know, his work centered largely on the contribution of sex in the aetiology of the neuroses. It is less well-known that he worked tirelessly on this subject for decades having given up sex quite early in his life.

Alternatively there can be an almost obsessive concentration on sex and sexual conquest. This pattern fits better with the image of the rapacious satyr of myth that aggressively pursued the object of his lust until he succeeded in his aim, only to immediately begin pursuing another target. For the male shadow, such behavior fits well with the more macho demands of the culture, but in recent times even females can be sexual predators quite openly without fear of reprimand. Of course, predatory vamps have been recognized for many years, but only in recent times have sexually aggressive females been sanctioned to any extent.

Either way, the voracious sexual appetite of the Satyr shadow is frequently hidden, more especially where it is linked with the more exotic forms of sexual expression. Of all the shadows this is the one that is most likely to be involved in fetishism, S&M, and other means of control expressed sexually. The shadow may play either part in these games, obviously enjoying having control over others, but sometimes finding relief through relinquishing control to someone else. S&M in particular has been described paradoxically as an intellectual form of sex, so it will come as no surprise to find in this type the combination of Air and Fire expressed as intellect and power, most especially where Water, in the form of emotional expression, is minimized.

This is not to say that this shadow is not sexually aggressive. He is actually quite aggressive and hostile generally. At times he can be prone to direct displays of violence because of his constant anger. Fortunately his urge for control will usually mean that he keeps a lid on it, but he can nevertheless be irritable, difficult company. Although Fire, because it relates most closely to passion, is apt to be blamed for this, it is actually the undeveloped Water that provides the motive for the angry disposition. This is because the emotions are less understood when Water is weak, and because they nevertheless continue to operate in an unconscious way.

The psychological defense mechanisms that relate to Water include *devaluation*, which refers to the demeaning of one's self or others by exaggerating negative attributes, ridiculing competence, and generally destroying the sense of self-worth. *Introjection* refers to the incorporation of the values or traits of others in order to prevent conflict with them, or reduce the sense of threat from them. Introjection also serves to defend against loss, usually following a death. In this event, a living person begins to express qualities belonging to the dead person. Doubtless some cases of possession are actually instances of introjection.

Reaction-formation is a means of preventing the expression or even the experience of unacceptable desires by exaggerating the very opposite desire. A disgust of all things sexual that is frequently and powerfully expressed may in fact conceal a sexually voracious appetite. The stereotype of the uptight librarian who suddenly becomes sexually unrestrained following a little bit of encouragement is a good example of this. *Regression* to more infantile modes of behavior is a common means of avoiding stress and of forcing others to adopt a caring role. *Isolation of affect* refers to the separation of painful emotions from associated events. An example would be the distress felt by soldiers when they have to kill. *Repression* is the exclusion from consciousness of distressing feelings or ideas. It is not the same as *suppression*, which refers to deliberate avoidance of disallowed thoughts and behavior.

Consequently, although the shadow often appears emotionless and cold, he is in fact plagued by feelings that he does not fully recognize and that operate largely outside of his awareness. To him the most reasonable cause of this emotional tension is other people, rather than his own needs and attitudes. The primary Air can either help or hinder this process by providing a strong capacity for personal insight, or by providing a spurious rationale to maintain the self-delusion. This shadow type is more likely, however, to give vent to hostile and aggressive feelings because the primary Fire makes these feelings more readily expressed.

This shadow is characteristically secretive because of a lack of trust in other people, which again is partly explicable as a consequence of the undeveloped Water, making emotions, and hence relationships, less easy to fathom; and partly by the developed Fire ensuring that the individual is competitive. The more socially astute individual will exhibit aggressive tendencies covertly in the form of jealousy and cunning vindictiveness. Due to his competitive and self-protective instincts, he will also have a penetrating manner that presupposes hostile intent in others.

This mistrust and hypersensitivity tends to push him away from others except insofar as he needs to dominate them. Despite the primary Air, there is a tendency to paranoia that can lead to unnecessary confrontation. At the same time his insensitivity can make him unpopular, with the net result that people avoid him. He is, in fact, most at home with other aggressive types like himself, because he knows where he stands with them—in a constant struggle for supremacy. Less-competitive, less-aggressive people are not so likely to get his respect because he regards them as weak. He is intolerant of weakness and believes firmly in the survival of the fittest. He is not likely to shrug and refer to individual differences when faced with, say, a mild-mannered Unicorn. The Satyr shadow is judgmental, opinionated, and cynical.

Small wonder, then, that this type is often lonely despite the strong Fire component, for although Fire is one of the social elements it is primarily concerned with directive relationships and competition. The Satyr shadow can therefore be something of a loner who moreover is given to morbid fantasy and brooding. There is also a strong self-destructive urge that can surprise many people who regard him as destructive of other people, if anything. This attitude overlooks the sense of isolation in terms of inner emotion and outer relation experienced by this type, and the frustration that attends it. Sometime, when the outward expression of the aggressive drive fails, it may turn inward instead.

The negative attributes that characterize the Satyr shadow are therefore a mixture of the unconscious qualities associated with the undeveloped elements Earth and Water (in that order), plus aspects of the primary elements that are being defended against during periods of stress. Which of these attributes is most salient depends very much on the learning experiences of the individual coupled with prevailing circumstances. Although the negative qualities of the primary elements are unpleasant when they come to the fore, they are usually transient and will be the focus of guilt feelings later. The effects of the undeveloped Earth and Water are more insidious, because they are unconscious and so work indirectly and constantly to influence feelings, thoughts, and behavior.

The negative qualities associated with Earth and Water tend to be fairly entrenched because they remain unconscious and undeveloped. The defenses listed above exist to safeguard the integrity of the personality as a whole, and can be difficult to dislodge. One of the positive features of Earth is to stabilize and contain the positive features of Water. Water reciprocates by giving feeling to the less-sociable Earth. Together these elements provide the basic conditions for growth. With both these elements undeveloped, they cannot be mutually supportive in this way. How this disparity affects magical practice will be outlined below.

The less-attractive features associated with the primary elements Air and Fire tend, on the other hand, to be relatively transient and mostly activated at times of extreme tension and stress. Even so, the associated behavior and motivation for acting badly are often unconscious because they are in themselves defense strategies and are consequently characteristics of the shadow. The fact that these behaviors are usually transient can mean that they exert a very damaging effect on interpersonal relations, especially if they are sudden and very much out of character. Of course, some people are chronically stressed and consequently exhibit shadow qualities most of the time. In these cases it can seem out of character if the usual sources of stress are removed and their behavior becomes less offensive.

While the primary elemental influences found in the shadow are on the whole temporary, traces of these characteristics may be evident all the time. Deformation of personality is not all-or-nothing—it exists as a continuum, ranging from severe to very mild. The patterns that derive from the primary elements manifest in the shadow in the following ways, depending on the primary type.

The Firebird with a Satyr shadow has Air as the primary element. When the elements of the primary type submerge into the shadow, the main effect is increasingly bizarre ideas, particularly revolving around the notion of threats. The principal reality-testing feature of Air becomes compromised under stress, and distorted reasoning is used to uphold the belief in people working behind the scenes or even of major organizations being involved in malicious plans. This paranoia is accompanied by hyperactivity and an anxious attempt to focus on too many things at once in order to keep ahead of the opposition. The result is failure to complete anything because of an inability to maintain focus, plus increasing alienation of even friends and relatives. The individual may sleep less while trying to do more, and eventually become exhausted.

The Dragon with a Satyr shadow has Fire in primary position. When the elements of this primary type submerge within the shadow, the individual becomes increasingly aggressive and irritable to the point that physical violence is more likely. He becomes more impulsive and less bound by social rules. Consequently both personal and work relationships become strained as the individual engages in more and more deceitful and antagonistic behavior while expressing no remorse for the obvious damage they are doing. The negative aspects of Fire are clearly evident from apparently self-destructive activities such as drinking excessively, gambling, driving too fast, and so on. Eventually he may become apathetic and morose.

All of these weaknesses can represent powerful limitations to successful magical outcomes. Since Earth is the weakest element in this shadow, it exerts the strongest negative influence. The most important of these for the Satyr shadow is a weak affinity for this undeveloped element. The problems associated with poor affinity with Earth concern failure in the final stage of the process to produce the manifest changes that magic is designed to achieve. As previously stated, the sphere of the Earth element is the beginning and the end of magical activity. The magician brings into a carefully chosen, specifically designed working area ritually significant aspects of the physical world, like the wand and the athame, and manipulates them using sounds and gestures to effect desired changes in the physical world. This starting point is also the end point. Recall what was said about performing magic as if it was already accomplished. One stands in the Earth sphere at the beginning and the end of the process simultaneously.

The problem with the weak Earth now becomes apparent: poor organization, disregard for ritual procedures, lack of connection with the forces of Earth, or being too bogged down in technique. Disregard for ritual procedures often includes a disregard for the postoperative grounding and sealing, and consequently being left open to the disruptive effects of incomplete connection from the Otherworld.

Of course, the biggest problem produced by a negative Earth is the very earthiness of the element. Earth is characteristically skeptical, pragmatic, hard-nosed, and literally too down-to-earth to believe in magic in the first place, and this skeptical attitude can work unconsciously to undermine your efforts. If you can't suspend disbelief for a while and open yourself up to the possibilities, then naturally you will have major difficulty progressing to the final stage and succeeding in your aims. Without conviction that you will bring about your desired aims, your performance is literally empty ritual. The paradox here is that in order to work effectively with earthy forces, you need to transcend them.

More insidious than these considerations are the unconscious beliefs that you don't actually deserve the things you aim for, or that it's wrong to be self-indulgent, selfish, and so on. Or a common underlying belief for people from a Judeo-Christian background is the fear of tampering with nature, or offending God, or doing deals with

Satan. Some people simply fear success and the responsibility and other changes it brings. For these people, to succeed at what they want would be worse that to fail constantly, so they are unconsciously motivated to undermine their own attempts and to bring about their own failure. Constant failure despite your best efforts is frustrating, but at least you can avoid change. These are some of the reasons why an undeveloped Earth can spell failure for the magical enterprise. You will have others that are personal to yourself, but their effects are the same.

There is also a weakness in the intuitive link due to the undeveloped Water. Water provides the intuitive, nonverbal receptive link with psychic forces and the emotional strength and maturity for the magical enterprise. Emotion provides a channel and a focus with which to direct the accumulated energy down toward the Earth sphere, where the magical effects are to manifest. Emotion is one of the central keys of successful magic, and if the emotional component is weak then the operation is compromised.

The unconscious effect of the undeveloped Water also goes beyond poor affinity with the magical qualities of that element to include unconscious self-sabotage. In the first place, the emotional realm is submerged in this type and, as powerful, upsetting forces, the emotions are guarded against. It follows that an activity such as magic, which makes special use of emotion, is difficult to engage in. Thus the first problem is fear of the emotions, one of the central tools of the magician's art.

Secondly, there is a fear of magic itself. That a magician should fear magic sounds odd at first, but remember that we should all be wary of it and cultivate a healthy respect. Further than this, however, is the deep-rooted moral admonition against "playing God." A lifetime of conditioning has to be overcome before this particular limitation can be uprooted. Another lifetime of conditioning concerns the fear of the Otherworld, of ghosts, demons, and all the other occult things that fall outside the sphere of the "good." If you intend to practice magic, you have presumably made a conscious decision that it is not of itself evil, and that you will not be pursued and destroyed by devils. Unconsciously, however, you may continue to believe these things and will therefore want to fail in order to maintain your sense of security.

These elemental shortcomings and preoccupations may reveal themselves in dreams and fantasies involving symbols of Earth such as a sense of inertia, of being trapped, buried alive, unable to move, or of strange beasts that lurk within the earth waiting to reach out and devour you. Alternatively there can be dreams about earthquakes, unstable houses, volcanoes, and landslides. Similarly there can be preoccupations with and dreams about water, particularly drowning, but also of thirst, and often as mysterious creatures from the hidden depths. You may dream of being on a sinking ship or of being unable to swim. There may also be dreams or waking preoccupations about other people, especially of feeling threatened by them.

Centaur Shadow

Earth with Water

Keywords: Controlled, undermining, irritable,
unstable, cold, lazy, neglectful

In myth, there were two branches of the centaur family. One branch was considered wise and good, the emphasis being on the human aspect; the other was wild and bestial. Robert Graves refers to the centaur tribe as being the most warlike of the Pelasgians. These centaurs ritually ate the hallucinogenic fungus fly-agaric and thereby became powerfully strong and sexually rampant. To the Greeks, the centaur was a symbol of the grotesque, animal side of human beings. Where the wise centaurs were famed for their skills as healers, the very blood of the other centaurs was poisonous. Myth tells of how Hercules was killed by wearing a shirt that had been dipped in the blood of the centaur Nessus.

The Centaur shadow has a number of things in common with his neighbor the Satyr shadow, one of which is a need for control. However, where the Satyr shadow needs control over self and others, the Centaur shadow attempts to predict and control everything. This type suffers from a chronic sense of insecurity regarding the unknown. That which is hidden is regarded with suspicion as a source of threat, so everything must be revealed and categorized. Much of this shadow's hostility can be traced to this deep sense of insecurity and the consequent need to erect barriers against people and the world generally in order to remain safe.

Various unconscious defense strategies have been identified, and these can be related to the elements. The psychological defense mechanisms that relate to Water include *devaluation*, which refers to the demeaning of one's self or others by exaggerating negative attributes, ridiculing competence, and generally destroying the sense of self-worth. *Introjection* refers to the incorporation of the values or traits of others in order to prevent conflict with them or reduce the sense of threat from them. Introjection also serves to defend against loss, usually following a death. In this event a living person begins to express qualities belonging to the dead person. Doubtless some cases of possession are actually instances of introjection.

Reaction-formation is a means of preventing the expression or even the experience of unacceptable desires by exaggerating the very opposite desire. A disgust of all things sexual that is frequently and powerfully expressed may in fact conceal a sexually voracious appetite. The stereotype of the uptight librarian who suddenly becomes sexually unrestrained following a little bit of encouragement is a good example of this. *Regression* to more infantile modes of behavior is a common means of avoiding stress and of forcing others to adopt a caring role. *Isolation of affect* refers to the separation of painful emotions from associated events. An example would be the distress felt by soldiers when they have to kill. *Repression* is the exclusion from consciousness of distressing feelings or ideas. It is not the same as *suppression*, which refers to deliberate avoidance of disallowed thoughts and behavior.

Since Water is the least-developed element in this shadow, this most particularly concerns the emotions. Because Water is undeveloped, emotions are often unrecognized, and so their effects on thoughts and behavior are not appreciated. For this shadow, as for the Satyr shadow, feelings are mysterious, random forces that swim up from the vast depths of the unconscious, threatening to devour the individual or drag him down with them. As a result, this type exerts great emotional control so as not to risk falling into the depths and being overwhelmed by these frightening beasts. He often rationalizes his own emotional reactions as being the result of other, external factors that need to be controlled, usually other people.

Because Fire is a primary element, the emotions of anger and lust are most readily expressed openly. As we have observed, other people are frequently seen as the cause of his emotional discomfort, so they are either kept at arm's length or treated as tools to specific ends. This type can, therefore, be quite ruthless in his treatment of others, using them when they appear to be useful, tossing them aside when they are not. Paradoxically for someone with a poor understanding of his own emotional states, he is often astute with respect to others' feelings and can be quite skilled at emotional manipulation. Hypersensitive and insensitive, he is hard-nosed and competitive. Everyone is a winner or a loser, and he most definitely wants to win.

Another feature that this type has in common with the Satyr shadow also stems from the combination of primary Fire and the repressed emotion of undeveloped Water. This relates to sex, and the Centaur shadow may also sublimate his sexual urges into art or competitive enterprises and therefore appear prudish and inhibited, even anti-sex. More often, however, he will use sex as an outlet for the emotions and as a substitute for genuine emotional closeness. For this reason, his sexual appetite can be voracious and often competitive in nature. The dominance issues here are marked as they are with the Satyr shadow, but the urge for secrecy is less pronounced.

Defense strategies related to Earth include *projection*, the unconscious rejection of unwanted thoughts and personal traits by ascribing them to others. The Phoenix shadow also exhibits *denial*, an unconscious refusal to acknowledge external realities because to do so would be too painful; and *somatization*, a preoccupation with physical symptoms that represents a psychological reaction to stressful situations. Denial of the physical self can also be seen among shadows that have a prominent Earth, Centaur among them.

Earth is also undeveloped, so the physical is either denied or abused. This type has a particular fear of losing control, hence a fear of becoming a drunk or drug-addicted down-and-out. It has been pointed out, however, that one of the features of the mythical centaur was ritual drug use leading to loss of self-control. This may in fact be the only means of escaping his fear of impending chaos other than by using sex. By the controlled use of mind-altering substances, he may find temporary release from the tension resulting from the constant battle against chaos. The problem, of course, is that drug use can easily get out of hand and any one experiment holds unknown risks. He is therefore effectively in a potential negative spiral of using more to escape more, with the effect that he is more completely ensnared.

The other risks associated with a weak Earth include failure to eat properly, often rationalized as a necessary dietary regime. As with his Satyr shadow cousin, the primary Fire can also encourage him to combine this nutritional self-neglect with excessive exercise, both of which constitute forms of extreme self-control. An associated byproduct of this behavior is that it permits him to feel superior to others who are evidently too self-indulgent and weak to be as self-disciplined as he. Other common features of the weak Earth are a denial of genuine illnesses, on the one hand, and hypochondria, on the other.

This type is self-centered as a necessary feature of a neurotic urge for self-preservation. He fears emotional disintegration, in particular, but may also worry about physical deterioration, either of his body or of his financial security. The obsessive-compulsive nature of this type as a means of controlling the unknown has been established, and this can extend to possessions. Order and cleanliness are not usually associated with weak Earth as much as total disorder, but here the striving for order is extreme and even pathological. He also has a reputation for parsimony, being not only mean with money and his other possessions but grasping as well. Once again, this is actually a sign of his sense of insecurity combined with his habit of treating people as commodities.

One further characteristic of this type that does little to endear him to other people is a know-it-all attitude. This habit of denigrating others represents the poisonous blood of the Centaur shadow. Whomever comes into sustained contact with him is slowly but surely ground down by his destructive undermining of their abilities and natural urge for self-development. His constant smug and superior denigration of all their efforts reveals his inability to tolerate autonomy in others. Autonomous people are a threat because they are potential competitors, and this self-contained loner does not want to have to deal with people except as minions. He fears their spontaneity because it makes them unpredictable and free. Better by far to poison their spirits, and keep them weak and in their place.

The negative attributes that characterize the Centaur shadow are therefore a mixture of the unconscious qualities associated with the undeveloped elements Water and Earth (in that order), plus aspects of the primary elements that are being defended against during periods of stress. Which of these attributes is most salient depends very much on the learning experiences of the individual, coupled with prevailing circumstances. Although the negative qualities of the primary elements are unpleasant when they come to the fore, they are usually transient and will be the focus of guilt feelings later. The effects of the undeveloped Water and Earth are more insidious because they are unconscious, and so work indirectly and constantly to influence feelings, thoughts, and behavior.

The negative qualities associated with Water and Earth tend to be fairly entrenched because they remain unconscious and undeveloped. The defenses listed above exist to safeguard the integrity of the personality as a whole and can be difficult to dislodge. One of the positive features of Earth is to stabilize and contain the positive features of Water. Water reciprocates by giving feeling to the less-sociable Earth. Together these elements provide the basic conditions for growth. With both these elements undeveloped, they cannot be mutually supportive in this way. How this disparity affects magical practice will be outlined below.

The less-attractive features associated with the primary elements Air and Fire tend, on the other hand, to be relatively transient and mostly activated at times of extreme tension and stress. Even so, the associated behavior and motivation for acting badly are often unconscious because they are in themselves defense strategies, and are consequently characteristics of the shadow. The fact that these behaviors are usually transient can mean that they exert a very damaging effect on interpersonal relations, especially if they are sudden and very much out of character. Of course, some people are chronically stressed and consequently exhibit shadow qualities most of the time. In these cases it can seem out of character if the usual sources of stress are removed and their behavior becomes less offensive.

While the primary elemental influences found in the shadow are on the whole temporary, traces of these characteristics may be evident all the time. Deformation of personality is not all-or-nothing—it exists as a continuum, ranging from severe to very mild. The patterns that derive from the primary elements manifest in the shadow in the following ways, depending on the primary type.

The Firebird with a Centaur shadow has Air as the primary element. When the elements of the primary type submerge into the shadow, the main effect is increasingly bizarre ideas, particularly revolving around the notion of threats. The principal reality-testing feature of Air becomes compromised under stress, and distorted reasoning is used to uphold the belief in people working behind the scenes or even of major organizations being involved in malicious plans. This paranoia is accompanied by hyperactivity and an anxious attempt to focus on too many things at once in order to keep ahead of the opposition. The result is failure to complete anything because of an inability to maintain focus, plus increasing alienation of even friends and relatives. The individual may sleep less while trying to do more, and eventually become exhausted.

The Dragon with a Centaur shadow has Fire in primary position. When the elements of this primary type submerge within the shadow, the individual becomes increasingly aggressive and irritable, to the point that physical violence is more likely. He becomes more impulsive and less bound by social rules. Consequently both personal and work relationships become strained as the individual engages in more and more deceitful and antagonistic behavior while expressing no remorse for the obvious damage they are doing. The negative aspects of Fire are clearly evident from apparently self-destructive activities such as drinking excessively, gambling, driving too fast, and so on. Eventually he may become apathetic and morose.

All of these weaknesses can represent powerful limitations to successful magical outcomes. Since Water is the weakest element in this shadow, it exerts the strongest negative influence. This represents a weakness in the intuitive link with the magical forces that have hopefully been contacted previously. Water provides the receptive, nonverbal link with these psychic forces, and the emotional strength and maturity for the magical enterprise. Emotion provides a channel and a focus with which to direct the accumulated energy down toward the Earth sphere, where the magical effects are to manifest. Emotion is one of the central keys of successful magic, and if the emotional component is weak, then the operation is compromised.

The unconscious effect of the undeveloped Water also goes beyond poor affinity with the magical qualities of that element to include unconscious self-sabotage. In the first place, the emotional realm is submerged in this type and, as powerful, upsetting forces, the emotions are guarded against. It follows that an activity such as magic, which makes special use of emotion, is difficult to engage in. Thus the first problem is fear of the emotions, one of the central tools of the magician's art.

Secondly, there is a fear of magic itself. That a magician should fear magic sounds odd at first, but remember that we should all be wary of it and cultivate a healthy respect. Further than this, however, is the deep-rooted moral admonition against "playing God." A lifetime of conditioning has to be overcome before this particular limitation can be uprooted. Another lifetime of conditioning concerns the fear of the Otherworld, of ghosts, demons, and all the other occult things that fall outside the sphere of the "good." If you intend to practice magic, you have presumably made a conscious decision that it is not of itself evil, and that you will not be pursued and destroyed by devils. Unconsciously, however, you may continue to believe these things, and will therefore want to fail in order to maintain your sense of security.

The other important consideration for the Centaur shadow is a weak affinity for the undeveloped Earth element. The problems associated with weak Earth concern failure in the final stage of the process to produce the manifest changes that magic is designed to achieve. As previously stated, the sphere of the Earth element is the beginning and the end of magical activity. The magician brings into a carefully chosen, specifically designed working area ritually significant aspects of the physical world, like the wand and the athame, and manipulates them using sounds and gestures to effect desired changes in the physical world. This starting point is also the end point. Recall what was said about performing magic as if it was already accomplished. One stands in the Earth sphere at the beginning and the end of the process simultaneously.

The problem with the weak Earth now becomes apparent: poor organization, disregard for ritual procedures, lack of connection with the forces of Earth, or being too bogged down in technique. Disregard for ritual procedures often includes a disregard for the postoperative grounding and sealing, and consequently being left open to the disruptive effects of incomplete connection from the Otherworld.

Of course, the biggest problem produced by a negative Earth is the very earthiness of the element. Earth is characteristically skeptical, pragmatic, hard-nosed, and literally too down-to-earth to believe in magic in the first place, and this skeptical attitude can work unconsciously to undermine your efforts. If you can't suspend disbelief for a while and open yourself up to the possibilities, then naturally you will have major difficulty progressing to the final stage and succeeding in your aims. Without the conviction that you will bring about your desired aims, your performance is literally empty ritual. The paradox here is that in order to work effectively with earthy forces, you need to transcend them.

More insidious than these considerations are the unconscious beliefs that you don't actually deserve the things you aim for, or that it's wrong to be self-indulgent, selfish, and so on. Or a common underlying belief for people from a Judeo-Christian background is the fear of tampering with nature, or offending God, or doing deals with Satan. Some people simply fear success and the responsibility and other changes it brings. For these people, to succeed at what they want would be worse that to fail constantly, so they are unconsciously motivated to undermine their own attempts and to bring about their own failure. Constant failure despite your best efforts is frustrating, but at least you can avoid change. These are some of the reasons why an undeveloped Earth can spell failure for the magical enterprise. You will have others that are personal to yourself, but their effects are the same.

These elemental shortcomings and preoccupations may reveal themselves in dreams and fantasies involving symbols of water, particularly drowning, but also of thirst, and often as mysterious creatures from the hidden depths. You may dream of being on a sinking ship or of being unable to swim. There may also be dreams or waking preoccupations about other people, especially of feeling threatened by them. Similarly there can be preoccupations with and dreams about symbols representing Earth, such as a sense of inertia, of being trapped, buried alive, unable to move, or of strange beasts that lurk within the earth waiting to reach out and devour you. Alternatively there can be dreams about earthquakes, unstable houses, volcanoes, and landslides.

Wodwose Shadow

Earth with Fire

Keywords: Depressed, burdened, apathetic,
cowardly, unmotivated, lazy, neglectful

In folklore, the wodwose is a nature spirit concerned very much with the growth and preservation of the natural world. In its negative aspect, this spirit loses his dynamic power and becomes stagnant. The process is best described in Greek myth where Cronus, originally the Titan associated with a golden age of plenty, castrated his father Uranus and devoured his own children through fear of being usurped. His wife Rhea, the earth goddess, helped their son Zeus escape; Zeus returned to overthrow Cronus, who became Lord of the Underworld.

Cronus is thus associated with old age, death, and with the crushing effects of time and inertia. He had counterparts in myths from all around the world, including Saturn, Kali, and Bran. As with the phoenix, the wodwose is closely associated with change and transformation as a natural process. Where the negative Phoenix spells the end of the process and death, the negative Wodwose refers to stagnation and a hopeless kind of living death.

Not surprisingly, then, this type is plagued by a sense of inertia and stagnation that cannot be overcome. As a result he feels hopeless and depressed by what seem to be circumstances characterized by insuperable limitation. Where the Phoenix shadow fears death as an inevitable and final conclusion, the Wodwose shadow would regard death as a release from the endless, dark night of the soul.

The Wodwose shadow is oppressed by a burden that may be real, such as a unhappy marriage or an unsuitable job, but it is always psychological as an attitude of defeat. Often the more concrete problem of, for instance, a job characterized by grinding routine, follows as a consequence of this fatalistic attitude. Having said that, this shadow does not believe in luck except for bad luck. He is pessimistic and prefers to guard against every eventuality, for which reason he is overcautious and a hoarder—because you never know when you'll need the moose-head plaque, or whatever. Feeling essentially insecure and unsafe, he needs to have control over himself and over his environment as far as possible. As a result, he can be caught in not one but a series of ruts affecting different aspects of his life. He is deeply mistrustful of things turning out well.

He is also suspicious of other people and is just as overcautious with them. Because he is so effectively armored, he is in fact extremely difficult to understand and get to know. This is also the case where Water is the primary element, for even relatively warm Merfolk will be strangely aloof and distant if the shadow is particularly strong. This type is therefore a mysterious creature that seems never to be completely revealed but stays secretively in partial darkness. Naturally this behavior can have the effect of making him unpopular, ironically, because he seems furtive and untrustworthy.

In fact, he is often guarded and aloof because he is easily taken advantage of and has been badly treated in the past. Unfortunately his primary elements, Water and Air, are partly to blame for this, because of the caring disposition of the former and the idealism of the latter. Hard lessons may have been learned early in life that had the effect of activating the shadow as a necessary means of defense against further injury. The result is a "burnt child" who does not easily open up to people until he feels safe to do so. In the meantime, he is isolated and lonely, although rarely friendless. Paradoxically he can feel further burdened by guilt at being so aloof, yet he can't get out of the habit of being so defensive.

There is at the same time good reason to be wary of the Wodwose shadow because he can be as autocratic and downright tyrannical as the people he tries to avoid. When he is not feeling thoroughly ground down and hopeless, he can be effectual but alienate people in the process. He sometimes has an ulterior motive for doing things for people, and he can be quite ruthless in his attempt to achieve his ends. He can be so convinced that he is right that he will not accept that other people have equally valid alternative viewpoints, and expects everyone to bend to his will. He is then intolerant of opposition and will freeze out those he doesn't accept. Ultimately, of course, this strategy may fail, and he is once again in the position of feeling hopeless and alone.

The Wodwose shadow is naturally frustrated by this self-fulfilling prophesy, and he inevitably feels that there is no point in trying to change things since the evidence of his experience is that nothing works. He is unaware of the extent to which his failure to progress is caused by self-obstruction of one sort or another. It's not simply a case of ruining his own efforts through being tyrannical; in fact, this is much less of a problem than his self-imposed duties. The Wodwose shadow believes that it is up to him to carry the burdens seemingly imposed by life but that are more often dumped on him by others. Here, for instance, we see the child caring for the aged parent or struggling with the ailing family business while the rest of the family live their lives. The Wodwose shadow is stoic in the face of these challenges, and plods on wearily as if there was no alternative to a life of drudgery.

He is just as controlled with his feelings as he is with all other aspects of his life. It has already been noted that this type is prone to depression, but it is less obvious that he is also prone to mood swings that include mania. This is something he shares with his cousin the Phoenix shadow, because both types are composed of the same undeveloped elements. The Wodwose shadow is also prone to grandiosity and ego-inflation so that at times he believes himself to be supremely gifted, even literally heaven-sent. At these times his pessimism is replaced, however briefly, by optimism and expansiveness. Finally, however, his golden vision is once again replaced by a bleak one, and he slides again into hopeless drudgery.

Various unconscious defense strategies have been identified, and these can be related to the elements. Psychological defense mechanisms that stem from Fire include *acting out*, the direct expression of feelings such as rage without reflection, guilt, or regard for consequences. Like the other defense strategies, this is a means of coping with stress and inner conflict. Deliberate self-harm in its various forms, including drug abuse and self-mutilation, can be recognized as essentially acts of aggression against the self in order to affect others in some way. *Displacement* is easier to understand. This involves directing pent-up rage onto others who are weaker and hence less dangerous than yourself. Kicking the cat would be an example. *Splitting* is an alternation between idealization and devaluation. Here the other person is seen as either all good or all bad. *Devaluation* involves demeaning oneself or another by exaggerating perceived negative attributes, ridiculing competence, and so on. *Idealization* involves exaggerating your own virtues or more commonly those of another in order to avoid recognizing bad aspects of yourself.

Identification is similar to idealization, and the two may coexist. Identification refers to the unconscious modeling of another person's attributes in order to increase your own sense of self-worth. Identification with an aggressor is a common method of reducing one's fear of him or her. The belief here is that the potential threat will diminish if the aggressor recognizes the similarities. *Introjection* is similar in that it involves the incorporation of another's values or personal traits in order to prevent conflict with or threat from them, but it does not have to uphold self-esteem. It is seen following loss, however, when the characteristics of the departed person (most commonly the case) are expressed by a living person as a defense against the loss.

The weakest element here is Fire, hence constant irritability plus periodic outbursts of anger are likely to attend perceived threats to his carefully maintained, self-protected state. More usually, however, he will use passive-aggressive strategies such as being late, forgetting important things, and doing things wrong or not doing them at all in order to remove perceived threats or to punish people. People who are weaker than him are more likely to experience direct aggression in the form of bullying.

Even in mild cases, where the elements are relatively well-developed and the shadow is consequently weak, there can be a characteristic lack of energy, drive, and passion. Obviously the problem becomes much worse if the elements of the shadow are very undeveloped. Then the power to project himself effectively and to make his presence felt is reduced, and his belief in his ability to effect change is correspondingly less. Clearly this can be a great handicap to any venture since it amounts to a failure of ambition, a problem complicated here by hopelessness that can be characteristic of the

Wodwose shadow's life generally. Similar problems beset other shadow types with weak Fire, but the problem is greatest for Wodwose and Phoenix shadows because of the associated drag of the undeveloped Earth.

Defense strategies related to Earth include *projection*, the unconscious rejection of unwanted thoughts and personal traits by ascribing them to others. The Phoenix shadow also exhibits *denial*, an unconscious refusal to acknowledge external realities because to do so would be too painful; and *somatization*, a preoccupation with physical symptoms that represents a psychological reaction to stressful situations. Denial of the physical self can also be seen among shadows that have a prominent Earth, Phoenix among them.

The shadow often provokes a sense of apathy and pointlessness that undermines the more optimistic outlook associated with the more-developed elements, as we have seen. Both Wodwose and Phoenix shadows are especially prone to apathy and listlessness because of the combined effects of weak Fire and negative Earth. Because their influence is unconscious, the cause of any consequent depression will often be unknown; indeed, the depression itself may go unrecognized and manifest as physical weakness, lack of appetite, and so on, such that a physical illness is suspected. Unfortunately the subject will also deny physical illness due to characteristic negation of the physical self. He can therefore reach a pitiful state before admitting to a problem, typically long after other people have begun openly worrying about his well-being.

Confusion due to the undeveloped Earth can show itself in various ways. He may negate his physical self to the extent of feeling dissociated, literally disembodied and no longer part of the physical world. Alternatively he may overcompensate and become preoccupied with somatic dysfunction to the extent of being a hypochondriac. He may be convinced that he is too substantial and fat, and actually attempt to diminish his physical self by dieting and, if the energy provided by Fire is not too weak, by exercising to extremes. Another effect of the undeveloped Earth that is likely to afflict the Wodwose shadow particularly is the sheer leaden weight of physical existence. This sense of being burdened by his very body may provoke the behavior described above.

The negative attributes that characterize the Wodwose shadow are a mixture of the unconscious qualities associated with the undeveloped elements Fire and Earth (in that order), plus aspects of the primary elements that are being defended against during periods of stress. Which of these attributes is most salient depends very much on the learning experiences of the individual coupled with prevailing circumstances. Although the negative qualities of the primary elements are unpleasant when they come to the fore, they are usually transient and will be the focus of guilt feelings later. The effects of the undeveloped Fire and Earth are more insidious because they are unconscious, and so work indirectly and constantly to influence feelings, thoughts, and behavior.

The negative qualities associated with Fire and Earth tend therefore to be fairly entrenched because they remain unconscious and undeveloped. The defenses listed above exist to safeguard the integrity of the personality as a whole and can be difficult to dislodge. One of the positive features of Fire is to enhance the positive features of Earth by galvanizing the potential qualities into action and by inspiring the individual. One of the positive features of Earth is to direct Fire's energy toward practical ends. With both these elements undeveloped, they cannot be mutually supportive in this way. How this disparity affects magical practice will be outlined below.

The less-attractive features associated with the primary elements Air and Water tend, on the other hand, to be relatively transient and mostly activated at times of extreme tension and stress. Even so, the associated behavior and motivation for acting badly are often unconscious because they are in themselves defense strategies, and are consequently characteristics of the shadow. The fact that these behaviors are usually transient can mean that they exert a very damaging effect on interpersonal relations, especially if they are sudden and very much out of character. Of course, some people are chronically stressed and consequently exhibit shadow qualities most of the time. In these cases it can seem out of character if the usual sources of stress are removed and their behavior becomes less offensive.

While the primary elemental influences found in the shadow are on the whole temporary, traces of these characteristics may be evident all the time. Deformation of personality is not all-or-nothing—it exists as a continuum, ranging from severe to very mild. The patterns that derive from the primary elements manifest in the shadow in the following ways, depending on the primary type.

The Unicorn with a Wodwose shadow has Air as the primary element. Consequently behavior that may become prominent during times of stress relates to distortion of the rationalism that is so much a feature of this element. Hence the individual may begin to behave in an increasingly eccentric, even bizarre, manner as the integrity of the intellectual and cognitive functions become compromised. They may become vague in their speech and unable to concentrate. At the same time they can become focused on insubstantial matters as though they were of major importance. They can become paranoid and lose touch with reality, thereby exacerbating the problems associated with the weak elements of the Wodwose shadow. They will be less and less inclined to be with other people and increasingly withdrawn as pressure mounts. The saving grace of the Air primary is the high degree of personal insight afforded by this element, such that the individual is able to recognize the need to break off and recuperate and thus stall the negative spiral before it goes too far.

The Mermaid with a Wodwose shadow has Water in primary position. This makes it unlikely that the individual will become socially isolated. However, during times of stress and tension, the less-attractive features associated with this element emerge as part of the shadow. In many ways these qualities represent a worsening of the basic pattern of the shadow and are mostly evident when the individual's hard-won social position is under threat. Hence he can become increasingly grandiose and boastful, full of a sense of his own importance. This outrageous conceit and snobbery is, however, usually based on nothing more than wish fulfillment. He does not pay attention to the facts but is guided entirely by the theme of his own grandeur and self-importance.

Interpersonally he becomes increasingly obnoxious and aggressive. He is self-assured, self-centered, and increasingly dominant and overbearing. He becomes more and more demanding of attention and admiration, and less and less patient and relenting. Other people are merely vassals to serve his ego. He feigns concern and interest in others only in order to exploit them, and is otherwise utterly disdainful of everyone. It is evident that the distortion of reality that is involved here follows the subsuming of the secondary Air element within the shadow. The individual concerned is both insensitive to others and hypersensitive regarding himself. Any attempt at contradiction of his inflexible and mistaken views is regarded as a personal attack, and is rewarded with explosive rage.

All of these weaknesses can represent powerful limitations to successful magical outcomes. Since Fire is the weakest element in this shadow, it exerts the strongest negative influence. The most important of these for the Wodwose shadow is that with a weak affinity for Fire, the magician loses the source of energy that magic depends on. Fire refers to the actual energy we call magic. This is the drive, the passion, and the very power that you want to direct. It goes without saying that in the absence of this passion and drive, the enterprise is doomed to failure. This energy is stirred up by the application of the will at the point in the process during which the magician attempts to petition the entities that have hopefully been contacted already. If, because of the makeup of his personality, the magician has a poor affinity with this element, the associated magical qualities will not be readily available. A limited disposition toward Fire can be very limiting indeed, not least because success depends in part on the conviction that the goal is already attained. Fire provides this conviction, the desire, and the will.

There can also be unconscious self-sabotage at work. Fire relates to morals and religious feeling, so the underlying belief that magic is an affront to God or just plain wrong can be a major factor leading to failure. Among the contradictions of Western society is the urge to succeed coupled with the admonition for being successful. The socioeconomic system encourages pursuit of worldly success, while the Church condemns it. We grow up trying to reconcile the elements of this paradox and cannot assume that it does not continue to exert an unconscious effect, even if we consciously reject it.

The problems associated with poor affinity with Earth concerns failure in the final stage of the process to produce the manifest changes that magic is designed to achieve. The sphere of the Earth element is the beginning and the end of magical activity. The magician brings into a carefully chosen, specifically designed working area ritually significant aspects of the physical world, like the wand and the athame, and manipulates them using sounds and gestures to effect desired changes in the physical world. This starting point is also the end point. Recall what was said about performing magic as if it was already accomplished. One stands in the Earth sphere at the beginning and the end of the process simultaneously.

The problem with the weak Earth now becomes apparent: poor organization, disregard for ritual procedures, lack of connection with the forces of Earth, or alternatively being too bogged down in technique. Disregard for ritual procedures often includes a disregard for the postoperative grounding and sealing, and consequently being left open to the disruptive effects of incomplete connection from the Otherworld.

Of course, the biggest problem produced by a negative Earth is the very earthiness of the element. Earth is characteristically skeptical, pragmatic, hard-nosed, and literally too down-to-earth to believe in magic in the first place, and this skeptical attitude can work unconsciously to undermine your efforts. If you can't suspend disbelief for a while and open yourself up to the possibilities, then naturally you will have major difficulty progressing to the final stage and succeeding in your aims. Without the conviction that you will bring about your desired aims, your performance is literally empty ritual. The paradox here is that in order to work effectively with earthy forces, you need to transcend them.

More insidious than these considerations are the unconscious beliefs that you don't actually deserve the things you aim for, or that it's wrong to be self-indulgent, selfish, and so on. Or a common underlying belief for people from a Judeo-Christian background is the fear of tampering with nature, or offending God, or doing deals with Satan. Some people simply fear success and the responsibility and other changes it brings. For these people, to succeed at what they want would be worse than to fail constantly, so they are unconsciously motivated to undermine their own attempts and to bring about their own failure. Constant failure despite your best efforts is frustrating, but at least you can avoid change. These are some of the reasons why an undeveloped Earth can spell failure for the magical enterprise. You will have others that are personal to yourself, but their effects are the same.

These elemental shortcomings and preoccupations may reveal themselves in dreams and fantasies involving symbols of Earth such as a sense of inertia, of being trapped, buried alive, unable to move, or of strange beasts that lurk within the earth waiting to reach out and devour you. Alternatively there can be dreams about earthquakes, unstable houses, volcanoes, and landslides. Similarly there can be dreams and obsessions with fire, such as the threat of being burned, or of wandering in deserts, or alternatively of being very cold and in need of warmth. There may also be dreams of fierce animals, such as lions, that are associated with hot countries and the sun.

Gryphon Shadow

Earth with Air

Keywords: Materialistic, unreliable, confused,
irrational, irritable, neglectful, lazy

In myth, the gryphon was the enormous beast of the goddess Nemesis, the daughter of hell and the night. Nemesis was the goddess of vengeance and the gryphon was her instrument of retribution. Nemesis has come to refer to an enemy or difficulty that cannot be overcome and that is associated in some way with retribution for past misdeeds.

Where Pegasus shadows derive a sense of personal security from being valued by other people, Gryphon shadows derive a sense of security from having physical things of value. This shadow does not trust other people, and so places his faith in objects. As an Earth type, this element is especially important, and here it is weak. Consequently the shadow unconsciously places undue emphasis on the physical world and will typically overvalue the more damaging and unhealthy aspects of the physical while undervaluing the healthy. Hence, he is lazy, indolent, and lacking in ambition. This can still be evident even with a well-developed Fire in the primary pair. In these cases, energy is misdirected and wasted on things in a way that is designed to maintain a sense of security. Other people can be amazed at how little the person does, considering how active he is.

He is prone to dismiss or ignore anything that he doesn't like or that threatens his sense of security. This can extend to his own physical self, for although he will place a high value on luxuries and will overindulge himself in shopping for nonessential material items, he will at the same time eat badly or not at all. At the same time as pampering himself, he will fail to take care of his physical health. And at the same time as dismissing "inconvenient" illness and injuries, he will be continually worrying about alleged life-threatening tumors and heart attacks.

Even despite the expansive nature of Fire and the imaginative quality of Water in primary position, he can exhibit an underlying lack of faith in the mystical, or relationships, or anything that is not firmly grounded in the manifest world of form. In this sense he can still be boring and rigid in his outlook, even with strong primaries. If Fire is strong, his religious and moral attitude will be fanatical and intolerant. If Water is strong, his interest in such things as the occult and dreams will be undermined by his underlying pessimism and thus be unsatisfying. If he does get involved in these pursuits, it may be a cynical involvement and just for the money.

He believes that to pay a high price for something means that it has a high value, and this carries with it the implication that the more that is spent on him, the more valuable he is. As a result, he is extravagant, grasping, and opportunistic. He will use people in order to obtain this sense of personal worth. Hence he is attracted to glitzy, glamorous people and their world as a hanger-on. He may even become romantically involved with people just because they have money and a wealthy lifestyle. He may even expect payment for services rendered and as proof of his worth. Relationships on another level would simply be confusing for him. Affection expressed physically and especially for a physical reward not only seems right to him, it may be the only possible type of exchange, given his lack of trust in others.

Various unconscious defense strategies have been identified, and these can be related to the elements. The unconscious defense strategies associated with Earth that we can see operating in the case of the Gryphon shadow include *denial*, an unconscious refusal to acknowledge external realities because to do so would be too painful; or *somatization*, a preoccupation with physical symptoms that represent a psychological reaction to stressful situations. Denial of the physical self can also be seen among shadows that have a prominent Earth, Gryphons among them.

Earth being weak also means that this type has a poor sense of being grounded. Without the all-important home he has no anchor, no compass, no sense of direction or belonging, and consequently feels as if he is adrift in an open boat. Not only is he unrealistic, he lacks adequate foresight. He therefore feels aimless and lethargic. The paradox is that although he places a heavy emphasis on material things, he does in fact need people, for it is only by comparison with others that he can feel valuable. Ultimately it is other people who give him a sense of value, not the things he owns. This is indeed his nemesis, for it is in the social world of other people, and more particularly the intimate expression of love and affection between himself and another, that he will find his true worth.

Defense strategies associated with weak Air include *fantasy*, the excessive preoccupation with daydreams and the imagination as a means of escaping from life's problems and one's own internal conflicts. This is also known as schizoid or autistic fantasy because in its most extreme forms this defense mechanism has the effect of removing the person from the social world. *Intellectualization* refers to the overuse of abstract thought in order to avoid psychological discomfort. This is evident from the attempts by some people to split hairs and argue over precise definitions for their behavior, as if they can thereby argue that their maladaptive behavior is in fact acceptable.

Rationalization refers to the pathological use of apparently plausible reasons to justify your behavior. *Projection* is the unconscious rejection of your own thoughts and character traits. Recognition of these ideas and traits would not fit with the self-concept, and consequently they are ascribed to others. *Repression* is fairly well-known to most people as the exclusion from consciousness of distressing feelings or ideas. It is not the same as *suppression*, which is a deliberate pushing away of unacceptable thoughts and behavior.

The defense mechanisms associated with Air often come into play to uphold the self-destructive behavior attributable to Earth. Inactivity will be rationalized as a need for rest, or even as due to illness. At the same time, genuine illness will be explained away as simple tiredness or as due to the weather, or some such thing. Poor diet and other types of physical self-neglect will be excused on the grounds that they are healthy, as in the claim that he is cutting down on fat or avoiding colds by not keeping warm. Vague references to recent research are often made to back up these claims. Thus, although he will ridicule scientific theories as a matter of course, he will expediently use these defensively to their own advantage.

Because Air is the least-developed element, Gryphon shadows often appear irrational to others, and while this scatterbrain appearance can be endearing in the short term, eventually it becomes annoying. The Water primary ensures that he will experience powerful emotional reactions, but because Air is weak he can neither understand them nor express them to others. Consequently the pleasantly amusing eccentric is eventually perceived as the crazy person who takes offense where none was intended, and who sees malicious intent behind every action. Since he has difficulty recognizing and accepting his own negative emotions he represses them, only to have them surface as physical illness or as emotional instability and even psychosis.

He therefore becomes argumentative and aggressive, often jumping to conclusions because his reasoning is distorted by his powerful emotions. In his case, the heart truly rules the head, because the head is unable to accurately perceive the facts of the matter and is therefore unable to understand what's actually happening. With the emotions in control, the sense of threat is rationalized retrospectively, sometimes in the most bizarre way.

Unfortunately he may be right part of the time because his indiscriminate, impulsive associations with questionable people leave him open to abuse. There is fertile ground here for a self-fulfilling prophesy. Because of poor discrimination, he gets involved with people that genuinely abuse him and about whom he is justifiably guarded. This sense of threat and mistrust is then generalized to everyone around him. Add to this his self-seeking and manipulative tendencies, and the scene is set for interpersonal chaos.

His career can suffer for the same reasons. He is seen as unreliable, absentminded, and impractical. He is also lazy and disregards accepted rules as if they do not apply to him. As we have seen, he can be socially disruptive in the short and long term, first by being a pleasant distraction, later by being a paranoid siren. His paradoxical combination of self-indulgence and lack of self-care puts him off work with real and imaginary health problems. Finally he sees work as hindering his quest for comfort and sense of security. Only a very highly paid position will fit with his notions about being properly valued; basic pay for routine work only reinforces his fundamental belief in himself as worthless.

Thus, the negative attributes that characterize the Gryphon shadow are a mixture of the unconscious qualities associated with the undeveloped elements Air and Earth (in that order), plus aspects of the primary elements Fire and Water that are being defended against during periods of stress. Which of these attributes is most salient at any given time depends very much on the learning experiences of the individual, coupled with prevailing circumstances. Although the negative qualities of the primary elements are unpleasant when they come to the fore, they are usually transient and will be the focus of guilt feelings later. The effects of the undeveloped Air and Earth are more insidious because they are always unconscious, and so work indirectly and constantly to influence feelings, thoughts, and behavior.

The negative qualities associated with Earth and Air tend therefore to be fairly entrenched because they remain unconscious and undeveloped. The defenses listed above exist to safeguard the integrity of the personality as a whole, and can be difficult to dislodge. One of the positive features of Earth is to enhance and stabilize the positive features of Air. One of the positive features of Air is to give inspiration and direction to Earth. With both these elements undeveloped, they cannot be mutually supportive in this way. How this disparity affects magical practice will be outlined below.

The less-attractive features associated with the primary elements Water and Fire tend, on the other hand, to be relatively transient and mostly activated at times of extreme tension and stress. Even so, the associated behavior and motivation for acting badly are often unconscious because they are in themselves defense strategies, and are consequently characteristics of the shadow. The fact that these behaviors are usually transient can mean that they exert a very damaging effect on interpersonal relations, especially if they are sudden and very much out of character. Of course, some people are chronically stressed and consequently exhibit shadow qualities most of the time. In these cases it can seem out of character if the usual sources of stress are removed and their behavior becomes less offensive.

While the primary elemental influences found in the shadow are on the whole temporary, traces of these characteristics may be evident all the time. Deformation of personality is not all-or-nothing—it exists as a continuum, ranging from severe to very mild. The patterns that derive from the primary elements manifest in the shadow in the following ways, depending on the primary type.

Wyverns with a Gryphon shadow have Fire as the primary element. Their personal relationships become unstable and the sense of self becomes unclear. Consequently the individual exhibits extreme moodiness and lack of restraint, often related to fear of being abandoned by others. They are therefore highly sensitive to any indication that others do not value them. They themselves veer between idealizing others and denigrating them. They are torn between fiery rage against others and the Water-based need to be accepted and wanted by them. However, manipulative behavior and selfish attention-seeking undermines their essential sociability and they begin to bring about the very abandonment they are attempting to avoid. With an ever-increasing sense of insecurity, their attempts to elicit care from others become more desperate and they may be prone to vituperative outpourings that further damage relationships. The negative spiral continues until the external pressures are removed, allowing a gradual return to usual functioning.

Chimeras with a Gryphon shadow have Water as the primary element, so emotionalism is more pronounced. Corresponding behaviors that may be emphasized during periods of stress include a compulsive need to be the center of attention, and they may be given to dramatic, over-the-top displays of affection that are essentially exaggerations of their usual behavior. They can become more than usually entertaining and very popular, at least initially. This new behavior can have a slightly manic feel to it, though, and there is an increased tendency to enhance their own popularity at the expense of others, who are the butt of their jokes. As the tension mounts, this aggressiveness becomes more marked and is directed against everyone, eventually including close friends and family. From this point on, the individual becomes more openly sarcastic and hurtful, and the popularity falls away to be replaced by dislike, sometimes extreme.

All of this is difficult for the Wyvern or Chimera primary, because both are extremely sociable types who like to be liked and appreciated by others. They can't bear to be alone, but at the same time they can be highly unpleasant if the shadow is too powerful in its effects. One aspect of the shadow, however, relates to the primary type, and this relates to pride. Wyverns and Chimeras like to be helpful to others and sometimes arrogantly assume that they can handle any problem that others present them with. This can be dangerous if the help being offered falls short of what the other person desperately needs. When the shadow becomes powerful, however, then everyone can suffer.

If the Gryphon shadow emerges during times of stress, or if the character is chronically neurotic, then he can become more withdrawn, lose touch with reality, and become increasingly eccentric, even psychotic. He continues to deny his loneliness and sense of rejection while refusing to accept his own feelings as the life-saving bridge that connects him with others on an intimate and meaningful level. He needs to overcome his fear of engulfment and give up his isolated freedom in order to be intimate and free. However, he tends to devalue others except insofar as they give value to him. His primary Fire can make him aggressive and spiteful, while his primary Water can make him sickeningly full of self-pity. His weak Earth makes him feel rootless and unsafe, so he overcompensates by being avaricious, lustful, and socially destructive.

All of these weaknesses can represent powerful limitations to successful magical outcomes. Limitations associated with undeveloped Air are poor skills of visualization, poor focus, and imprecise statements in the form of goals, affirmations, and incantations. These block the capacity for communication with the occult forces upon which successful magic depends. By the same token, weak affinity with the Air element results in inhibition of divinatory abilities.

This last is in itself a major limiting factor, since it refers directly to psychic power. Even if you are not going to make much use of divination (and what occultist doesn't?), you will want oracular guidance in formulating goals and uncovering barriers to success. In this event, a reduced capacity for seership is a serious handicap that means having to work blind. Finally, there is the question of ethics, or lack thereof. Undeveloped Air can mean that the magician believes that he knows what's best for everyone else, and as a consequence does not hesitate to work magic for or even against others "for their own good." Needless to say, this should be resisted, which is why the magician should fully understand the motivational basis of his own actions.

Additional unconscious factors associated with Air are likely to be more insidious and limiting. The very rationalism and logic that Air symbolizes militates against the very notion of magic. Since the inception of the Age of Enlightenment, when superstition was swept away and rationalism became our creed, the mechanical, clockwork universe replaced the occult universe that had preceded it. As we have seen, modern science now cleaves more to an apparently irrational model, with which ordinary people are still not entirely familiar. We have all grown up imbued with rationalist principles and the scientific endeavor. This lifetime of obeisance to rationalism can be difficult to dismiss entirely, no matter how fully you may disregard it on a conscious level. At the back of your mind there lurks a man in a white coat, shaking his head at magic—and you believe he is right.

Weak Earth threatens failure in the final stage of the process, the production of the manifest changes that magic is designed to achieve. The sphere of the Earth element is the beginning and the end of magical activity. The magician brings into a carefully chosen, specifically designed working area ritually significant aspects of the physical world, like the wand and the athame, and manipulates them using sounds and gestures to effect desired changes in the physical world. This starting point is also the end point. Recall what was said about performing magic as if it was already accomplished. You stand in the Earth sphere at the beginning and the end of the process simultaneously. Consequently, a poor affinity with this element represents a major limitation of the whole process.

Poor organization, disregard for ritual procedures, lack of connection with the forces of Earth, or alternatively being too bogged down in technique are all indications that this important affinity is minimal. Disregard for ritual procedures often includes a disregard for the postoperative grounding and sealing, leaving you prone to the disruptive effects of the Otherworld.

Of course, the biggest problem produced by a negative Earth is the very earthiness of the element. Earth is characteristically skeptical, pragmatic, hard-nosed, and literally too down-to-earth to believe in magic in the first place. With Earth as the least-developed element, this skepticism will operate unconsciously to undermine your efforts, which is why the pre-ritual baths and other preliminaries are necessary. These procedures are designed to cancel out the limiting factors of your own personality. If you can't suspend disbelief for a while and open yourself up to the possibilities, then naturally you will have major difficulty progressing to the final stage and succeeding in your aims. Without conviction that you will bring about your desired aims, your performance is literally empty ritual. The paradox here is that in order to work effectively with earthy forces, you need to transcend them.

More insidious than these considerations are the unconscious beliefs that you don't actually deserve the things you aim for, or that it's wrong to be self-indulgent, selfish, and so on. Or a common underlying belief for people from a Judeo-Christian background is the fear of tampering with nature, or offending God, or doing deals with Satan. Some people simply fear success and the responsibility and other changes it brings. For these people, to succeed at what they want would be worse that to fail constantly, so they are unconsciously motivated to undermine their own attempts and to bring about their own failure. Constant failure despite your best efforts is frustrating, but at least you can avoid change. These are some of the reasons why an undeveloped Earth can spell failure for the magical enterprise. You will have others that are personal to yourself, but their effects are the same.

These elemental shortcomings and preoccupations may reveal themselves in dreams and fantasies involving symbols of undeveloped Air, such as falling or trying to fly, or of being threatened by huge birds or even of the gryphon himself in his aspect of agent of retribution; or there can be a threat of powerful entities in the sky, symbolized by thunder and lightening. Symbols of undeveloped Earth can include inertia, being trapped, buried alive, unable to move, or of strange beasts that lurk within the earth. Alternatively there can be dreams about earthquakes, unstable houses, volcanoes, and landslides. On the other hand, you may dream of being insubstantial, a ghost.

8

TECHNIQUES FOR
DEVELOPING WEAK ELEMENTS

Most people have one, more usually two, sometimes three, but rarely four strong elements represented in their personality. Two is most usual, with the other two remaining relatively undeveloped. The implication of this is that the personality is characterized principally by these strong elements and subconsciously by the weak ones. If your Q score is high—i.e., there is a large degree of differences between elements—then the very strengths derived from these highly developed elements actually become weaknesses. The reason for this is that the bigger the difference between elements, the more exclusive the reliance on the main characteristics and the less likely it is that the weaker ones will be drawn upon consciously. These may continue to exert an effect, but this will operate subconsciously. This chapter offers some methods for developing these weaker elements and thereby increasing the extent to which their respective qualities can be utilized consciously, both in magic work and in life generally.

This is not to say that by performing these exercises you will be able to rid yourself of personal problems. If you think that you have problems of a psychological nature, you would be better advised to seek the services of a qualified professional. If you have mental health problems, or worry that you may have mental health problems, you should not be practicing magic. Psychotherapy is advisable for anyone who intends to follow an occult path because it offers a structured and contained way of enhancing self-knowledge and hence creating a more balanced personality. Two models that are likely to appeal to the student of the occult are the Jungian analytical psychology and psychosynthesis, because of their emphasis on spirituality as a main feature of human experience and development. Just be sure that the practitioner you choose is qualified and reputable.

Developing weak elements can be a lengthy process, and you should not assume that application of these techniques on a few occasions will rectify huge deficits. Personal development is a lifelong process, some aspects of which take longer than others. Even the aging process can be helpful; Jung, for instance, was of the opinion that differences between temperaments are reduced naturally over time simply as a consequence of greater maturity. At the same time, one's life experiences can have the effect of forcing the development of weaker elements. A lot of people find themselves growing up in an environment that is antithetical to their nature—one such stereotype is the dreamer with potential to become a gifted writer who is obliged to do routine, boring work to help keep the family fed.

This tends on the whole to make for a rather frustrating, unfulfilled life, but there can be a good side to it. You may be highly imaginative and intuitive, possibly even to the extent of being psychic. These are all Water qualities. However, your parent(s) may have frowned on these characteristics and constantly pushed you into more practical, here-and-now (earthy) activities. If so, this would have made you feel frustrated, but at least your potential earthiness will have been developed to some extent instead of being left relatively dormant. I speak from personal experience in this regard. I have always been dreamy and intellectually inclined (a Unicorn with a Wodwose shadow), but I was obliged from an early age to help out with the family business, unloading lorries, conducting sales, etc. The net effect of this was to ground me somewhat, to push me to interact with other people more than I would have done, and to build me up physically. Although I resented the work at the time, I can look back and appreciate the clear benefits from having done it.

It is advisable to make use of a range of techniques, including others that you may discover elsewhere. In this way you stand a better chance of enhancing the element in question. Also, bear in mind that your preferred techniques will inevitably reflect your principle elemental makeup, so try the techniques that have less appeal as well. Working with crystals, for instance, is an Earth technique, and you may have little interest in crystals because you need to develop your Earth element—so try crystals!

From an occult perspective, the meditation exercises are probably the most direct method of enhancing elements, if you believe that you have actually entered the Otherworld with the intention of contacting the relevant beings for help. If you prefer to regard this as a purely psychological technique, such as is employed within psychosynthesis, then you are deliberately accessing your subconscious in order to effect changes that will manifest in your conscious life. Either way, if you have read the description of each temperament, you will be familiar with the associated qualities. In these meditations you will immerse yourself in the raw element as far as possible, and the symbolism will affect you subconsciously to enhance these qualities in your conscious life. You do not need to remind yourself of the specific qualities of each element during the exercise.

I have offered two meditations for each element, one involving a trip to the realm of the element itself, and one that is more traditional. Use either or both, as you wish. Alternatively, you may like to meditate on the fabulous beast that represents the qualities of the type that you would like to develop. If, for instance, you have a Dragon shadow, you could meditate on the image of the dragon itself. Try to become this creature and to experience its primary qualities. You should eventually find that they become more evident in your own makeup.

In any case, observe the following: Ensure that you have the time to perform the meditation, and that you will not be disturbed. Try to ensure that you have environmental conditions that are conducive to the work—you can't do much about external noise but you can wear headphones and play appropriate music or natural sounds. Dim the lights, light a candle and incense if this seems appropriate, and perhaps use something that symbolizes the element, such as a photograph of the sea, the sky, a mountain, the sun.

Wear appropriate colors and assume the magical persona if you feel inclined. Adopt a comfortable position—upright in a comfortable chair is frequently best for Western-ers. Breathe slowly and deeply and go through the process of progressive relaxation. After the meditation, stretch and ground yourself. Do something that will bring you back to earth, such as eating or drinking. Write up your experiences. Above all, remem-ber that you are in no danger during these exercises. You cannot be harmed by beings you encounter during the meditations, and you can end the exercise at any point just by opening your eyes and getting up. The immediate effect of these exercises should be a sense of relaxation and peace. If you don't enjoy them, discontinue and try something else.

Meditations

Earth (1)

See before you a cave mouth. Walk into the cave. Feel the temperature drop as you walk farther in. Walk deep into the heart of the mountain. Notice the various crystal struc-tures of different colors embedded in the tunnel walls and ceiling. Feel the immense age and heaviness of the rocks and stones. When you reach the heart of the mountain, find yourself standing in a huge cavern, the intricate crystal stalactites and stalagmites creat-ing the effect of a subterranean cathedral. Enthroned in the center of this palace that glows softly with its own fluorescence you see Gheb, queen of the Earth elementals. State your purpose and ask that she assist you in developing the earthy part of your character. You may see gnomes throughout the cavern, emerging from the rocks. Stay with them awhile, see what they have to show you, and listen to what they say. They may give you a gift, such as a rune stone, to indicate that your earthiness is being enhanced. Bring this back with you. Thank the gnomes and Queen Gheb before leav-ing. Later, you may want to offer them a gift in return, such as a crystal. Bury this some-where while offering thanks.

Earth (2)

Place before you something that represents the Earth element. A stone is an obvious choice, but you may like to vary the exercise and use other things such as a symbol or a picture of a mountain. Focus on the stone. Familiarize yourself with its features, then close your eyes and visualize it as fully as possible. Now become the stone. Become aware of your density, your weight, your inertia, your great age. Experience as fully as possible the different attributes of the stone/chosen item and understand them as aspects of yourself. When you are ready, stretch and ground yourself.

Air (1)

You are on a cliff top. Ahead of you, barely visible, is the faint outline of a castle and of a shimmering bridge leading over to it. You step confidently onto this bridge and walk to the castle in the clouds. You walk through the pale but mighty doors and on into the great hall with its high walls of refracted light, rainbows like stained glass. Enthroned high in the center of this palace you behold Paralda, king of the Air elementals. State your reason for visiting his domain and request assistance in developing the airy qualities of your personality. You may then see hundreds of sylphs in the air around you. They will carry you on the four winds to the distant reaches of the universe, to knowledge and understanding of all things, and to the wisdom of the ancients. Pay close attention to what the sylphs show you, and listen to what they teach. They may offer you a gift, such as a feather, to indicate that your airy nature has begun developing. Bring this back with you. When you are once again in the castle of air, thank King Paralda and his sylphs before leaving. Later you may wish to offer them a gift in return, such as some incense that you can burn in the open air while offering thanks.

Air (2)

Place before you something to represent the Air element. A stick of burning incense is ideal, but you may wish to vary the exercise by using symbols of the Air element, such as a skyscape. Familiarize yourself with the incense as it curls gently round in the air. Close your eyes and visualize it as fully as possible, then become it yourself. Experience your airy qualities, your weightlessness and grace, your expansiveness, limitlessness, clarity, and ability to penetrate into the things around you. Understand these things as aspects of yourself. Then open your eyes, stretch, and ground yourself.

Fire (1)

You are standing at the gates of a castle of fire. The gates open to admit you. Inside the castle you seem to be standing in the very heart of a furnace. You walk into this intense heat with confidence. In the great hall—the walls of which are red, yellow, and blue soaring flames—Djinn, king of the Fire elementals, is enthroned on white heat at the heart of the inferno. State your purpose for entering his fiery realm and ask for assistance in developing your fiery qualities. You may then see salamanders scurrying among the flames. Race with them with unbounded energy and an exhilarating sense of freedom. Revel in their expansiveness and speed. Take note of everything they show you and listen closely to what they say. They may give you a gift, such as a small stone glowing brightly with its own natural light. Bring this back with you. Thank King Djinn and the salamanders before you leave their domain. Later you may wish to give them a gift in return; you may burn an entire fresh, red candle and offer thanks to them.

Fire (2)

Place before you something that represents the Fire element. A candle is an obvious choice, though you may like to vary the exercise and use other things, such as a symbol or a picture of the sun. Focus on the candle. Familiarize yourself with its features (do not stare too long at the flame), then close your eyes and visualize it as fully as possible. Now become the flame. Become aware of yourself as pure energy manifesting as heat and light. Experience as fully as possible the different attributes of the flame/chosen item and understand them as aspects of yourself. When you are ready, stretch and ground yourself.

Water (1)

You are at the side of a sacred pool with a waterfall opposite you. The water is so clear and pure that you can easily see the bottom of the pool, the colored pebbles lying on the bottom, the small fish swimming near the surface. Walk into the beautiful, cool water until you are completely submerged. You find as you walk that the pool has great depth, many times greater than was apparent on the surface. Eventually you find that you have to swim down into the sunlit depths where you are able to breathe the water without difficulty. You realize that you have entered a watery palace, at the deepest part of which you find Necksa, queen of the Water elementals. State your purpose for entering her watery realm and request that she assist you in developing your watery qualities. You may then see undines emerge from the water around you. Feel yourself immersed in love for all the people and all the things, and feel the joy of perfect balance and harmony. Know that you are connected to everything through the shared medium of water; as it touches you, so it touches everything. The undines may give you a gift, such as a shell, to help you to develop your watery characteristics. Bring this back with you. Thank Queen Necksa and the undines before leaving them. Later you may wish to offer a gift of your own, such as a few drops of perfume that can be sprinkled in a pool or stream, as you give thanks to them.

Water (2)

Place before you something that represents the Water element. A small bowl of water is an obvious choice, though you may like to vary the exercise and use other things, such as a symbol or a picture of the sea. Focus on the water. Familiarize yourself with its features, then close your eyes and visualize it as fully as possible. Now become the water. Become aware of your clarity and purity, your life-giving, life-sustaining nature. Feel your immense depth and all the different attributes of the water/chosen item, and understand them as aspects of yourself. When you are ready, stretch and ground yourself.

Behavioral Techniques

These techniques are designed for use in everyday life as a means of enhancing weak elements.

Earth

The principle virtues of Earth are practicality, steadiness, etc. It follows from this that the best thing to do to strengthen earthy qualities is to practice them, hence do practical things. This is easier if you can combine practical activities with something you are interested in. If you have an interest in healing, for instance, you might consider making your own herbal remedies, learning about and using aromatherapy, and so on. Tend the garden. Learn to cook. Pay attention to your body and your physical needs—try exercising more, doing yoga, having a massage. Learn to play a musical instrument, or even make one. Learn to paint or sculpt, or make clay pots. Make your own magic tools and robes. Remember that the aim is not to be good at these things but to make a habit of doing something practical. Learning social skills is a good idea, and one way to approach this is through learning a language. Doing formal courses not only allows you the chance to get feedback about your performance from an expert, you would also be acquiring useful skills.

Air

For some people this will be the most difficult element to enhance through behavioral means because in order to develop the somewhat dry, intellectual, and theoretical skills associated with this element, the most direct way is *to practice* these somewhat dry, intellectual, and theoretical skills. The best examples of these are found in academic texts on philosophy, comparative religion, the law, logic, and mathematics such as algebra or trigonometry. The exception is the study of magical and occult theory itself. For a good examination of occult matters from a scientific perspective, I recommend *Where Science and Magic Meet* by Serena Roney-Dougal. Or try reading scientific articles, some of which focus on metaphysical matters. Psychology may be of interest, particularly Jung's extensive writings, most of which is fascinating to the student of the occult. An analysis of opposing arguments will allow you to hone your own ability to argue in a calm, logical way, and to get to the facts of a matter. Try also to examine the various factors that lead to a given outcome—historical analysis of the events that led up to World War I, for example. Practice making formal plans for yourself, including timetables. Obviously the reason for doing these things is to enhance your mental clarity, powers of logic, and other airy qualities.

Fire

While you can't plan to be impulsive, which is a characteristic of this element, you can try to be less routine in your habits. Try to do something entirely different at intervals throughout the day. Vary your activities as much as possible. Practice talking to people. Get into the habit of starting conversations, even just casual exchanges about the weather. Practice thinking on your feet. Brainstorm something, then summarize your conclusions. You might even try acting a small part in amateur dramatics, singing, or whatever. Consider taking up some form of competitive sport, especially a martial art. Or try dancing more often—in other words, cultivate the energetic feature of fire that you are trying to enhance. Not only will you go some way to developing this element, you will enjoy yourself and become physically and psychologically healthier in the bargain.

Water

This is a particularly difficult element to cultivate because qualities like empathy, sociability, and psychism can't be learned easily. You can begin just by observing other people's behavior and considering why they do what they do. The subtle reactions expressed through body language can be particularly informative. Try putting yourself in another person's shoes. Admittedly this is easier said than done, and it may be easier if you can identify with a character in a book or a film and experience things vicariously through these characters. Or try to experience the emotions expressed in songs as if you had written them yourself—then remind yourself that these are the expressed feelings of another person.

Write songs, stories, or poems. Keep a diary in which you reflect on things that have happened during the day. Try imagining someone else having your feelings—it can come as a surprise to some people that others can feel the same way, although they often do. People who need to develop watery qualities especially need to understand that individual differences are just that—differences, not faults. Finally, try to develop your intuitive powers; practice methods of divination such as scrying, or methods that employ the kind of pictorial images found in the tarot. Study your dreams, the language of symbols. Meditate. Consider how different atmospheres, colors, sounds, the weather, etc., affect you—and others.

Affirmations, Crystals, Colors, Symbols

Affirmations

In this section I will refer to several methods of enhancing elemental qualities, beginning with affirmations. Affirmations are important for two reasons: They exert a positive psychological effect on you, and they attract the type of forces that help bring about the changes you aim for. Recent research confirms the power of a positive attitude. It seems that "lucky" people tend to be those who expect to be lucky, while good fortune does not on the whole favor people who expect to fail. You need to repeat an affirmation at least six times in order to make sure that it penetrates deep into the unconscious. These do not need to be complicated—in fact, the simpler the better. Try something like "My earthy (or fiery/airy/watery) qualities become stronger by the day," and repeat this daily. This is done within seconds, so it is hardly a chore, and it can be very effective.

Crystals

The notion of having several bodies corresponding to different aspects of being is ancient, and is most extensively described by the Indian concept of kundalini, or "divine force," and its associated system of energy points, called chakras. This system describes seven bodies, each of which is attuned to a different vibrational frequency. The first is the physical, followed by the etheric, the astral, the mental, the atmic, the monadic, and finally the divine. For the purposes of this book I will refer only to the first four because they relate to the elements. As you can tell, the first four bodies correlate with the elements Earth, Fire, Water, and Air. The physical body correlates with Earth because the physical body itself is part of the Earth plane. The etheric body is closely connected to the physical, and indeed dies with it. This is because the etheric body has the function of transferring life energy from the universal source to the physical. The etheric is therefore the energy body and corresponds to Fire. The astral body is also known as the emotional body, and naturally corresponds to Water. Given what has been said about the creative power of thought and the centrality of psychology to magical practice, it is notable that the mental body, corresponding to Air, is the outermost of the four.

If you would like to know more about kundalini and the chakras, try a comprehensive text such as Paulson's *Kundalini and the Chakras* (1998). You can influence the power flow through the chakras by meditating on them or by using appropriate crystals. The correspondences are as follows:

Earth base of the spine (Maladhra Chakra); tiger's-eye, red jasper

Water just below the navel (Manipura Chakra); citrine, yellow jasper, calcite

Fire center of the chest (Anahata Chakra); malachite, jade, rose quartz

Air between the eyebrows (Savikalpa Samadhi Chakra); amethyst, sodalite

In order to activate dormant chakras, you can either meditate on them or use appropriate crystals. If you don't have the correct crystal, use clear quartz. Clear quartz is the most highly prized crystal among shaman the world over, who refer to them as "stars of the earth." The crystal should be round at one end and pointed at the other. If you are meditating you need only visualize the desired changes. If you prefer to use a crystal, hold it about two inches above the chakra and move it in a circular fashion. Visualize brilliant light of the appropriate color (see list below) flowing down from the crown chakra at the top of your head and up from the base chakra at the base of your spine. These meet in the crystal and are directed into the chakra you are working on by placing the tip of the pointed end against your skin.

It may be necessary to clear a blocked chakra before activating it. Once again, use meditation or a crystal if you prefer. The process is largely the same; hold the crystal about two inches above the chakra, round end toward the body, and move it in a circular fashion. Visualize the blocked energy as a dark cloud being drawn out of the chakra and into the crystal. Bury the crystal afterward overnight so that the energy thus collected can be returned to the earth. Activate the chakra using the process described above.

These are merely suggestions for treating the chakras that correspond to the elements, but there is always the danger of neglecting the other chakras and producing an imbalance elsewhere. I recommend that you find a good introductory text that will allow you to gain some understanding of the chakras and of kundalini. Then you may wish to consider joining a class and learning about the practical application of these ideas. Wearing the appropriate crystals or having them about your person is also useful for enhancing elemental qualities. Again, there are numerous books on the market that will inform you of which crystals are most appropriate for different reasons. I recommend *Cunningham's Encyclopedia of Crystals, Gems, and Metal Magic* (1998) as good, comprehensive text.

Color

The psychological power of color has been recognized for millennia. Color has been used in ritual and as a means of signalling rank and royalty down through the ages. The colors associated with each element are as follows:

Earth green

Air yellow

Water blue

Fire red

Diagram 7: Colors associated with the twelve types

Each of the twelve types has a corresponding color that is a variation of the main color (see diagram 7). Other colors worthy of mention include white, which represents a perfect balance of all colors and traditionally has associations with purity. Black tends to have bad associations in Western culture, but it should not necessarily be regarded as "bad" since it too can represent balance and receptivity. Black can be a heavy, draining influence, however, and care should be taken as to the extent to which it is used. Brown and russet are colors closely associated with the earth and can be used in this connection with good effect. Pink is traditionally associated with love and harmony and can be used in connection with Water for this reason. It is also associated with Fire through the red aspect of the color, so it may be used specifically for energizing, caring, and nurturing qualities. Grey is a useful color because it is neutral. Purple is traditionally associated with spiritual qualities, and can be used during meditation in this connection. Gold and silver are divine colors traditionally representing the sun–moon and male–female principles respectively.

Color can be used to enhance the undeveloped elements via meditation and visualization in the following way: Arrange things so that you have the time and space to perform the exercise. You do not want to be rushed or disturbed. Prepare yourself for meditation by adopting a comfortable position and ensuring that you are neither too hot nor too cold. Go through the progressive relaxation procedure, then when you are fully relaxed imagine that you are breathing the appropriate color into your lungs and feel it imbue your whole being with its positive energy. You can do this as often as you like, and you may also wish to try the technique as a means of relieving ailments. Find a good book on color therapy for details.

Another method of tapping the positive qualities of color is to surround yourself with the color you are working with. One way to do this is to use a colored light, or alternatively have materials of the appropriate color around you. Wearing the color as much as possible is a particularly good method because clothes are such a major expression of personality and individuality. By wearing the right colors, you will not only benefit from their vibrational frequencies but you will also go some way to identifying with them as part of your being.

Symbols

The astute reader will have noticed that much of the preceding material has been large-ly related to symbolism. Symbols are powerful representations of complex ideas that often take the form of a single glyph. The hexagram called the Star of David is a good example. This simple arrangement of two equilateral triangles represents the Jewish peo-ple, the Judaic religion, the State of Israel, and inevitably recalls the Holocaust. Similarly, the British Union flag is composed of the crosses of the patron saints of the British Isles superimposed onto each other as a striking symbol of the British people and all that they represent, including, it has to be said, imperialism. Nothing has the same kind of immediacy and power to convey a set of complex ideas. Even individual colors have powerful symbolic associations—red is not simply a particular vibrational frequency on the visible part of the spectrum, it is also blood, war, life, energy, drive, enthusiasm, anger, danger, and power, depending on context. This does not take into account the associations and symbolism that this one color may have for a given individual.

Symbols are like living entities from the Otherworld. In *The Way of Wyrd* (1983), Brian Bates describes runes as being cast into the mystical sea in order that they may bring back messages. Runes (the word means "secret") form just one powerful set of symbols that you can draw on. You may be familiar with numerous other systems, and many more are waiting for you to discover them. Just a few of the more common ones include astrological symbols, the tarot, and the animal spirits of the Native American medicine wheel.

As I have said, symbols have a personal as well as a collective significance, so it is up to you to choose the symbols that resonate with you and your needs. Don't feel obliged to follow a system in particular just because someone says you should. You may even want to create some symbols of your own. I devised my own symbols for the elements because I was not very impressed by the traditional geomantic symbols used by most magicians. These may have accumulated energy and a powerful link with the Other-world over time as simple function of being widely used, quite apart from any intrinsic power they may have. I still prefer my own versions. Feel free to use my symbols or to devise your own. Either way, the idea is to make use of the chosen symbols to enhance your undeveloped elements by wearing them, meditating on them, or having them in your immediate environment.

Probably no one has written as much on symbols than Jung, and it would be well worth reading some of his writings or perhaps an introduction to Jung by someone such as Fordham (1959). For Jung, symbols are analogues of things that are difficult to verbalize and that therefore find their best means of expression nonverbally. A symbol is therefore a nonverbal, pictorial statement regarding particular concepts. We have already seen how collective symbols are recognized and used. Personal symbols typically emerge in dreams, as I discussed in regard to the unconscious effect of undeveloped temperaments. Pay close attention to your dream symbols, and keep a diary to see what symbols arise most frequently in your dreams. These can give you a clue as to which symbols and associated influences you should take notice of.

9

RITUAL

There are numerous ways of performing magic, from the relatively simple to the highly elaborate. One thing all forms of magic have in common is that they involve trance. Trance is necessary in order to allow the magician to stand "between the worlds." In order to influence this world, it is necessary to psychologically remove oneself from it, to some extent, and enter the Otherworld. There it is possible to transcend time and space and to effect changes that would otherwise be impossible.

In order to induce this trance, the magician engages in a set of ritualized actions. These can appear quite superficial and inane to the casual observer. Sympathetic magic, for instance, involves things like the insertion of pins into a wax effigy in order to make the intended victim suffer in some way. It is a mistaken belief that the wizard believes the effigy to be the victim; he is actually using these things as an aid to trance. It is the process being worked out in the Otherworld that has the power, not the wax or the pins.

The same is true of the more extensive operations performed by the ceremonial magician in his circle. No one should believe that the simple recitation of magic formulae combined with the waving of wands is going to change anything in this world, although the burning incense will make it smell nice. All the words, sounds, colors, smells, and indeed the whole operation inclusive of visualization is designed to induce trance so that the magician's intent can be conveyed to the Otherworld and worked out in this one.

The importance of trance to magical work is evident from the trance journeys of shamans the world over, and even from the work of educated and respected Westerners in our own epoch. The Irish poet and occultist W. B. Yeats wrote a wonderful collection of folktales between 1898 and 1902 in which he several times makes reference to the importance of trance for magical work. On one occasion he was walking with a man and a young girl on a shore somewhere in the west of Ireland. The girl passed into a trance as they walked and stated that she could hear distant music coming from the rocks and see the fair folk themselves. The man, and finally Yeats himself, became entranced by the spirit of the place, and together they communicated with the fairies.

Yeats also discovered for himself the dangers inherent in occult work. In one story he relates how he went with two sorcerers to witness them communicating with spirits, and he states that he deliberately would not allow himself to become entranced in order to better tell whether the spirits could be observed by the ordinary senses. He relates that even though he fought against trance he did indeed witness dark clouds about the room, and that he felt the presence of grotesque shapes for some days after. The sorcerers apparently affirmed that had Yeats gone into a trance, he would have been possessed. Fortunately for him, however, Yeats had not crossed the line and entered the space between the worlds where he would have been vulnerable.

The actual words and gestures of magical practice are rather like a performance celebrating the success of the venture. These components of the ritual do not by themselves bring about the desired changes. This is because the practice of magic is a psychological process that demands the full engagement of the magician on a personal level, hence the necessity of trance. Magic is a state of mind. The main point of this book is that individual differences predispose us to succeed with aims that reflect our personal psychological makeup, and to have a greater or lesser affinity with the different aspects of ritual.

This sounds contradictory. If the success of the magical aim does not depend on the ritual, why bother to perform one? Why not just do the magic and dispense with the useless ceremony? Actually, some very gifted natural magicians can do just that because they are able to step between the worlds quickly and easily and produce the desired effect. These people are the geniuses of magic. Merlin would have been one of them, as Mozart was a genius in the field of music.

The rest of us, however, need assistance. Ritual serves to induce and maintain the trance, not to bring about the desired end. The Otherworld is not bound by temporal constraints like this one. The Otherworld is all time or no time, a constant now. To step into the Otherworld is to step out of the ordinary temporal flow. That is why the beginning and the end of the ritual coexist. That is why the ritual is like a song that celebrates what already exists. Yet to communicate this message to the world, the song has to be sung and the ritual performed.

You may like to regard it as a journey, specifically a trance journey. It is a journey round the circle and through the elements. Our personal affinity with these elements is what keeps the different aspects of ritual alive and the trance unbroken. The problem of weak elements in magic work is this lack of affinity and the risk of trance failure. The mystical energy of the elements is the same but they express different qualities of the Divine. When we begin our journey in the Earth sphere, we are in the company of gnomes. Then we progress into the company of sylphs, then salamanders, then undines, then to gnomes again. The energy is transformed from element to element, rather like the colors of the rainbow, each of which is derived from a single source. Thus, although the journey begins and ends in the realm of Earth, the desired changes are not fixed in this world until the trance journey is complete and the circle is whole.

The phases of ritual that correspond to elementary powers are as follows: The gathering of materials into a chosen space followed by their manipulation via gesture and the like corresponds to Earth, since here we are working on the Earth plane with earthy materials. This too is where the magical trance begins; indeed, it may well have begun already during the preliminaries. If so, it now deepens and becomes gradually deeper as the magician moves into the Air sphere and contacts the relevant powers via invocation and visualization. The power builds to a peak in the sphere of Fire as the force merges with the will of the magician. In the Water sphere, it literally pours like a torrent through a channel of emotion that directs the power back to the sphere of Earth, where it effects the desired change.

In practice, of course, this process is a seamless progression, otherwise the all-important trance stalls and the whole enterprise fails. This is why the elements of your personality are important, not just because of the particular goals but because of the need for an unbroken trance. It isn't difficult to see how someone with a weak Earth will be out of tune with that element and trip over the various practicalities. Or how people with a weak Air will not believe in the process and thereby undermine their own efforts. Or how someone with weak Fire will be unable to accommodate the power raised. Or how someone with weak Water will not be sufficiently psychically or emotionally engaged to direct the power.

There are some important preliminaries before the ritual begins, and some important post-ritual activities. The most important preliminaries involve reducing your own negative influences. These offer an indirect means of combating your own psychological weaknesses that may serve to undermine your magical aim. They are designed, in effect, to bind your shadow. First make positive statements regarding your magical ability. The exact wording doesn't matter as long as you follow the general rules for affirmations. Second, take something physical to represent your limitations and use it to absorb their negative influence. Watson (1996) advocates the use of a black stone and some sea salt that you should take into a bath with you. I recommend Watson's book as an invaluable magical text. In it she gives various procedures for enhancing positive and reducing negative influences, but in general use whatever seems appropriate in this regard.

During the ritual, use all the methods and techniques (except mind-altering substances) that will help you to achieve and maintain the trance state. The five sensory channels should be engaged by using the appropriate sounds, colors, scents, fabrics, and flavors. Rituals should have a fairly dramatic beginning, such as the beating of a drum or sound of a gong, to formally mark the commencement of a special event. Rituals usually begin with the casting of the circle and the invocation of the elemental monarchs. The middle section involves the actual incantations, gestures, and so on. The end is marked by thanking the monarchs and by another dramatic flourish, using a drum or whatever, to mark the end of the ritual and the return to ordinary life.

During the course of the ritual, use whatever helps to induce and maintain trance. A constant rhythm is particularly effective, so use a drummer (or tape of one) and dance or simple gestures, whatever suits you. More importantly, use rhyme and rhythm together to make your utterances hypnotic. It's a good idea to compose your own ritual so that it's in your own words and therefore more personal, which is why I haven't offered one here. Memorize it as a complete piece before starting so that you don't have to stop and read it. Perform the whole ritual to yourself, for your own benefit and pleasure.

The most important follow-up activities are the grounding and sealing. Grounding is a psychological exercise in which you "bring yourself back to earth," or more accurately back fully into this world. This involves standing and imagining that you are literally taking root in the ground beneath your feet. Sealing the aura involves visualizing a protective flame surrounding your body. An example of this is the *Ritual of the Lesser Pentagram* (Conway 1974), but for examples of both grounding and sealing, see also Watson (1996). Finally, a sound way to ground and seal yourself is to do something physical, such as eat and drink something light. It has been conjectured that the Wiccan practice of cakes and ale at the end of ritual work serves just this purpose.

After this come the positive affirmations that are designed to maintain a positive frame of mind so that your underlying negativity does not work against your goal before it has a chance to manifest. These should be phrased positively *with absolutely no negatives* ("I am well" is positive; "I will not get ill" involves the negative word "not"). They should be phrased in the present, even for future-directed aims, because the unconscious and the Otherworld are timeless—the idea that something will happen in the future automatically implies the possibility that it may not. Affirm that the desired outcome has already occurred ("I am well" even if you are not yet recovered, for instance). Repeat the affirmations for at least three months, and repeat them at least six times per day in order that they penetrate the unconscious.

10

MAGICAL APPLICATIONS OF PERSONALITY: THE FETCH

One magical technique that is closely connected to personality is the creation of a fetch. The word "fetch" is of unknown origin but refers to one's double as a sort of wraith. I think it is an appropriate word to describe a simple spiritual entity that is deliberately designed and created for a specific purpose. I will take this opportunity to define various terms that can lead to confusion, since this type of creature is frequently referred to as an "elemental." Strictly speaking, an elemental is a nature spirit associated with one of the four elements. We have met these before, but at the risk of repetition I will reiterate. The associations are:

Gnome	Earth
Sylph	Air
Salamander	Fire
Undine	Water

The fetch is also variously referred to as an elementary, a fith-fath, an homunculous, a familiar, or genie. "Genie" gives the best indication of the nature of the fetch. Genies are familiar from Arabian magical lore as spirits that have been created or entrapped by magicians in order to serve their master. You can refer to them as genies if you prefer, but I will retain the term "fetch" because its meaning clearly indicates that it is, in some sense, a wraith or double of the magician who conjures it rather than a truly independent entity.

A fetch, then, is a representative of the magician, usually in miniature. It is composed of a mixture of all the elements, as indeed is the magician who creates it. A fetch is constructed from aspects of the magician's own personality in an unequal, unstable mix. This instability means that the fetch has a narrow range of applications, and in practice it is usually restricted to a single, well-defined task. This task is reflected in its elemental makeup. The instability that is due to the unequal mixture of elements also ensures that its existence is finite and predetermined by the magician.

This may sound familiar, and indeed it should. Are we ourselves not composed of an unequal mixture of elemental components that incline us to particular interests and equip us for particular activities? Are we not also transient life forms that are born to die once our allotted span is worked out? If you want to take this similarity to its logical conclusion, then we seem much like fetches that have been created by the Supreme Magician. The ancients held to the view that an imperfect mix of elements produces an unstable, hence transient, existence. Animals thus generally live shorter lives because their elemental composition is even less stable than that of humans; from a Christian viewpoint, they do not harbor the divine spark.

So a fetch is a short-lived being of our own creation that is designed to perform tasks for us. The range of possible applications is vast as long as the task is specific and relatively simple. A fetch could not be charged to bring about world peace, although one could be designed to influence a world leader. On the whole it would be best to resist the urge to mess with global politics and to stick to healing, finding lost objects, protection, and so on.

The technique for creating a fetch is fairly simple, but like all magic (and indeed any skill) it takes practice to produce the best results. First you need to decide exactly what you want your fetch to do. A fetch does not have much intelligence, so be very clear about this. It is not unlike deciding what to teach your dog. You can teach the dog to bring your slippers by using very clear, unambiguous commands. Anything else will simply confuse the animal. You can, however, train one dog to do numerous things, but you will need one fetch for each task.

Having decided exactly what you want to achieve, the next thing is to decide on the elemental makeup of your fetch. This ought to follow fairly clearly from your chosen aim. Imagine that you want to do some healing. Fire is appropriate as a curative primary element, but it needs Air in order to breathe, so that's secondary. Earth acts as a stabilizing factor and provides fuel, and Water naturally comes last because it cools and soothes, and also because it might otherwise interfere with the action of the primary Fire. The elemental constituents of the fetch are in this way linked closely with the chosen task. Another example might be for the fetch to guard an object or room. Here the order might be Earth (object), Fire (protection), Air, and finally Water. You can use the descriptions of the different types as a guide if you are unclear about the required elemental makeup for a given task.

Having decided the order of the elements, you now need to decide what form the fetch should take, how long it should live, how often it should work, and where it should reside. The form is up to you, but ideally it should reflect the nature of the task. Dragons, cats, and so on can be used as protectors, for example. Don't forget to name it. Its life span should allow it enough time to complete its task. It's a good idea to use naturally occurring cycles, such as lunar or seasonal, for this because it's tidy and can coincide with optimum working times.

Try a span of a month from new moon, building to a peak at full moon, then winding down again to expire at the next new moon. Or winter solstice to winter solstice. The only exception to this rule relates to guardians. These remain dormant unless activated by unwelcome visitors. It's advisable not to allow a fetch an indefinite life, nor to continue its existence beyond the time set for its dissolution, otherwise it may try to resist its demise and become unruly. Certainly your first attempts should aim at short life spans.

Instruct the fetch to spend specified periods at work and then to rest and recharge. This is to prevent it from doing too much too soon, and to prevent it from dying prematurely from exhaustion. The duration of its working periods can vary from a few minutes to a few hours each day or all day once weekly, or whatever seems appropriate. Finally the fetch needs somewhere to live and recuperate. This can be any suitable

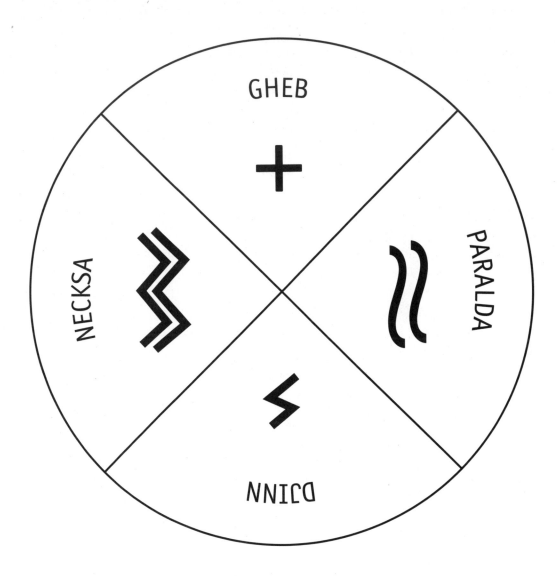

Diagram 8: The geomantic disk

container such as a bottle, box, room (if it's designed to protect a room), crystal, ring, or whatever. Whatever you choose to house your fetch, consider the suitability of the correspondences. Do not house your fetch in a red, Fire-related crystal if its primary element is Water, for instance.

The following example illustrates the process. My friend Kim had lost a set of rune stones that she kept about her at all times in a small leather bag. She had carved these herself and wanted very much to recover them. She decided to create a fetch to locate them.

Creating the Fetch

Cast the circle using your preferred method. Make sure you have something in which to house the fetch. Kim used a small, four-sided bottle. On each side she had used glass paint to illustrate the elements in the same order: Earth, Fire, Air, Water, and included runic inscriptions for good measure. Having placed the bottle in the center of the geomantic disc (see diagram 8—you can inscribe this on the floor, within the circle, and physically sit inside it, if you have room; alternatively, a smaller disc that is large enough to accommodate the ring, bottle, or whatever can stand on this for the ritual's duration), she faced north to invoke Gheb, the queen of the Earth elementals. Using the meditations described earlier in this book, Kim first attuned herself to the earthiness of her own character, then visualized Gheb and petitioned her to send gnomes to help in the quest. Then she faced south and invoked Djinn, king of the Fire elementals. She attuned herself to the Fire aspect within herself, visualized Djinn, and petitioned him for help from the salamanders. She followed the same procedure facing east to invoke Paralda, and west to invoke Necksa.

Facing north again, Kim concentrated on the bottle and visualized the fetch within it. This, she decided, would take the form of an earth dragon to reflect the principle elements Earth and Fire. She named it Othel (the name of the rune that represents possessions) and visualized it urgently moving around in its glass home. Then she charged it with Earth, then Fire, then Air, and lastly with Water. (Note that charging requires the magician to access his or her own elements via meditation and visualization, then direct each type of energy into the object, where they will exist collectively as the fetch.) She called it by name and instructed it to find her lost runes for her. She commanded that it should search on alternate hours throughout the day and return to its bottle to rest and recharge between times. She gave it life for one month from that time (it was a new moon), at which time its constituent elements would return to her.

She then forgot about Othel, so as not to interfere with her work. Three weeks later her mother visited and gave her a present of a ceramic box with a Chinese dragon carved into the lid. Inside the box was the small leather bag containing the lost runes. Her mother had bought the box as an early birthday present because she knew Kim liked dragons. She wanted to find something to go inside it, and had come across the runes in a bric-a-brac stall in Kim's neighborhood and bought them because they fitted nicely inside the box. She did not know that she was completing Othel's job for her.

11

THE LIMITS OF MAGIC

The limitations of magic fall into two categories, the external and the internal. This book is mostly about the latter, and indeed the internal, personal factors can be seen to be the most important. The limits of magic are therefore to be found mostly within your own psychology. Although in theory the things that can be achieved with magic are without limit, in practice the limitations are pretty clear. Magic is a means of effecting change outside the known laws of time and space, yet these laws cannot be overturned at will.

Recent thinking has meshed with ancient ideas to dispel the illusion that what you see is all there is. This old/new philosophy, combined with modern psychology, is very much the basis of modern magical theory. Despite the infinite possibilities implied by this theory, we still find that our efforts to bring about desired changes are curtailed.

The first and most obvious advice is to be realistic. People are often doomed to disappointment and failure because they set their sights too high. One way around this problem is to think of alternative ways to your chosen aim. Few would be so vain as to attempt to use magic to produce unaided flight. A more realistic alternative would be to magically obtain a ticket on a scheduled flight, or the money with which to buy the ticket. This is a facetious example, but it illustrates the point. I know someone who tried to gain the affection of a well-known actor, even though she had never met the man! It would have been more realistic to effect a meeting, at least to start with.

Some goals are more easily achieved than others, and these small steps can lead eventually to the desired outcome. It's rather like tipping rocks down a hill. Small rock, little effort. A big rock, on the other hand, can be moved either by gradually removing the earth that holds it in place or by inserting smaller rocks underneath it until it tips over.

This brings us to the idea of "fast" and "slow" magic. There are two distinct ideas associated with magical speed. First, consider the analogy of moving a large rock by inserting smaller rocks underneath it. The numerous small steps leading to the eventual goal means that more time is required. Small goals can generally be achieved with greater speed. Second, things happen when the time is ripe for them to happen. People often expect instant results and are disappointed to find that, having performed the appropriate ritual on Sunday, they are not promoted by the boss first thing Monday morning. The I Ching deals with the problem of time factors most eloquently. This astounding text describes the cyclic nature of time and the favorable or unfavorable aspects of current time conditions with respect to your query.

Third, the forces that are called on in magic differ from each other in both influence and manner of operation. They do not react well to impatience. Fourth, it may be that you are not ready to succeed in your aim. If your guides and other powers that have your best interests at heart have good reason for making you wait, then there is a good reason for it. Imagine, for instance, that you have a desire to work in another country. You perform rituals in an effort to facilitate this, but fail utterly. Then you meet the love of your life, an event that would not have occurred if you had succeeded in your aim. It isn't difficult to imagine other scenarios like this one. Again, if you find that you are not succeeding even at realistic, modest aims, consult your favored oracle for guidance.

In summary, the physical limitations that you encounter relate mainly to what is or is not reasonable about your intention. Of course there are occasions when the unreasonable is possible. We are all familiar with stories in which people acquire superhuman strength that allows them to lift crashed cars off injured children, and the like. There will be times when everything is right for you to succeed beyond your usual expectations, especially if your sense of urgency is great enough to produce the extra emotional force required.

Temporal limitations are related, in part, to the nature of the ultimate goal. A series of small steps takes longer than one massive stride. You also need to take account of natural development. Cress grows overnight, trees take years, and there's nothing you can do to alter this. Some forces take longer to exert their effects, and you can't change that either.

Finally, and from the perspective of this book most importantly, there is the matter of your own psychology. The main premise outlined in this book is that by virtue of our personalities, we all have greater or lesser degrees of resonance with particular forces, and hence we have a corresponding greater or lesser chance of success with associated aims. The aim of this book is to reveal just how your personal psychology affects your magical ambitions and how you can go about correcting your shortcomings.

What Should Be Achieved?

Earlier I made reference to some magical intentions that appear questionable from an ethical perspective. These are goals that involve manipulating other people or doing things either without their consent or even against their wishes. There is a lot of truth in the old adage that power corrupts. This is true of all kinds of power, whether it be social, financial, or magical. If you have power, you must learn when not to use it. Once again I would recommend use of an oracle such as the I Ching as a guide.

The ethics of magic are generally not referred to in most books on the subject unless it is implicitly via reference to the Rule of Three, which states that whatever you do will be returned to you threefold, so beware! This is often associated with the Wiccan Rede that states "An ye harm none, do what ye will." Why your magic should be revisited on you with three times the force of the original spell has never been explained as far as I know, but the notion is a useful one to bear in mind because it warns against unwise or malevolent deeds. The essential message here is that you reap as you sow, bad for bad, good for good. Unfortunately the Rule of Three is more a frightener than a set of ethics.

Many learned tomes have been produced on the subject of ethics, and I have no intention of doing more than summarizing two outstanding schools of thought, deontology and utilitarianism. Deontology is an ethical system that refers to duty as a guide to morality. From the deontological perspective, certain things must always be done or never done. Within the medical arena, for instance, it is always a duty to relieve suffering as far as possible. On the other hand, even voluntary euthanasia must never be performed. It should be obvious from this example that in order to conform to a pre-set moral standard, the individual must yield up some of his or her rights, in this case the right to die.

Utilitarianism is a moral philosophy that considers actions to be right or wrong according to the outcomes produced. Thus, given a choice, an action is deemed morally correct if it brings about the most happiness out of the different possible choices, and morally wrong if it produces the greatest unhappiness. In this system, voluntary euthanasia becomes a moral necessity if it leads to a reduction of avoidable suffering. One of the main criticisms of utilitarianism is that it is concerned entirely with outcomes and pays no heed to intention.

The practice of magic is condemned on both grounds. From a Christian deontological viewpoint, for instance, magic of any description is simply "wrong" because it conflicts with the will of God (and of course the Church). Since we have a duty to obey God's will, we cannot practice magic as to do so is not just unethical, it's evil. Thus we find even healers lumped in with black magicians.

Magic falls foul of the utilitarians when the outcomes are judged to be productive of unhappiness. Obviously this is most likely to be the case if black magic is the cause of the outcomes, but since utilitarianism does not consider the magician's intention, even white magic can be considered unethical if the outcome is different to that intended.

Happily, there are versions of both moral approaches that come close to agreement. Rule utilitarianism, for instance, propounds the idea that there is a best set of rules by which to bring about the most happiness and the least unhappiness, and it is clear that this moral outlook resembles that of deontology in essence.

From the foregoing it would seem that the practice of magic does not fit well with either moral position. Occultists tend to be freethinkers who are not attached to established organizations and the moral strictures thereof. The magical intention of the individual for each spell cast determines the moral tenor of the magician's practice, and since you can't guarantee that the actual outcome will be the one you intended, the Wiccan Rede is easier to say than it is to adhere to.

A position midway between the two major schools, such as rule utilitarianism, therefore seems to be the best compromise, but this requires lone practitioners in particular to establish their own set of moral protocols. This is good in a way because it forces individuals to think for themselves and to question established verities. Why, for instance, is it supposed to be wrong to use magic to pursue material wealth? We use every conventional means at our disposal to the same end. Why not magic?

My own belief is that we can and should if need be. The reason for the prohibition against magic for this end seems to lie in the remote past. The dualism that has plagued Western thought for millennia had its inception in the Zurvanist offshoot of Zoroastrianism in Persia circa 1400 B.C.E. The fundamental idea that the world of matter was created by an evil demiurge to confound the all-good Creator of the spiritual universe found its way into the philosophies of several religions, including Christianity. Hence the Christian ethic that we should labor but ask for no earthly reward, since our true reward awaits us in paradise. Hence the "sins of the flesh" and the renunciation of the same by religious orders of monks and nuns.

To be fair, Christianity is not alone in steering people away from earthly delights. Buddhism also considers the world of form to be a snare because it is an illusion, and to become enamored of it is to be lost to the spiritual reality beyond. Note, however, that Buddhist thinking does not portray the world of matter as inherently evil. For the Buddhists, to be ensnared by the lure of the material world is foolish rather than sinful.

This, then, is the basis of the prohibition against the magical pursuit of earthly things. Since we are spiritual entities trapped in gross physical bodies, we should follow spiritual goals and avoid the material. As a pantheist I disagree with the idea that the physical world is not part of the divine, and thus disagree that it is in any way evil or that it should be avoided. I do, however, agree that the world of matter is transient and illusory and that we can become ensnared by it, or more accurately by our own gross desires. Our spiritual nature is, on the other hand, eternal and consequently more in need of our full attention. As the Buddhists have pointed out, this is the real problem of the physical world—that it can too easily distract us from what is truly important.

I know a multimillionaire whose stated aim in life is to make as many millions as possible. That's his business, of course, but it seems to be a sterile goal. After all, he can't take it with him, and he's already extremely rich. His attitude is a reflection of the Western paradox. Capitalism congratulates people for acquiring as much wealth as possible, while the Church states that you shouldn't enjoy it.

I do not therefore advocate self-aggrandizement for its own sake any more than I endorse greed or cruelty. On the other hand, I would not criticize someone who casts spells that are designed to meet his or her physical needs. Why should anyone live in poverty if there is a way out of it? Why should anyone suffer privation or deprivation unnecessarily? Remember that most people in the world do not have the means to haul themselves out of poverty using orthodox methods. Often the moral imperative is to feed and clothe your family, not to adhere to the dictates of rich organizations such as the Church.

In magic, as in all things, there is intention and outcome. Before casting spells, you need to consider your motives. If you think you may be on the wrong path, get off it. At the very least consult someone else about it, or the I Ching. If you truly believe that your motives and your methods are above reproach, consider the potential outcomes. Of course you can't be held responsible for what other people do. If you know someone who desperately needs a car in order to work and you get one for them, you have succeeded in your aim. If he gets drunk and crashes it, that's his fault, not yours. You can know your own motives and hopefully the immediate, desired effects of what you do, but that's all. It reminds me of the conundrum about having the choice of saving a child from drowning or of letting him drown. Surely you would do your utmost to save him. But what if the child was Hitler and you knew that he would then live to devastate Europe and murder millions? Would you save him then? Yes, because happily you would not have this knowledge of the future. You would do the right thing and save the innocent child. What he does later in life is his doing, not yours. In short, you act for the best as far as you can.

If you're wondering why I am concentrating so much on ethics it is because in considering this area that we return to the original question that led to the writing of this book, namely the difference between black and white magicians. The main thesis of this book is that magic is essentially a psychological enterprise, and consequently your own psychology is of central importance to what you want to do, what you can do, and what you actually do. In describing people in terms of the four elements split into two types, I am attempting to underline the fact that we all have a bright and a dark side. These different aspects of the self determine what interests and values we have, and subsequently with what aims we are most likely to succeed.

Most of us know ourselves through the bright, primary side, and this is the side of ourselves that we like to present to others. This is the part of ourselves that has positive strengths that allows us to do worthwhile and constructive things. At the same time, however, there is the dark side of the shadow. This is the side of which we are often unaware and which disposes us, particularly during difficult times, to wrongful, destructive acts. We are in effect simultaneously black and white magicians. Which of these holds the wand of power at any given point decides whether we will be constructive or destructive in our aims. Which of these has most control of the wand is determined by the degree of self-knowledge we possess. Any one of us can submit briefly to the dark urges of the shadow. Some of us risk becoming the shadow more permanently.

If this is to be avoided, then we must know and understand ourselves as well as possible, both to appreciate our strengths and to beware our weaknesses. This is why, if you do not have a set of ethical rules to follow, you should establish some and stick to them at all times. In this way you stand a better chance of avoiding behavior that can hurt others and yourself. A set of ethics can also act as a personal barometer. If you feel an urge to disregard your own morality due to anger, jealousy, or whatever, then you will know that the shadow is rising. At these times you should adhere to your beliefs concerning what is right and work on yourself to stay on the bright side.

Remember that the shadow does not make you do things at these unfortunate times. You are the shadow.

Bibliography

The American Psychiatric Association. *The Diagnostic and Statistical Manual of Mental Disorders, 4th Ed.* The American Psychiatric Association: Washington, D.C., 1994.

Andrews, T. *How to Meet and Work with Spirit Guides.* Llewellyn Publications: St. Paul, Minn., 2000.

Arroyo, S. *Astrology, Psychology, and the Four Elements: An Energy Approach to Astrology and Its Uses in the Counseling Art.* CRCS Publications: Sebastopol, Calif., 1975.

Bates, B. *The Way of Wyrd.* Arrow Books Ltd.: London, England, 1983.

Brown, S. *The Principles of Feng Shui.* Thorsons: San Francisco, Calif., 1996.

Capra, F. *The Tao of Physics.* Shambhala: San Francisco, Calif., 1975.

Castaneda, C. *The Teachings of Don Juan: A Yaqui Way of Knowledge.* University of California Press: Berkeley and Los Angeles, Calif., 1968.

Chetwynd, T. *A Dictionary of Symbols.* Paladin: London, England, 1982.

Conway, D. *Magic: An Occult Primer.* Mayflower Books Ltd.: Frogmore, St. Albans, Herts., England, 1974.

Conway, D. J. *Animal Magic: The Art of Recognizing and Working with Familiars.* Llewellyn Publications: St. Paul, Minn., 1995.

———. *Magical, Mythical, Mystical Beasts: How to Invite Them into Your Life.* Llewellyn Publications: St. Paul, Minn., 1996.

Coxhead, N. *The Relevance of Bliss: A Contemporary Exploration of Mystical Experience.* Wildwood House: London, England, 1985.

Cunningham, S. *Cunningham's Encyclopedia of Crystals, Gems, and Metal Magic.* Llewellyn Publications: St. Paul, Minn., 1998.

Farrar, S. *What Witches Do.* Peter Davies Ltd.: London, England, 1971.

Fordham, F. *An Introduction to Jung's Psychology.* Penguin Books Ltd.: Harmondsworth, Middlesex, England, 1959.

Ferrucci, P. *What We May Be: The Vision and Techniques of Psychosynthesis.* Thorsons: Hammersmith, London, England, 1995.

Gettings, F. *The Arkana Dictionary of Astrology.* Arkana: London, England, 1990.

Graves, R. *The White Goddess.* Faber & Faber Ltd.: London, England, 1961.

Hampson, S. E. *The Construction of Personality,* 2nd Ed. Routledge: London, England, 1982.

Harner, M. *The Way of the Shaman.* Harper & Row: New York, N.Y., 1990.

Johns, J. *The King of the Witches.* Pan Books Ltd.: London, England, 1971.

Jung, C. G. *Psychology and Alchemy.* Routledge: London, England, 1966.

———. *Analytical Psychology: Its Theory and Practice.* Routledge: London, England, 1976.

Mathews, J. *The Elements of the Arthurian Tradition.* Element Books Ltd., Longmead, Shaftesbury, Dorset, England, 1989.

Mathews, J., and C. Mathews. *The Western Way: A Practical Guide to the Western Mystery Tradition.* Penguin Books Ltd.: Harmondsworth, Middlesex, England, 1994.

Noel, D. C. *The Soul of Shamanism: Western Fantasies, Imaginal Realities.* The Continuum Publishing Co.: New York, N.Y., 1997.

Paulson, G. L. *Kundalini and the Chakras.* Llewellyn Publications: St. Paul, Minn., 1998.

Reinhart, M. *Chiron and the Healing Journey: An Astrological and Psychological Perspective.* Penguin Books Ltd.: Harmondsworth, Middlesex, England, 1989.

Roney-Dougal, S. *Where Science and Magic Meet.* Element Books Ltd., Longmead, Shaftesbury, Dorset, England, 1993.

Sakoian, F., and L. S. Acker. *The Astrologer's Handbook.* Penguin Books Ltd.: Harmondsworth, Middlesex, England, 1973.

Watson, N. B. *Practical Solitary Magic.* Samuel Weiser: York Beach, Maine, 1996.

Wing, R. L. *The I Ching Workbook.* Doubleday & Co. Inc.: Garden City, N.Y., 1983.

Yeats, W. B. *The Celtic Twilight: Myth, Fantasy & Folklore.* Prism Press: Bridgeport, Dorset, England, 1990.

Glossary

Common Psychological Defense Strategies

[text in brackets refers to examples of behavior indicated by the strategy]

Acting Out: a means of coping with stress that involves doing things impulsively without regard to the longer-term consequences [smashing crockery].

Denial: unconsciously ignoring factual aspects of the world because to recognize them would be too disturbing [partner is having an affair].

Devaluation: attributing to oneself or others excessive negative qualities [jealousy makes you ridicule your sister's abilities].

Displacement: directing emotions (typically anger) at substitute targets, usually because the real target is too powerful to attack [kicking the cat].

Fantasy: when used to excess, the avoidance of the harsh realities of life by retreating into make-believe [pretending to have connections and friendships with famous people].

Idealization: attributing to oneself or to others excessive positive qualities [regarding your father as a wonderful person so that you don't have to see him as a drunken bully].

Identification: adopting, or finding in oneself, the personal qualities of another person in order to enhance one's self-esteem by being like that person [trying to act like an older, socially successful friend].

Intellectualization: the overuse of abstract thinking in order to reduce emotional discomfort [justifying the tendency to steal by referring to social inequality].

Introjection: the incorporation of another person's values or personal traits in order to "keep" them [especially to ward off a sense of loss, e.g., bereavement; or to be safe from a potential aggressor on the basis that "If I'm like that person, he will not want to harm me"].

Isolation of Affect: disconnection of one's feelings from one's behavior in order to safeguard the sense of self [soldiers "shelving" their feelings in order to engage in combat].

Projection: attributing your own "bad" traits to other people [you don't trust anyone, so you accuse everyone of not trusting you].

Rationalization: unconscious self-justification using apparently plausible arguments [not eating properly on the basis that particular foodstuffs are bad for you].

Reaction-Formation: avoiding distressing feelings that arise because of a particular personal trait by adopting the (usually exaggerated) opposite of that trait [you fear your own aggressive potential so much that you always appear meek and mild].

Regression: a means of dealing with stress by adopting behaviors more suited to earlier periods of development [thumb-sucking].

Repression: unconscious avoidance of ideas, feelings, etc. in order to escape the distress that would otherwise result [a man hates his mother].

Somatization: concern with physical illness as a means of dealing with psychological distress [frequent complaints of physical illness].

Splitting: an alternation between idealization and devaluation [you regard your brother as entirely good or as entirely bad, depending on how you feel at any given moment].

Suppression: the conscious avoidance of disturbing ideas, feelings, etc. [mounting debts].

Index

☽ REACH FOR THE MOON

Llewellyn publishes hundreds of books on your favorite subjects!
To get these exciting books, including the ones on the following pages,
check your local bookstore or order them directly from Llewellyn.

Order by Phone
- Call toll-free within the U.S. and Canada, 1-877-NEW-WRLD
- In Minnesota, call (651) 291-1970
- We accept VISA, MasterCard, and American Express

Order by Mail
- Send the full price of your order (MN residents add 7% sales tax)
  in U.S. funds, plus postage & handling to:

  Llewellyn Worldwide
  P.O. Box 64383, Dept. 0-7387-0187-4
  St. Paul, MN 55164–0383, U.S.A.

Postage & Handling
- **Standard** (U.S., Mexico, & Canada)

If your order is:
    $20.00 or under, add $5.00
    $20.01–$100.00, add $6.00
    Over $100, shipping is free

(Continental U.S. orders ship UPS. AK, HI, PR, & P.O. Boxes ship USPS 1st class. Mex. & Can. ship PMB.)
- Second Day Air (Continental U.S. only): $10.00 for one book + $1.00
  per each additional book
- Express (AK, HI, & PR only) [Not available for P.O. Box delivery. For
  street address delivery only.]: $15.00 for one book + $1.00 per each
  additional book
- International Surface Mail: Add $1.00 per item
- International Airmail: Books—Add the retail price of each item;
  Non-book items—Add $5.00 per item

Please allow 4–6 weeks for delivery on all orders.
Postage and handling rates subject to change.

Discounts
We offer a 20% discount to group leaders or agents. You must order a minimum of 5 copies of the same book to get our special quantity price.

Free Catalog
Get a free copy of our color catalog, *New Worlds of Mind and Spirit*.
Subscribe for just $10.00 in the United States and Canada ($30.00
overseas, airmail).

Visit our website at www.llewellyn.com for more information.

Write Your Own Magic
The Hidden Power in Your Words

R<small>ICHARD</small> W<small>EBSTER</small>

This book will show you how to use the incredible power of words to create the life that you have always dreamed about. We all have desires, hopes and wishes. Sadly, many people think theirs are unrealistic or unattainable. *Write Your Own Magic* shows you how to harness these thoughts by putting them to paper.

Once a dream is captured in writing it becomes a goal, and your subconscious mind will find ways to make it happen. From getting a date for Saturday night to discovering your purpose in life, you can achieve your goals, both small and large. You will also learn how to speed up the entire process by making a ceremony out of telling the universe what it is you want. With the simple instructions in this book, you can send your energies out into the world and magnetize all that is happiness, success, and fulfillment to you.

- Send your energies out into the universe with rituals, ceremonies, and spells
- Magnetize yourself so that your desires are attracted to you, while the things you do not want are repelled
- Create suitable spells for different purposes
- Produce quick money, attract a lover, harness the powers of protection, win that job promotion
- Learn the ancient and powerful art of paper-burning, used in the Far East for thousands of years

0-7387-0001-0
5³/₁₆ x 8, 312 pp. $9.95

To order, call 1-877-NEW-WRLD
Prices subject to change without notice

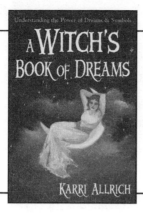

A Witch's Book of Dreams
Understanding the Power of Dreams and Symbols

KARRI ALLRICH

Watch your respect for dreams deepen as you start to witness the wisdom and foresight of your subconscious, which often predicts outcomes before the waking mind can conceive them. In *A Witch's Book of Dreams,* you will begin by understanding archetypes and the language of dream symbols. You will be introduced to your soul twin and your dream lover. You will encounter your shadow self, and see the patterns of belief and behavior that hinder you in subtle ways. By creating your own dream journal and personal dream dictionary, you will come to a greater understanding of the power of symbols.

The author illustrates Jungian concepts in an unclouded style, spiced with humor and compassion. Her merging of Jungian concepts with the path of the Witch weaves a spell of dream magick that carries you on an inner journey toward understanding and personal growth.

The extensive dream dictionary is a treasure in itself, with hundreds of symbols and interpretations to help you immediately in your dream work.

- Begin a Dream Journal
- Cast a Dream Spell
- Work with symbols both psychologically and magickally
- Create a personal Dream Dictionary
- Find correspondences in tarot, chakras, colors, and herbs to enhance the power of understanding and healing

1-56718-014-0
6 x 9, 240 pp., illus.

$12.95

To order, call 1-877-NEW-WRLD
Prices subject to change without notice

Dreams—Working Interactive

*with Software for Journaling
& Interpretation*

STEPHANIE JEAN CLEMENT, PH.D.,
AND TERRY ROSEN

Dreams is the only complete and interactive system for helping you determine the unique, personal meaning of your dreams. What does it mean to dream of the house you grew up in? Why do certain people appear in your dreams again and again? How can you tell if a dream is revealing the future? Together, the book and software program provide everything necessary to effectively record and analyze whatever message your subconscious throws your way.

Absent in *Dreams* is the psychological jargon that makes many dream books so difficult. Examples of dreams illustrate the various types of dreams, and each chapter gives information about how to identify and work with dream symbols. The software program gives you the capacity to print out your dreams, incorporating the symbol definitions you select. What's more, the program will facilitate further exploration of your dreams with suggestions and questions.

With the PC-compatible Interactive Dream Software you can:

- Record your dreams, visions or waking experiences
- Get an immediate listing of your dream symbols that are included
  in the electronic dictionary
- Add your own new definitions to the database
- Answer questions to facilitate more in-depth exploration of your dreams

1-56718-145-7

7½ x 9⅛, 240 pp., CD-ROM software program for PC format with Windows $24.95

To order, call 1-877-NEW-WRLD

Prices subject to change without notice